STEVE WAUGH'S

1997 ASHES DIARY

STEVE WAUGH'S

1997 ASHES DIARY

Foreword by Lynette Waugh

HarperSports
An imprint of HarperCollinsPublishers

COVER PHOTOGRAPHY
FRONT: AUSTRALIAN PICTURE LIBRARY/ALLSPORT
BACK: MAIN PHOTO AND CENTRE - AUSTRALIAN PICTURE LIBRARY/ALLSPORT
LEFT AND RIGHT: STEVE WAUGH

Harper*Sports*
An imprint of HarperCollins*Publishers*

First published in Australia in 1997
by HarperCollins*Publishers* Pty Limited
ACN 009 913 517
A member of HarperCollins*Publishers* (Australia) Pty Limited Group
http://www.harpercollins.com.au

HarperCollins*Publishers*
25 Ryde Road, Pymble, Sydney NSW 2073, Australia
31 View Road, Glenfield, Auckland 10, New Zealand
77–85 Fulham Palace Road, London W6 8JB, United Kingdom
Hazelton Lanes, 55 Avenue Road, Suite 2900, Toronto, Ontario M5R 3L2
and 1995 Markham Road, Scarborough, Ontario M1B 5M8, Canada
10 East 53rd Street, New York NY 10032, USA

National Library of Australia Cataloguing-in-Publication data:

Waugh, Steve, 1965-.
  Steve Waugh's 1997 Ashes Diary.
  ISBN 0 7322 5870 7.

1. Waugh, Steve, 1965- - Diaries. 2. Cricket players - Australia - Diaries.
3. Test matches (Cricket) - Australia. I. Title. II. Title: Ashes diary.

796.358092.
Printed in Australia by Southbank Press on 115gsm Gallery Matt.

5 4 3 2 1
01 00 99 98 97

*~ **Dedication** ~*
To my daughter, Rosalie,
whose smile makes me feel as if
I've scored a double hundred every day.

ITINERARY

FOREWORD, BY LYNETTE WAUGH

INTRODUCTION, BY JUSTIN LANGER

ACKNOWLEDGEMENTS

Special thanks to all the members of the 1997 Australian cricket touring squad for their support, friendship, understanding and input during the tour.

Thanks also to . . .
Lynette, for her continued support, love, friendship,
foreword and, most of all, for being a great mum to Rosalie.

Phil and Ethel Doughty, for looking after and keeping company to Lynette and Rosalie during their stay and for giving me their continuing support and love.

Scott Grant and Toyota, for the use of a sponsored car during my family's stay in the UK and their continued support back home in Australia.

My lucky scorer, Mike Walsh, who, without fail, again provided me with endless statistics and information after each day's play.

Bill Brown, one of cricket's true gentlemen, for giving me the opportunity to interview him at Lord's.

Geoff Armstrong, for his continued belief and guidance in this project, and his honesty and integrity in all matters.

Errol Alcott, for those dressing-room photos that I feature in.

Justin Langer, for his introduction and text in the book. Lang, your attitude towards cricket continues to be an inspiration to all around you.

Kodak and Canon, for their support.

FOREWORD

by Lynette Waugh

WHEN I MET STEPHEN 13 years ago in high school, if anyone had asked me to predict what lay ahead for us I definitely wouldn't have guessed that it would evolve into a life together dominated by cricket. I was 17, and you could say that I was very uninterested in the game. I come from a family of two girls and, at that age, we knew nothing about cricket, only that it was a terrible drone that endlessly occupied my grandfather's TV during our summer holidays. That, of course, all changed very quickly when Stephen was selected for New South Wales and then thrust into the Australian team. My education of the game began (and continues today), but now it is accompanied with enjoyment and immense pride in Stephen and his achievements.

I was asked to write the foreword by Stephen and, initially, I was extremely nervous and unsure. Since the birth of our daughter Rosalie just over a year ago, the most I've had to write has been a scratchy postcard or a shopping list. I thought, why would anyone want to know about me? My life to all seems pretty obvious — looking after our baby and watching cricket.

I never view our life as anything but ordinary. Some aspects of it may seem quite bizarre to others but to us they are just normal. I suppose that it's because we know no different, it's been our life together from the start and we've just grown into it. I imagine that's one of the benefits of beginning a cricket career together rather than arriving on the scene after it's established.

On so many occasions after Stephen has been asked for an autograph, the autograph seeker will turn to me and ask if I'm Steve's wife. After a positive reply this is nearly always followed by, 'So, what's it like being married to a famous cricketer?'

I love married life and I love being married to Stephen, although I'm sure I would enjoy it even more if he was home more often. The most difficult part of our relationship is the long separations, not only are they long but frequent too. As time goes by the separations don't become any easier. In fact, I think they become more difficult, especially since the birth of Rosalie.

Each time Stephen leaves, I feel really sad for him because he's missing time with his daughter — and anyone who's a parent can understand how children can literally grow before your eyes. The quality of time rather than the quantity is definitely more important to us now, especially to Rosalie. Contact with Stephen is priority number one, so Rosalie and I spend countless hours — and many dollars — talking to him on the phone. From the age of 10 months, Rosalie already recognised the sound of the phone ringing as something special. She is very good at listening and chatting on the phone to her daddy.

However, nothing can replace being with him so in mid-June of this year we set off for England. It was Rosalie's first big tour — although she'd already had 10 plane trips in her first 10 months — and it was my third Ashes tour.

Life touring with a cricket side is no easy task. I remember my first Ashes Tour in 1989. I left Australia waved off by family and friends wishing me a fantastic holiday, and that's what I truly believed — that I would spend endless days with Stephen: watching cricket, sightseeing and enjoying the UK.

Boy, was I mistaken. I didn't realise how demanding it would be. There were plenty of days where Stephen was occupied with cricket, training and team functions and very few days spent with me. I remember I was there nearly eight weeks before Stephen got a match off.

I spent three months away on that tour and I'd have to say it was my biggest learning curve yet. I did have a fantastic time but I had to make huge adjustments to the way I perceived a cricket tour to be: all work and some play! I also became very independent — Stephen says 'fiercely independent' these days! — because in 1989 the players' wives and girlfriends weren't allowed to stay with the team until the last two weeks of the tour. We couldn't even step foot inside the team hotel. Finding accommodation and transport to complement the cricket matches we watched became as much a preoccupation for us as the sights we wanted to see.

Prior to departing for this year's Ashes tour, I anticipated spending three months touring England with our baby daughter, who would then be 10 months old. I don't know whether some would consider me to be brave or crazy. I had travelled on the 1989 tour with Pip Boon and 15-month-old Georgina, and in 1993 with Helen Healy and 2-year-old Emma — so I knew what would be ahead.

I was lucky to have my parents accompany me on this tour. They were keen to see some cricket in the UK and also couldn't bear to be apart from their granddaughter for three months. So they were my constant companions. Their help with Rosie, their numerous baby sitting stints and their fantastic company was a blessing which I am so thankful for.

Unlike previous tours, for the Test matches we could stay with the team at the team hotel — even in the same room. So things were looking bright for the touring prospects of Rosalie and Lynette Waugh. It was a big adjustment for all of us. Firstly, Stephen had to adjust to having two extra people in his already tiny and very messy hotel rooms! Each night he would come home from cricket to a dark and quiet room, as his arrival home was always past Rosalie's bed time.

My adjustments were those of a mum — trying to feed your baby with unfamiliar food from non-child friendly hotel menus (with unfriendly prices too!) and pacifying a crying baby to quick silence so she wouldn't disturb Stephen or any other player who was in the next room. Rosalie's adjustments were major and we did expect a lot from her. She went from sleeping 12 hours a night at home to waking 4–6 times a night from the first night we were away. She often just didn't know where she was when she woke, something which Stephen could sympathise with after his many travels.

Travelling in the car was something we also became proficient at. My father was the expert packer of our bulging Toyota Picnic. Our journeys from one part of England to another were many and often long; an average trip was around 2–4 hours every few days — a very long time for a little girl to have to sit still.

My father and I shared the driver/navigator role and my mother became Rosalie's entertainer. On many occasions my mother virtually did a cabaret act to keep Rosalie amused as we chewed up those motorway miles. By the end of the tour Rosalie's favourite songs were 'Postman Pat' and 'Mickey Mouse Club'. I think my parents would be very happy never to have to hear those two songs again! One trip I did without my parents was from Scotland to Birmingham and then to Wormsley for a one-day match. The longest leg was Edinburgh to Birmingham — six hours straight — and, to my amazement, it was easy because Rosalie slept all the way.

The benefits to be found on such a tour as this year's Ashes series undoubtedly outweigh the negatives. One such benefit was the organisation at the various cricket grounds. They were definitely expecting us. The facilities for wives with children at Lord's and Manchester were outstanding. To the wives' joy and the children's pleasure they had set up rooms which we could use for ourselves and the children. The rooms were stocked with food, a television to watch the cricket and, in the case of Manchester, even toys and colouring in books — a mini creche for the kids. It was just fantastic. I know it may sound strange to say we went to the cricket ground and watched it on TV, but cricket grounds are definitely not child-friendly places.

It is completely unrealistic to think you can pack small children into rows of seats with nowhere to move or play without driving their mothers to distraction or disturbing the spectators. Such facilities are a necessity to players and their families today as the game is thrust further into professionalism, involving more games and more time away.

Children often only see their dads at the cricket — even when the match is in their home state, as there are fewer days between games these days. Such facilities enable us to have the children grouped together to play and watch the cricket on TV (which they are very good at). It also allows the wives to take turns and slip away to watch their partners from the stands.

To my extreme disappointment and embarrassment though, such facilities are non-existent in Australia. The only time in the cricket year when children feel welcome is at the Christmas Test. Other than that there is nothing available. Instead, we are offered on some occasions, such as in Sydney, a row of seats — with no carpeted area for babies or toddlers to play. I really don't see why it is such a difficult task to provide families with a private, comfortable room to watch cricket from.

Mark Taylor's wife, Judi, summed up the situation when we were in the UK. On one occasion, a disgruntled spectator, who wasn't happy about Judi's boys being at the cricket, asked her, 'How did you all get in here?' Judi pointed out clearly to him that when your husband is a player, you come as a package deal. After all, who else would be crazy enough to take small children to the cricket unless you had to?

The highlights for adults travelling are nearly always the attractions they see. For children though, it is more the actual 'experience' of travelling. Travelling exposes them to a wide range of new and different experiences. Rosalie grew up so much when we were away. We took away a shy and quiet little girl and returned with an outgoing and confident one. She developed a wonderful friendship with the Healy children and, although Helen Healy and I were already good friends, the enjoyment Rosalie had with Emma, Laura and Tom on tour and the help I received from Helen was not only a highlight but a blessing. The Healys made our trip fun, 'survivable' and full of wonderful and special memories. Rosalie's time with them has left a lasting impression, even now when she sees a photo of Emma, Laura and Tom she is filled with smiles and giggles.

Although I had intended to stay in the UK for three months, after eight weeks I decided I had to be realistic. I had to admit to myself that yes, it had become a struggle and I had probably been a bit too ambitious to think I could survive three months in hotels with a baby. Helen had returned a week earlier and my parents would be returning a month earlier than me. Rosalie and I were already missing the Healys a lot and I knew I would be lost without my parents. Rosalie was not settling down at night and Stephen was being forced to write his diary in the hotel bathroom, using the vanity as his desk and the toilet as his seat. So I decided to come home early.

We'd had eight fabulous weeks filled with a mixture of life experiences. Rosalie and I spent time with Stephen and the cricket had been fabulous. It had been more than worthwhile to travel all that way to see Stephen score his two hundreds at Manchester. I remember thinking after Stephen had scored his hundreds that life couldn't get much better than this.

I was sitting in the front row at Old Trafford clapping as Stephen scored his second hundred, holding Rosalie as, for the very first time, she watched her daddy score a hundred. It seemed better still when I thought I could have been at home at 3am, alone with a cup of tea, watching Stephen's achievement on TV and clapping very quietly so as not to wake a sleeping baby.

INTRODUCTION

What is Mental Toughness?
by Justin Langer

YOU OFTEN HEAR STATEMENTS that cricket at the top level is a mind game, a mental battle with one's self, a game played as much between your ears as it is with the opposition. Some people even attempt to estimate what percentage of the game is mental and what proportion is technical or physical. This is a tough but interesting question — the truth is that success is generally achieved by getting all three of these facets right.

Professional sport today features players, administrators, coaches, computers, video feedback, fitness advisers, nutritionists and sports psychologists. The current-day professionalism in cricket has led to an increasing incentive for players to use every available resource to ensure that they maximise their potential and make the most of the opportunities now available.

Strangely though, sport psychology, 'the inner game', whatever you like to call it, seems to be the least studied of all cricket skills, even if it is widely accepted as being the most important ingredient of success.

There is no doubt that sports psychologists can be valuable, but in my opinion the best psychologists come from within the team, from the players — team-mates and ex-players alike. Much can be learnt from talking with the Waugh brothers, Mark Taylor and Ian Healy, Shane Warne and Glenn McGrath, Geoff Marsh and Allan Border. Invaluable lessons can be gained from these 'real life' psychologists who have experienced the heat of the cricket battle and have performed exceptionally under pressure over an extended period of time. These are sportsmen who have refined and mastered their minds and techniques to a point where their chances of consistent performance are maximised.

At present, the cricketer who best epitomises mental toughness is Steve Waugh. Since 1993, he has made a mountain of runs in Test cricket and his average is comparable with the greatest players who have ever graced the cricket fields around the world. His batting in the third Ashes Test in 1993, at Trent Bridge, when he helped save the game, seemed to be the turning point in what, up until that time, had been a sometimes spectacular but too often inconsistent career. Two years later, when Stephen stood up to the awesome Curtly Ambrose on a green pitch at Trinidad, where the ball was seaming and bouncing like a spitting cobra, he sent shivers down the spines of his team-mates who sat in the dressing-room searching for inspiration.

His double century in Jamaica on the same tour, where he partnered his younger brother in a stand that took Australia to the brink of a series victory, couldn't have been made by anyone but an extremely strong-spirited and determined person. On this Ashes tour, Stephen's centuries in each innings of the third Test, at Old Trafford, scored with a bruised right thumb and an Ashes series to rescue, were feats of exceptional skill, determination and concentration.

What is the key to his consistency and his outstanding record over the past four years? How has Steve Waugh transformed himself from a very talented cricketer to a player who will go down in our rich sporting history as a great Australian sportsman?

The 'text book' sport psychologists would put it down to key words such as 'Concentration', 'Goal Setting', 'Discipline', 'Dedication' and 'Belief'. Sitting on the famous Lord's balcony during this tour, I talked to the world's No.1 batsman about his personal pursuit of excellence, about mental toughness and generally what makes him tick. His thoughts make for very interesting learning for anyone looking to emulate his incredible deeds.

I have noticed that 'Tugga' tends to hit a large number of balls at practice leading up to a Test Match. So I asked him how important his preparation is for a game.

'Preparation and training are very important aspects of my game,' he replied. 'My practice sessions are very specific, designed to ensure that I feel as though I have done everything possible to be ready for the battle ahead. In simple terms, it is about feeling good about my game so that the odds of performing well weigh heavily in my favour. I give some thought to how the opposition are likely to attack me, then I relax totally and trust my instincts and preparation during the match.'

Next I quizzed him about his concentration and consistency. In a nutshell, the Steve Waugh philosophy and key to peak performance seems to be about single-minded, focused concentration. About having the ability to concentrate solely on the next ball and giving it your full attention with a totally clear mind. It is almost a 'meditative' state. Clear focus on the ball, without any thoughts hindering that pinpoint concentration on the only thing that matters … the very next ball.

'Talk to AB (Allan Border), Boonie (David Boon), they will tell you the same thing,' Stephen says. 'The next ball is the only important thing. The really good players give 100 per cent to every ball. I know the best way to enjoy success is to play every ball as well as I possibly can.'

Mark Taylor, who has played most of his career alongside his vice-captain, believes that one of the main reasons for his mate's success comes down to Discipline. He told me, 'It is as if Steve decided to trade flamboyance and flashiness for runs. No matter what the situation, he refuses to give his wicket away and is determined to make the bowlers bowl at him, no matter what level of cricket he is playing.'

Tugga admits, 'It doesn't matter so much how you look as how many runs you score. You have to work out what works best for you, trust yourself and discipline yourself to the task at hand. Even in my net sessions I discipline myself to play as if I am in a game. Not getting out is as much a habit as getting out can be.'

Steve's thoughts on goal setting are intriguing. 'I am not a big one for setting goals,' he claims. 'My only real goal is to give my full attention to the next ball bowled at me, 100 per cent concentration on the next ball. Obviously I have ambitions but not specific goals, except the one I have just described.'

Two days after our Old Trafford victory, Tugga confessed that one of the most pleasing aspects of the two centuries he scored in that game was being able to win a mental struggle. Leading up to the game he'd had to work very hard on his mental game, as his confidence was low and a few negative thoughts had crept in to his head. 'We all have them (negative thoughts), I guess it's just how we get over them. I kept talking to myself, prepared well and told myself not to be stupid, to get on with the job. This was a fantastic learning experience, another learning experience.'

In a way it is nice to know that even the world's best batsman has negative thoughts. At least we know he's human!!

A question often asked of the champions is 'What actually is Mental Toughness?'. At the end of the day it is about performing consistently in all conditions for an extended period of time. Steve Waugh's summation of this question is this: 'Believing that you are better than the opposition, being brutally honest with yourself and always looking to improve your game. These are the crucial factors in my success.'

Australian cricket has the best psychologists in the business. The Chappells, the Waughs, Rod Marsh, Dennis Lillee, Bob Simpson, Shane Warne, Ian Healy, Mark Taylor … the list goes on. Steve Waugh is a role model for tough, disciplined Australian cricket — a man who is following in the footsteps of great cricketers who themselves learnt many valuable lessons over the years.

THE 1997 AUSTRALIANS

CAPTAIN: MARK TAYLOR— TUBBY
VICE-CAPTAIN: STEVE WAUGH — TUGGA

MICHAEL BEVAN — BEVO
ANDY BICHEL — BIC
GREG BLEWETT — BLEWEY
MATTHEW ELLIOTT — HERBIE
ADAM GILCHRIST — GILLY
JASON GILLESPIE — DIZZY
IAN HEALY — HEALS
BRENDON JULIAN — BJ
MICHAEL KASPROWICZ — KASPER
JUSTIN LANGER — LANG
GLENN McGRATH – PIGEON
RICKY PONTING — PUNTER
MICHAEL SLATER — SLATS
SHANE WARNE — WARNEY
MARK WAUGH — JUNIOR

MANAGER: ALAN CROMPTON — CROMMO
COACH: GEOFF MARSH — SWAMPY
PHYSIOTHERAPIST: ERROL ALCOTT — HOOTER
FITNESS CO-ORDINATOR: STEVE SMITH —SMITHY OR TATTOO
SCORER: MIKE WALSH

THE VENUES

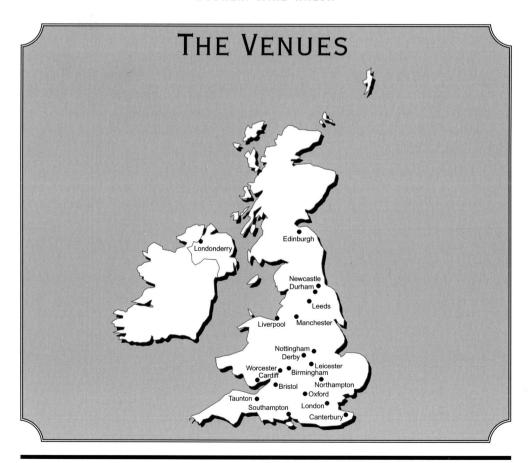

DAY 1 | MAY 10

Sydney to Hong Kong

EVEN AFTER 12 YEARS on the international cricket merry-go-round, encompassing countless overseas tours, I remain something of a novice when it comes to packing bags with any sort of authority. A final 30 minutes of mayhem invariably sees me scavenging through my compact discs to try to narrow the field down to my favourite 20 or so, followed by a double, and then triple-check on my cricket kit to make sure all the essentials are safely tucked away in my monstrously-proportioned, 'Coke'-emblazoned cricket coffin. Then there's the mad scramble to locate that always-elusive passport. And then there's a final scout around, which more often than not leads me to my toiletry bag, standing there all alone like a scorned child in the corner of the room, begging for a berth on the upcoming tour.

These final moments at home are always emotional ones. Hurried goodbyes to family are not exactly the way you want to part company, but life as a modern-day cricket professional is full of them. For me, each tour becomes a little more difficult, particularly as I am now the father of a nine-and-a-half-month-old daughter, Rosalie, who I miss desperately on each and every day I'm not with her. And, like me, my wife, Lynette, is no better at saying goodbye than when I first toured for Australia back in early 1986 (to New Zealand) and the tears still flow when it's time to head off.

Lynette doesn't come to the airport any more, where we don't get any sort of privacy, particularly with camera lenses everywhere sweating on players showing any affection to their loved ones. As well, there are countless interviews wanted and needed by the television and radio stations and a stream of autograph hunters desperate for a scribble on any piece of paper they can lay their hands on. This is a far from ideal environment to bid a proper farewell, especially for a tour that lasts longer than the usual winter season.

At the airport, I found the boys in a jovial mood, although the fun was tinged with a touch of apprehension and a dash of excitement. This, after all, is the ultimate tour, the pinnacle for any Australian cricket player — an Ashes tour. The group that assembled in front of the Cathay Pacific business-class check-in is the 33rd Australian touring party to the UK, and as such has a chance to enhance the legend of the lads in the baggy green caps. It is a huge honour to have this opportunity and I quickly realised that everyone on board appreciated this fact.

It was great to catch up with the lads once more. It almost feels as if the family is back together again. For some, this is a new test of their characters — Justin Langer, for example, is leaving his six-week-old daughter, Jessica, for the first time. Knowing how proud and doting he is of her, the initial week or two away will be torture for him. But Shane Warne has probably the most difficult situation to leave behind, as his wife Simone is only six weeks away from delivering their first child. Not long after we got through customs, he mumbled to me, 'Leaving this time was the hardest thing I've ever had to do.'

For Michael Bevan and Andy Bichel, this tour will be a new experience — they're travelling as married men. They have been sampling married life for just 13 and 14 days respectively. But, as we all know, we are also married to our profession and 'give and take' is essential for both marriages to prosper.

Marriage is not the only thing new to our squad; appearances have also changed. Fast man Jason Gillespie has returned to his 'Australia's Most Wanted' look, with the goatee making a reappearance, while Michael Slater has gone for a 'George Clooney' haircut. Slats has also added a couple of fashionable highlights that he thought wouldn't be discovered by the boys — how wrong he was! Brendon Julian's new short back and sides has given him an angelic choirboy look. And coach Geoff 'Swampy' Marsh has continued his remarkable weight loss campaign, which began during the just gone Australian season when a caring spectator asked, 'Hey, Marsh, have you swallowed a sheep?'

Without doubt, though, the biggest news of all came from Glenn McGrath, who informed the troops that he is now the proud owner of 34,000 acres (Pigeon said 'acres', not 'hectares') of terra firma, located about 100 kilometres north of Bourke, just short of the Queensland border. This, apparently, is a mere 1000ks from Sydney. Being a country boy, originally from Narromine, his love of the bush will only be enhanced every time he wanders till his heart's content. It is vitally important to get away from cricket during your time off, to clear your head and get back to reality. I find that it makes you refreshed and ready for the next challenge, and it also helps to put everything in perspective.

Pigeon has already asked Swampy whether or not we can have our pre-season camps out on his new property. However, this idea doesn't sit too well for the city boys — our 'living off the land' skills are about as good as Pigeon's cover drive.

In all, the squad has 79 pieces of luggage to be checked in and out throughout the tour. Plus there are our carry-on-board items, which all adds up to a major operation every time we move to a different venue. As for the flight to Hong Kong? The days of drinking and rowdiness on plane trips are long gone, so the journey was a tame affair. The only incident was Jason Gillespie's not insignificant nose bleed due to the change in air pressure, which needed a napkin as well as tissues to stem the flow.

DAY 2 | MAY 11

Hong Kong

THE REALITY OF TOURING life hit home once more as soon as I drew the hotel-room curtains back this morning. Outside was a mass of high-rise apartments and hotels, all jammed into every available square centimetre of land, and all enveloped by the blanket of pollution which hovered menacingly. Meanwhile, down at reception, our team management was experiencing their first problem of the tour, as the hotel porters were refusing to lift our cricket bags onto the luggage van because, it seemed, the coffins weighed more than they did. But eventually we headed off to the Kowloon Cricket Club to prepare for the colony's first-ever one-day 'international', against an 'International XI' including the South Africans Brian McMillan, Lance Klusener and Shaun Pollock.

We had been warned that the game was in jeopardy due to persistent heavy rain that had drenched the ground over the past three days. The playing area was indeed almost saturated in parts, but still in reasonable shape overall, so it was decided the game would be delayed by only half an hour and reduced from 45 overs to 40. The main objective of the fixture was to continue the build-up of some interest in cricket throughout the Asian region; Australia now has a responsibility in this area, as part of their obligations to the International Cricket Council. This game was to be beamed to over 30 countries, via pay television.

The only Australian player unavailable for this game was Michael Slater, who has a slight hamstring strain courtesy of a pre-tour training session. In these sorts of games the boys are all praying the captain wins the toss and bats, purely because it might rain later in the day and save us from fielding for the entire duration of overs.

Needless to say, Tubs wasn't very popular when he informed us 'we're batting second' but, thankfully, our 40 overs in the field went relatively quickly. And, more importantly, they were injury free. Without doubt, the most pleasing aspect of our time

STEVE WAUGH

MICHAEL SLATER AT KAI TAK AIRPORT IN HONG KONG, COMPLETE WITH HIS LATEST PURCHASE — THE NEW TEAM GHETTO BLASTER.

in the field was Greg Blewett's unveiling of a new slower ball, which is delivered in a similar fashion to one of Warney's backspinners. When it came out properly it was a real winner, and seems to be something quite capable of taking wickets.

Tubby's unfortunate recent run of outs continued when it came to our turn for a dig, but nothing much should be read into this. Our innings was a relaxing, carefree one, where luck plays a huge part. Brother Mark and I continued our good form of late, dispatching a few balls downtown. (Literally!!! The ground is miniature by international standards.) Victory was claimed with 10 overs to spare, to cap off a positive day all round for Australian cricket. We'd all had a taste of what lies ahead.

The early finish left us with a couple of spare hours to fill in, an easy task in a city where the shopping is among the finest in the world. I talked myself into buying a mini stereo system, while Slats was given the job of purchasing the team's 'ghetto blaster', in preparation for a few dressing-room celebrations. He didn't let us down; in fact, a few even commented that he might have gone a little over the top when they saw him stagger into the hotel foyer burdened with a box that could have contained a new microwave or possibly even a mini fridge. This, we were proudly told, was reputed to be the loudest, most powerful piece of machinery available. Slats sunk into the lounge chair a contented man, but then we realised that someone would be needed to haul it around. The consensus was that Steve Smith, our fitness guru, was the No. 1 candidate. After all, we argued, he is the one who is going to cause us the most anguish during this tour, so why not pay him back a little!

London

I FELT LIKE A rookie on my first overseas trip when we touched down at Heathrow, at 6.05am. Such is my excitement at being back for my third Ashes campaign. I must admit, the boys looked remarkably smart in their new dress suits, so distinct from the usual pin-striped blazers, as we made our way through customs accompanied by the ever eager press photographers. All were desperate for a

AUSTRALIAN PICTURE LIBRARY/ALLSPORT

A PENSIVE MARK TAYLOR DURING THE FIRST MEDIA CONFERENCE OF THE 1997 TOUR.

shot of Warney, who remains big news over here. I'm sure his every move will be monitored during the next four months, to the point that if he wants any privacy, he'll have to become a virtual prisoner in his own hotel.

It is good to be back at the Westbury Hotel, our home away from home for all of my Ashes tours. Just being here makes things that bit more stable for us. We know we can trust the staff and the management know what our requirements are.

Our first official duty was the traditional media conference, scheduled for 10am in front of every cricket-related journalist, presenter and commentator in the land. Each team member had been prepared for the obvious questions, thanks to a two-hour media training session in Sydney before we left for Hong Kong. Issues such as the captaincy and vice-captaincy controversies were bound to crop up, so Tubs and I had worked out our replies in order to prevent unwanted or unwarranted headlines. Surprisingly though, the normally voracious appetites of the notorious Fleet Street broadsheet journalists for ineffective answers to provocative questions weren't evident. The whole affair ran smoothly, partly perhaps due to the presence of Michael Parkinson, who handled proceedings. And he was clearly expecting the worst — when he declared question time was open, he remarked, 'Okay, let the bun fight begin.'

BRENDON JULIAN (LEFT), MARK WAUGH (CENTRE) AND GLENN MCGRATH GET AN EARLY TASTE OF THE ENGLISH AUTUMN.

The rest of the morning was spent shopping around London and getting our bearings. This was important, as we will be spending a fair proportion of our tour here and it's vital to know where all the good pubs are and, of course, where all the 'golden arches' are as well.

We knew, though, that it wouldn't be long before Mr Smith inflicted some anguish upon us. This afternoon we found ourselves sweating it out on the treadmills and bikes, barely a couple of hours after unpacking our suitcases. For me, the scariest thing was that I almost enjoyed the exercise, while the swim and spa definitely made me feel a tad rejuvenated. Mind you, there was no way I was going to let the human equivalent of an energiser battery know any of this!

This being our first night together in London, we all headed off for a feed at a favourite hang-out of previous tours — a Mexican restaurant called 'Break for the Border'. But what had initially sounded like a good idea turned out to be a somewhat foolish one. Jet lag was beginning to set in, and we all struggled to get through the meal without falling asleep at the table.

DAY 4 | MAY 13

London

I KNEW I DIDN'T feel that flash when I woke from a restless night's sleep. The answer was simple. I squinted at my bedside timepiece, which read 5.36am. Unfortunately, there was to be no more shut-eye, as my body insisted it was a reasonable hour back in Australia and, as such, my day had begun. I resigned myself to the fact I couldn't win the battle. Anyway, there wasn't much point considering fitness session No. 2 was scheduled for 7.30am. The routine this morning consisted of a 15-minute walk to Hyde Park, followed by a one-minute run, one-minute brisk walk, 10 push-ups, 10 sit-ups, each repeated eight times over.

A spot of breakfast was sneaked in before we headed off for our first training session at Lord's (a place that was totally foreign only to Jason Gillespie among our squad). It's always special to get back there and Geoff Marsh summed it up perfectly when he mentioned to me, 'I'm more excited to be here as a coach than when I actually played here.'

Training was low key, the idea was to get all the travel stiffness out and develop a feel for the tour and what lies ahead. These early sessions do have special significance for Tubby Taylor, though, as he has virtually told everyone that he has a month to get his batting right or else he'll drop himself. In this event, of course, I'd take over the No. 1 job.

That scenario is something I haven't given much thought to, which I'm sure many would find hard to believe. One thing I have learnt from playing at this level is that you can't think too far ahead. Nothing is ever guaranteed, so it's always best to play for the moment and not the future. Sure, I would love the top job, but I also hate seeing fellow players performing poorly, as I know how much playing and succeeding at this level means to them and what they've had to sacrifice to reach this level. And Mark Taylor has been not only a team-mate of mine for over 15 years, but a very good friend, too.

The way I hit the ball in my net session was a genuine surprise, considering that I hadn't picked up a bat in three weeks before the cameo in Hong Kong. Most balls found the middle in a morale-boosting session for me, but others were not so fortunate, especially Bevo, who turned in perhaps his worst net session ever. Not that this means anything, because the first week of a tour such as this is basically a period where you need time to adjust to the different conditions. But if, after a week or

AUSTRALIAN PICTURE LIBRARY/ALLSPORT

THE 1997 AUSTRALIANS LIMBER UP AT LORD'S.

two, you're still struggling … then you have to take notice and rectify things. One slight downer for me came afterwards — Smithy must have noticed the extra girth on my waistline after the three weeks I've just spent in the tuckshop and ordered me to undergo another visit to the gym for 25 minutes of bike work and a spot of swimming.

Tonight's team meeting provided an opportunity for the ground rules for the entire tour to be laid down, and for us to briefly discuss and clarify our team goals for the Test series. Everyone is in great spirits, particularly after this afternoon's individual meetings between players and the captain and coach, which from all accounts went exceptionally well. I believe this is potentially a great squad, not just because of the talent available but, more importantly, because all these guys are great blokes. I believe we can create a team spirit that will see us virtually unbeatable over here. Interestingly, today's press comments have been almost gushing in their praise for us. This was nice to read, though I couldn't help thinking that they are building us up, but hoping and praying they will get the opportunity to tear us apart at some stage in the near future.

The day's formalities weren't over just yet, as the tour sponsor, Coke, were hosting a function for us at the very hip 'Café De Paris' restaurant-nightclub in the centre of London. In booking this venue I'm sure the Coke management had more than admirable intentions, but the meal of Spartan proportions, backed up by unknown sauces and extravagant concoctions was not what the boys fancied. My fellow diner, Jason Gillespie, was mortified by the entree of raw tuna in a pepper-based sauce, and refused to even acknowledge its presence on the table. The side salad of 'Lord's grass clippings' and Parmesan cheese received a token stab of the fork before Dizzy dismissed it as being 'absolute crap'. Happily, the situation was somewhat saved by the main-course — fillet steak — although the quantity wasn't what us Aussies are used to. But it did satisfy the taste buds and that, on the night, was a first for most of us.

DAY 5 | MAY 14

London

TIMES HAVE CERTAINLY CHANGED since I began my international career back in 1985. This is typified by the fitness regimes that are now in place. There once was a time when all the players would be curled up in their sheets, dreaming of a nice English breakfast to start off their day, but not any more. Instead, we found ourselves in the foyer of the Westbury Hotel at 7.30am, marshalled together in preparation for a team workout involving running, walking, sit-ups and push-ups.

The greatest benefit from this exercise was just being out in the fresh air and open spaces of Hyde Park instead of the stale recycled air of our hotel rooms. Not everything has changed during my career though, I thought, as I tucked into the bacon and eggs on offer at the breakfast buffet. But then I noticed that most of the younger brigade were settling for muesli and a selection of fruits.

Training was once again on the 'hallowed turf' of Lord's, with all the boys trying to step it up a cog or two. I was disappointed with my own form today, and in particular my lack of concentration and application during my net session. I vowed to myself it wouldn't happen again, bad habits are like a cancer that can spread quickly and affect your whole game before you can get it under control. On a positive note, Mike Kasprowicz bowled with excellent rhythm and movement in an impressive spell that augers well for his tour prospects.

Tattoo continues to hammer me about my midriff, and demanded another extra session this afternoon — 25 minutes on the stationary bikes, followed by a swim and (thankfully) a spa to round off the occasion. When these tasks had been completed it was time to start preparing for tonight's MCC dinner, held in our honour at Lord's — a thought that didn't exactly have us all eager with anticipation. Most of the lads find these dinners hard work, as we are split up, one to a table, and required to entertain a circle of up to a dozen guests. The gents at tonight's function are a part of the elitist

Lord's membership, a club limited to males and with an average age on the wrong side of 55. Consequently, you feel like a school kid in their presence.

I was lucky to have a 'modern thinking' group who were quite entertaining. But the downside came after my nearest companions had extracted enough information about topics ranging from our tour prospects to the England side's make-up; they departed to be replaced by a new group who fired exactly the same queries at me. After three hours I was a shell of a man.

Some of the other lads copped a bit of a blast. Take Andy Bichel, whose table partners suggested, 'You Aussies take this sledging to a new level, you do it far too often.' Bic, of course, came back strongly on our behalf, but it was to no avail. 'It's always in the papers,' he was told, 'so it must be true!' This is always a topic that brings heated debate, and it's hard to break the stereotype that allegedly began back in the Chappell era. To be honest, I always find it amusing that people reckon we need to resort to these tactics. In my experience, sledging is born of desperation and we certainly haven't experienced too much of that sensation in recent times.

But the night was far from awful. Mark Taylor certainly won over the members with his tribute to the great Denis Compton, while our manager, Alan Crompton, gave a detailed account of the great significance of the Ashes in a speech that was probably one of his life's highlights. Crommo enjoys a genuine love affair with this game. The chairman of the recently-formed ECB (the England and Wales Cricket Board), Lord MacLaurin, then gave an insight into the future of English cricket in an eloquent and sometimes eye-opening address, before the audience got down to some serious cigar smoking.

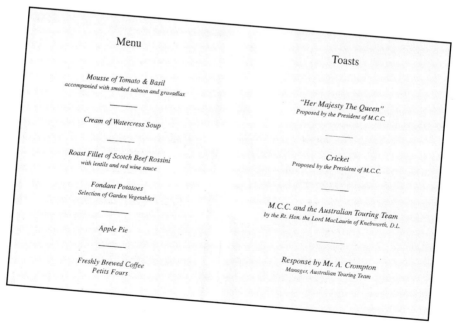

Menu

Mousse of Tomato & Basil
accompanied with smoked salmon and gravadlax

———

Cream of Watercress Soup

———

Roast Fillet of Scotch Beef Rossini
with lentils and red wine sauce

Fondant Potatoes
Selection of Garden Vegetables

———

Apple Pie

———

Freshly Brewed Coffee
Petits Fours

Toasts

"Her Majesty The Queen"
Proposed by the President of M.C.C.

———

Cricket
Proposed by the President of M.C.C.

———

M.C.C. and the Australian Touring Team
by the Rt. Hon. the Lord MacLaurin of Knebworth, D.L.

———

Response by Mr. A. Crompton
Manager, Australian Touring Team

THE MENU FOR THE MCC DINNER HELD IN OUR HONOUR AT LORD'S.

DAY 6 | MAY 15

Arundel

AUSTRALIANS 5–235 (MJ SLATER 50*, ME WAUGH 46, MA TAYLOR 45)
DEFEATED THE DUKE OF NORFOLK'S XI 122 (JN GILLESPIE 4–21)
BY 113 RUNS.

THE TOUR'S OPENING FIXTURE had us pitted against the Duke of Norfolk's XI at the majestically impressive ground located next to Arundel Castle. The only downside was the two-and-a-half-hour bus trip to get there, much of it on long winding roads that had our bus swaggering along like a drunk in the night.

Even at this early stage of the tour the guys have all laid claim to certain seats on the bus, with the front stalls being occupied by team management. Behind them is the '500' card school of Taylor, Warne, Bevan and Elliott, who are seated opposite Langer, Julian and S. Waugh. The remainder of the team are up the back of the bus, separated from the front by a fridge and a microwave. A toilet is down the back. The bus also has three televisions, which come in very handy on the long hauls, especially for those who aren't keen book readers or card sharks.

An Ashes tour always ignites British spectators' interest in the game, and this was quite evident by the mid-week crowd of over 10,000 that eagerly packed in to have first glimpse of the touring Aussies. Slats' impressive unbeaten half-century at the death of our innings signalled not only that he was 'back' but, more significantly, helped exorcise some personal demons that can prey on players who have to come back from being dropped. You never know, this innings may prove to be the singularly most important of the whole tour!

Ominously for England, Dizzy Gillespie claimed a wicket with his first delivery on British soil when he ripped out the off stump of a disbelieving county professional. Many more, I'm sure, will suffer the same fate, as this guy is something special.

Glenn McGrath and Dizzy may even form one of the great opening combinations.

Significant contributions also came from Tubs, who showed glimpses of a return to form, and Kasper, who bowled impressively. My innings was brief, but the 27 runs I scored were made with some authority and I was pleased with my efforts.

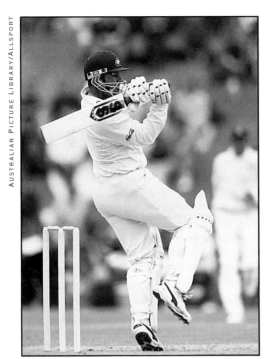

MARK TAYLOR DURING HIS INNINGS OF 45.

JASON GILLESPIE, WHO TOOK A WICKET WITH HIS FIRST DELIVERY ON ENGLISH SOIL.

MY FIRST INNINGS OF THE TOUR, A QUICK 27, WAS A SATISFACTORY START.

DAY 7 | MAY 16

Northampton

THE VICE-CAPTAINCY IS A huge honour for me. And with it comes a single room as a little perk on the side. However, with this extra privacy comes more time for contemplation and I am already finding I regularly flick through photo albums, and think of home and, in particular, my wife and daughter. There have been many times over the past few months, and especially in the past few days, when I've wondered whether it is really worth it all, whether being away from home so much and missing seeing my little girl learn new things is the right thing. But I guess you can't have it all. I am doing something I love and the thing I do best … and getting well paid for it.

On a positive note, when I do get home we inevitably spend a lot of full days together. For us this is quality time, and an opportunity that not many families get.

Back to the real world meant preparing for the first One-day International, which is less than a week away. Practice today was more like it — I was more switched on and came away from the net session feeling in control of my game. However, with this confidence boost came the disappointment of breaking my favourite bat. This bat was the one that scored 160 in the recent first Test against South Africa, in Johannesburg, so it was special to me. But all is not lost, as it will make the journey back to Australia and end up living in my memorabilia room at home.

Lord's came in for quite a shock this morning. During practice, a Los Angeles-based cricket team, made up of street kids possessing haircuts straight out of the Mad Max films, arrived. The story of this team, called the 'Homies and Pops' (after the gang terms 'home boys' and 'people of power') is quite an inspiring one. Their leader, Ted Hayes, is attempting to guide these youngsters to a better life via cricket. He believes cricket is a sport that requires discipline, character and patience, and it also asks you to work as a group. He wants to see these qualities develop among his team, which includes at least one cricketer who has had a friend die in his arms following a 'drive-by' shooting in LA. This is a noble project, but one that Ted Hayes thinks can lead to a USA team playing at Lord's within 10 years. I hope he's right.

In the afternoon, it was time to hit the asphalt again, as our bus, disguised as a Coke billboard, set off on the 90-minute drive to Northampton, which is home, among other things, to the famous Doc Martens boots.

A testimonial soccer match for the benefit of the former Coventry City defender, David Busst, was being played only 30 minutes away from our shack for the night (the salubrious Swallow Hotel). Busst had suffered a horrific double compound fracture of his lower leg while playing for Coventry against Manchester United 18 months earlier. In fact, so grotesque was this injury that players from both sides needed counselling to overcome the nightmares, while Busst has, to date, had to endure 15 operations just to enable him to walk again.

On a typical misty, icy cold evening, a packed crowd at Coventry's home ground, Highfield Road, saw the great Eric Cantona for Manchester United and 'Gazza' (Glasgow Rangers' superb but often controversial England international Paul Gascoigne), as a guest for Coventry, exhibit their freakish talents. Their displays left us (Taylor, Julian, Langer, Gilchrist and S. Waugh) feeling privileged just to be in the same stadium. There is something special about seeing geniuses in action, such as a Maradona, a Viv Richards or a Shane Warne. Invariably a hush comes over the crowd, with everyone anticipating a moment of greatness and no-one wanting to miss it, otherwise it will be lost forever.

Tubby safely navigated the boys home in pouring rain, as we continued to talk of the magic we had just witnessed. And as the windscreen wipers stayed at full speed, it became more and more apparent that a day off tomorrow is a distinct possibility.

DAY 8 | MAY 17

Northampton

AUSTRALIANS 232 (MA TAYLOR 76) DEFEATED NORTHAMPTONSHIRE 5–134
(IN 35 OVERS; MB LOYE 65*) BECAUSE OF THEIR FASTER SCORING RATE.

ONCE AGAIN, I WASN'T woken by the booked wake-up call but because my body thermostat had overheated due to the absence of air conditioning (instead, stifling hot air is continually being pumped out, to please the locals who seem to appreciate the extra warmth).

Outside, though, the temperature did look on the coolish side. A thick mist made it impossible for the sun's rays to penetrate — the type of day an Australian cricketer dreads. And I couldn't help but notice the abundance of rabbits darting about in the adjoining grassland.

Being one of the reserves for today's fixture meant that I, along with Blewey, Heals, Pigeon and Bic, had to make good use of the facilities available to keep us in good shape for the games ahead. So, while the playing team did their usual 20 to 30 minutes of stretching and warm-ups, we hit the nets. The practice wickets were excellent and the time spent on them was invaluable, particularly for we batsman who like to feel the bat on ball in a match-like situation, which can only occur when good true practice wickets allow it.

Years ago, the reserves would have put their feet up and completed no more than routine tasks, such as organising drinks, making sure the autograph bats were signed and generally just checking to see that the guys on the field were happy and ready to play at their best.

The reality of today, though, is that you must do extra work — whether it be in the gym, on the running track, a brisk walk or even some boxing or swimming. If you've completed these tasks you might be asked to go to a sponsor's box, to talk to some valuable clients, or perhaps do a spot of commentary for the television stations covering the game. I managed all three tasks today and have now come to the conclusion I'd much rather be out on the field playing than 'watching'.

The ominous looking weather finally did what it had threatened to do all day, and the game ended prematurely. On the day, though, the better side gained the win, which doesn't always happen in these situations.

One couldn't say we were convincing winners and, to be truthful, we made a lot of basic mistakes, including bad calling between the wickets and some sloppy fielding. Good performances were turned in on the batting front by Gilly, Slats, and Junior, but the most significant was from Tubs, who occupied the crease for 126 balls in scoring his 76. Statistically, this might be classed as a bit laborious, but it was compiled on a testing wicket. Tubs held the innings together, which was invaluable from our team point of view. When you are out of form there is only one way back and that is by occupying the crease until your feet movement, shot selection and timing gradually come back to you. Judging from today's efforts, our captain is on the way back.

Encouraging signs in the bowling department came from BJ, whose rhythm looks great at present, and Warney, whose tempo and control of delivery appear to be nearing the heights of 12 months ago.

Thankfully, our next destination of Worcester was only one hour away, but it did require a pit stop for food. 'Huey', our bus driver, pulled off the motorway and then gave us the bum steer of the year when he cheerfully told us, 'This place sells good food.' That may well be the case if you're looking to add a couple of thousand calories in one sitting, but that I do not need to do!

RICKY PONTING, ONE OF A NUMBER OF AUSTRALIAN BATSMEN FIGHTING FOR A PLACE IN THE AUSTRALIAN ONE-DAY LINE-UP.

DAY 9 | MAY 18

Worcester

WORCESTERSHIRE 5—123 DEFEATED AUSTRALIANS 121 (GR HAYNES 4—40, DA LEATHERDALE 5—10) BY FIVE WICKETS.

IT'S ALWAYS GOOD TO see a fellow Aussie professional cricketer over here and none is more popular than today's opposition captain, Tom Moody, a man who only a few months back was in national colours, playing in the Australian One-day team during the 1996–97 World Series.

Everything about today's game was typically English — from the cathedrals in the distance to the lush outfield, the manual scoreboard, the overcast dull conditions, the chicken curry at lunch and, devastatingly for us, the little 'dinky' medium-pace bowlers who combined to make us look like schoolboy novices.

Arguably the Australian team's biggest weakness in recent years has been our inability to adapt to variances in wickets that we're not used to. This was our nemesis here, as not even one of us came to terms with a seaming wicket against bowlers who on flat wickets would be classed as 'cannon fodder'. Today they were world beaters, or made to look so, due to some lazy and ill-advised strokeplay.

Only Justin Langer had any sort of excuse, for he was 'triggered' (as in, robbed by umpire). These types of decisions seem to follow some players around. It appears commonplace for a player of high standing to be given the benefit of the doubt while players who are trying to make names for themselves are given the rough deal. This is certainly a testing time for Lang, who is away from his newborn child and, after many overseas tours, still trying to force his way into the top XI. Mental strength will be needed for him to succeed on this tour.

We managed only 121, and the depth of our plight was highlighted by the knowledge that the destroyer for Worcester, David Leatherdale, wouldn't normally get a bowl in a Chinese restaurant. However, owing to injuries, he got a chance and tomorrow morning will be able to start filling up his scrapbooks with the newspaper reports of his miraculous deeds.

The news wasn't all bad, though. Kasper bowled beautifully, gaining regular movement in the air in much the same way Terry Alderman did in 1989, and we all know what Alderman accomplished with these attributes.

Big 'Moods' was the hero of the day and the town, leading from the front in compiling 32 and marshalling his troops for a famous victory. From the way the crowd was going off at the finish, you would have thought the Poms had won the Ashes, but when you've been starved of success it does make victory much sweeter when it happens. Hunger is something that will definitely motivate the England side this tour and could well be a crucial element in the overall outcome of the series. For the team that is the most desperate usually wins.

The English squad was announced today. It appears the selectors have changed their priorities and finally plumped for youth. The choice of Ben Hollioake in the squad, at just 19 years of age, after only half a dozen first-class games, is a watershed selection and signals that talent will be recognised and appreciated much earlier by the three 'Gs' (the new English selection committee: Mike Gatting, Graham Gooch and chairman David Graveney). Their squad is full of players I've never come across — Dean Headley, Ashley Giles, Graham Lloyd, Adam Hollioake, Ben Hollioake, Mark Ealham and Chris Silverwood. This probably gives the home team a slight advantage, as we don't know many of their players' strengths and weaknesses while our game is well known to them.

The full England squad is Mike Atherton (captain), John Crawley, Robert Croft, Phil DeFreitas, Ealham, Giles, Darren Gough, Headley, A. Hollioake, B. Hollioake, Nick Knight, Lloyd, Silverwood, Alec Stewart and Graham Thorpe.

After a week of full-on cricket and commitments it was time to let the hair down a bit. We began tonight's proceedings with a team feed at an Italian Restaurant, followed by a thirst quencher or two at a local establishment. It was there that I made my thoughts clear to Malcolm Conn, the journalist who is covering the tour for the *Australian*, who wrote only a couple of days ago that this series was no longer the ultimate for an Australian cricketer and that we were putting on a facade to try to enhance this 'myth'. How wrong he is. This is still the ultimate tour, steeped in history and tradition.

It will always be special.

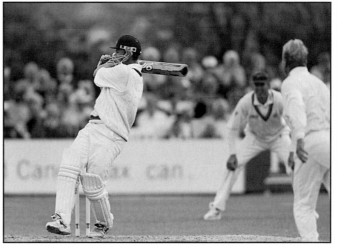

ADAM GILCHRIST AT WORCESTER. IN THE SLIP CORDON IS GILLY'S WA TEAM-MATE, THE WORCESTER CAPTAIN TOM MOODY.

DAY 10 | MAY 19

Durham

OUR FIRST TASK FOR the day was not to pay our room bill or to indulge in a spot of breakfast, but to sign 300 cricket bats for the Test series sponsors. I can assure you there is a distinct difference between the first signature and the 300th scribble. In fact, some players had resorted to initials only as they neared completion.

Our trip to the next port of call, Durham, in the north-east of England, presented us with the longest leg of our adventure so far — four hours from Worcester. Lang, as he always does, looked after the team and purchased a handful of videos that served as a saviour once boredom set in (about 20 minutes into a trip). Meanwhile, the quartet of Elliott, Bevan, Taylor and Warne had just about reached the stage where they would have been eyeing off a spot in the *Guinness Book of Records* — for continuous card playing. I can't recall a solitary moment of road travel that hasn't involved a hand or three. It was with some relief that we finally reached our destination, and once we had checked into our rooms, the lads all headed off in

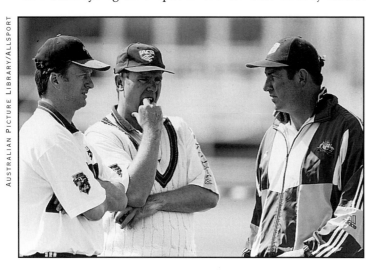

AUSTRALIAN PICTURE LIBRARY/ALLSPORT

THE TOUR SELECTORS — WAUGH, TAYLOR AND MARSH.

various directions for some R&R. Some took to the local golf course, which I viewed as a brave option considering the obscenely cold temperature, while others went walkabout down the cobblestone streets in search of a bargain or two. The toughest ventured to the gym for a workout with Steve Smith, who was going cold turkey after not pumping iron or wearing out a treadmill for the previous couple of hours. My task, along with Swampy and Tubs, was to pick the side for the first One-day International and to have a chat about our initial thoughts on the Test team line-up.

After lengthy deliberations on various options we eventually settled on a combination for the first One-dayer which I'm sure (as always) will leave at least some of the omitted players disappointed. We'll be keeping our decisions to ourselves until after our One-dayer with Durham tomorrow, in case someone puts up a big case for selection against David Boon's new side.

BRENDON JULIAN SETS ABOUT ADDING HIS SIGNATURE TO A ROOMFUL OF CRICKET BATS.

My situation as a selector is a little awkward, as Tubby's ordinary form over the past two years is a topic that just won't go away and one that must be discussed. As a good friend for over 15 years, I'm not comfortable with the fact that I may be the one to end it, as I will be a deciding vote if Tubs and Swampy don't agree on the right thing to do.

I really can't see how the team will benefit if, for instance, I leave Tub out of the One-day side. Then, two weeks later, Tubs will be captain again for the Tests and I will be his vice-captain. This, to me, is not an ideal working environment, as we are in positions where we have to not only trust each other, but also work closely and give each other support.

In my opinion, the selectors back home should be making these hard decisions. My great hope is that Tubs makes some runs and finally squashes all the repetitive talk about his form. The constant speculation is starting to damage the morale and spirit of the side, simply because the issue is one that nobody is able to dodge.

The bottom line is that we would all like to see Tubs play every One-dayer and Test — he's the tour captain and should lead the team.

There are always two sides to any argument. In this case, we have the world's best Test-match captain, who also possesses an outstanding personal record which includes

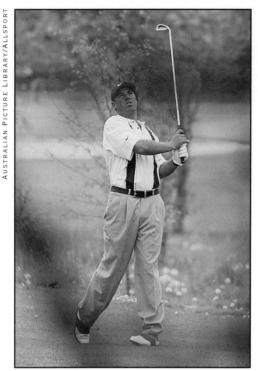

WARNEY ON THE GOLF COURSE ... NOT
FOR THE LAST TIME!

14 Test centuries. On the other hand, Tubs hasn't reached 50 in his last 20 Test innings. I know quite a few journalists think he shouldn't be playing Test cricket. The dilemma is not an easy one to solve. Realistically, Tubs is the only one who can do it — by scoring plenty of runs.

I hope he does.

Warney's tally of Margherita pizzas is mounting by the day, with another two added with ease tonight. Afterwards, it was great to catch up with David and Pip Boon for a quick drink in the bar. After his early-season efforts with the County Championship newcomers, Durham, Boonie has already been labelled a legend in these parts.

Apparently, he has already added some toughness and professionalism to the squad. In due course, I'm sure, he will also enlighten them on the merits of fine Australian red wine.

I JOINED GEOFF MARSH, DAVID AND PIP BOON, AND MICHAEL SLATER'S WIFE,
STEPHANIE, FOR A DRINK AND A CHAT IN DURHAM.

DAY 11 | MAY 20

Leeds

AUSTRALIANS V DURHAM,
MATCH ABANDONED.

AS SOON AS WE arrived at Durham's home ground, the impressive Riverside complex at Chester-le-Street, we knew that there would be no play today, despite the best efforts of the water guzzling 'super sopa' that was busily trying to devour the pools of water that lay all over the outfield.

For Durham, this was to be a day of celebration, with the revered soccer great, Kevin Keegan, due to officially open a new section of grandstand, while the local team would have obviously benefited from the experience gained in such a fixture. From our point of view, quite a few players needed a run to gather some momentum and form. But it was not to be, and the game was officially cancelled even before the scheduled starting time of 10.45am, much to the disbelief of the considerable crowd that had gathered.

It's quite amazing, though, what a few autographs can do to appease a crowd and one sensed that they were now all going home quite satisfied with the day's entertainment. I also felt I had achieved something out of the morning, after I confronted a well-respected journalist and former player, Simon Hughes, about a recent column he wrote, which I believed was out of line. In this article, he gave all the Australian team ratings for 'Style', 'Sledging' and 'Stamina'. It just so happened that I was labelled as not entertaining, a major sledger and not fit, leaving me as the only member to fail in all three categories. Initially, I saw the humorous side to this tongue-in-cheek piece, which, of course, duly found its way into all the Australian papers. I did take exception, though, to the non-entertaining tag and told him so when I spotted him at the ground. Looking very sheepish, he began to try to justify his ratings before changing tack and agreeing he was wrong. He ended up preferring to point the finger at the editor who had told him to spice the articles up a bit. I was glad that I had made my point and he seemed relieved to get his grievances off his chest. The end result, a form of truce if you like, was that I am now the proud owner of a signed copy of his just-released book, *A Lot of Hard Yakka*.

Confronting a journalist can be a hazardous exercise — generally there can only be one winner and that's the person with the pen in their hand. But sometimes I reckon it can be justified. These occasions are when the comments are not backed up by fact, or when the criticism is not constructive, but even then a player rarely comes out on top. As a rule, it is better to remember that one day the story will be wrapped around some fish and chips, while you'll still be out there batting on.

Upon our arrival in Leeds, we were greeted by sunshine overhead, so we immediately dumped our gear at the hotel and headed for the nets at Headingley. It's always nice to return to a ground where you have experienced success; it was here that I scored my first Test century, in 1989, and again reached three figures in 1993. So I made a beeline for the same position in the dressing-room I occupied for those two matches, to make me feel even more comfortable and confident.

Training today was excellent, with everyone realising it was time to up the ante and start switching on. This was best exemplified by Pigeon, who had easily his best-ever net session with the blade, keeping the lengthy queue of bowlers that always seems to congregate in his vicinity wicketless for the first time in his entire career.

Tonight's confirmation of the team for the game in two days time wasn't easy, reflecting the difficulties we faced when we first discussed the side in detail back in Durham. Very few of us are able to say we are in good form, and some are carrying a variety of ailments.

On the batting front, only Taylor and Slater have any runs on tour to speak of, so both became easy selections.

On the bowling side of things, Michael Kasprowicz has been the stand out so far, and he gained the third bowling position, just ahead of BJ, who has also been quite impressive but is carrying a niggling neck problem. Kasper, a laid-back gentle giant, has benefited from the enforced layoff imposed on Andy Bichel due to a back injury. Many say this is fair recompense for events at Bic's recent wedding, where Kasper performed the best man's duties with distinction.

Blewey was almost ruled out because of a dodgy knee, while Bevo hasn't bowled yet due to a cortisone injection he had in his groin before he came on tour. Consequently, we might have left ourselves a little exposed in the fifth bowler department and slightly underdone in our preparation, yet at least on paper we'll start as favourites.

The full team is Taylor (captain), S. Waugh (vice-captain), M. Waugh, Bevan, Blewett, Slater, Healy, Warne, Kasprowicz, Gillespie and McGrath. I'll be batting at No. 3.

It was off to the cinemas tonight for the boys to watch the cult hero of the team, Jim Carrey, starring in his new flick *Liar Liar*. He has been a favourite of ours since we watched *Ace Ventura* and *Dumb and Dumber* endlessly during our recent trips to the Indian subcontinent. Glenn McGrath reckons the Waugh boys are Dumb and Dumber, but I believe if they are looking to make a sequel they should base the story on Pigeon and Dizzy.

Well, perhaps not Dizzy!

DAY 12 | MAY 21

Leeds

THE FAMOUS SPORTS BOOKMAKERS, Ladbrokes, this morning offered the most generous odds ever posted on a sporting event when they quoted 'M. Walsh' at 5–1 to score the most runs for Australia tomorrow. Being the official Australian tour scorer, Mike Walsh is bound to score the most runs and all from the comfort of the scoreboard. But before anyone could cash in on this scam it was revealed to be a printing error — M. Waugh at 5–1 is correct.

Still not a bad bet.

This morning's practice session was conducted in moustache-snapping conditions that sent a burning sensation through our lungs with each intake of air. Each breath out was accompanied with a puff of mist, as we struggled in vain to get the circulation moving. Even Tattoo's warm-up routine didn't get the usual moans and heckles. It was so cold that we were revelling in his guidance and grateful for his input — maybe the cold had begun to affect our judgment.

As vice-captain, and therefore now part of the team 'hierarchy', I am now involved in more functions and meetings than when I was simply a member of the squad. Today it was the turn of the genial Ranjan Madugalle of Sri Lanka (the ICC Match Referee) to underline to both sets of management their responsibilities to the game and to discuss any points of conjecture regarding the playing conditions. This was all pretty straight-forward stuff, more a routine than a learning experience. The only unusual piece of information that came to light was the fact that the IRA may want to gain attention by way of a bomb threat at the ground, although it was stressed that such a situation was highly unlikely. In the case of this actually happening, the security staff would first be told of the threat, then the players and finally the crowd. To lighten the atmosphere, I suggested that a bomb threat wouldn't be a bad tactic if your team was in trouble. All you'd have to do, if things weren't looking good, is give your mate a call and tell him to phone the ground. But alas, it's not that simple — unless you know the IRA's secret code for genuine threats that has to be said before anyone takes any action.

My pre-game routine was pretty much as usual — a reasonable haircut (£12) and a massage (£25) to get me relaxed and feeling fresh for tomorrow. Blewey, though, wasn't so lucky in his search for a decent cut. In fact, he suffered the double blow of handing over £35 and then having to wear a style not unlike the one he had for his first day at school. Needless to say he copped a pasting from the lads all night, many of whom broke out into spontaneous laughter each time his new spiked crew cut came into view.

Generally, before a game the team dines together, just to get that bit closer and tighter as well as to enjoy each other's company. Would you believe it, tonight our chosen restaurant was also frequented by Messrs Atherton, Gough and Croft from the England side, who looked more than a little outnumbered by the 20 or so in our party. As luck would have it, we were seated right next door to them.

MICHAEL KASPROWICZ COMPLETES A FIELDING DRILL AT OUR FINAL PRACTICE SESSION BEFORE THE START OF THE TEXACO TROPHY ONE-DAY SERIES.

DAY 13 | MAY 22

The First One-day International, Headingley, Leeds

ENGLAND 4–175 (GP THORPE 75*, AJ HOLLIOAKE 66*; GD MCGRATH 2–34)
DEFEATED AUSTRALIA 8–170 (MG BEVAN 30, GS BLEWETT 28; D GOUGH
2–33, MA EALHAM 2–21, AJ HOLLIOAKE 2–22) BY SIX WICKETS,
WITH 9.5 OVERS TO SPARE.

BREAKFAST ON MATCH DAYS for me is generally a couple of juices, toast, tea, eggs (either scrambled or fried), tomatoes and baked beans — more than enough to see me through to lunch time in the game. As usual, the last of the tea had to be rushed down, as the bus was waiting …

Not unexpectedly, there were extensive queues already forming outside the ground by the time our coach pulled up at Headingley's gates nearly two hours before the scheduled starting time. That time went like a rocket — it was good to be back playing top-level cricket — and after Tubby called incorrectly, we found ourselves getting first opportunity to put a few runs on the board.

The simple act of tossing a coin has now developed into a major production, with everyone having to wait until the television cameras are in place before the coin can go skywards. Once the toss is won it's straight into a chat with the commentary teams of both BBC Television and then Sky Television, which invariably turns out to be a mini press conference. Only then are the captains allowed to go back and inform their prospective teams of the result.

Our batting performance was indicative of our preparation, with each player struggling to come to terms with the slow seaming pitch. My innings, despite the nature of the wicket, strangely felt like the first of the season, with the ball hitting the bat quicker than I expected. This was due to a couple of reasons — one being the pace of Darren Gough, which was much quicker than anything we'd come across on tour so far, the other was the grey sky and dark dreary colours the crowd were wearing. It all seemed to form a blurry picture. And just when I felt as if I was gaining some momentum and confidence, I played across the line of an outswinger from Mark Ealham and presented him with his first international One-day wicket.

It was much the same for all the batsmen. The statistics told the story — our top scorer was Michael Bevan with 30 as we stuttered to our final total, which was 50 runs short of what we had hoped for at the start of the day. For England, Gough and Robert Croft both impressed. It is already quite obvious that this whole summer is going to be much harder than many English critics would have led the public to believe.

With One-day cricket anything is possible and it appeared, especially when we reduced England to 4–40, that we might pull off a memorable victory. It was then that Adam Hollioake, a guy who learnt most of his cricket in Oz, strode to the wicket to partner the gifted Graham Thorpe. If there's one thing that gets an Australian side fired up more than a Pommie walking to the wicket, it's an ex-Aussie in Pommie colours walking to the wicket, but on this occasion his desire, application and determination proved too much for our attack. In a 'Boys Own Annual' finish he dispatched Dizzy for

THE HOTTEST
TICKET IN TOWN.

GRAHAM THORPE DURING HIS UNBEATEN 75.

ONE ENGLISH
VICTORY IN A
LIMITED-OVERS
GAME ... AND
THE TEST
SERIES IS
ALREADY
DECIDED.

a pulled six to win the match, before swiping the three stumps for souvenirs and careering into the ecstatic swarming crowd as he ran from the ground. To make it even sweeter, unbeknown to him or his brother Ben (who was left out of the starting XI), his Mum and Dad had flown over from Perth to see the game. One can only imagine how proud they must have felt.

Hollioake, was named the Man of the Match, but I was even more impressed by the composure and self-assurance of Thorpe, a guy who has always had immense natural talent without ever quite supporting these gifts with runs on the board. Hopefully this won't be his summer!

It's always at least a little disheartening to lose when playing for your country, but there is more than enough experience in our squad for us to get too down about it. Rather, we have to work on improving our game quickly, so we can fight back in the next two One-dayers, to be played in London on the weekend. To this end, we decided to make the four-hour journey back to the capital straightaway.

We're still all in good spirits.

DAY 14 | MAY 23

London

TWENTY FOUR HOURS CAN sometimes put a better perspective on things. I now realise that England held a slight advantage over us going into the first One-dayer. The fact that we hadn't seen a lot of their players in action, and as such didn't really know their strengths or weaknesses in order to exploit or avoid them, was a bigger plus for the home side than we first thought. Tomorrow we will be better prepared.

The numbers for training today, at The Foster's Oval, were down to 14, with BJ, Bic and Blewey all unable to take part. Blewey's knee flared up yesterday and is of great concern, especially for the moment, as it throws the balance of our One-day side out of kilter. He, along with Bev, has become our fifth 'bowler'.

Once again the practice wickets were painfully slow and once again the press were hounding Mark Taylor about his form. It must be like 'Ground Hog Day' for Tubs at the moment, with the same questions being asked, the same pressures being applied and the lack of privacy continuing on and on. Quite clearly, captaining your country and failing with the bat is not the ideal mix, because you always have to front the press. At the moment, we are trying to unburden him of some of the team's obligations by sharing the media responsibilities.

After training it was time for another selection meeting, with the urgent matter of a replacement for Blewey top of the agenda. And there was the ever-present matter of Tubby's form. It was decided that Adam Gilchrist would be given the nod, replacing Blewett on the back of his encouraging efforts in the One-dayers in South Africa. The remainder of the team has been given the chance to redeem themselves.

The main concern within the team for us at the moment is the constant conjecture and discussions about Tub's lack of runs in the big matches. I guess it's only human nature, considering it's always in the news, but it has to stop or else we'll self-destruct.

The best way for us to get things back on track is to make the senior players aware of their obligations to the team and make sure they kill off any whingeing and discussions of selections as soon as they hear them. The non-sighting of a member of the Australian selection panel, Steve Bernard, is a little intriguing, as we assumed that he would be around to have a chat and exchange ideas. Steve is following the cricket around and I was told he'd been informed by the chairman of selectors, Trevor Hohns, that he may be needed.

AUSTRALIAN PICTURE LIBRARY/ALLSPORT

GREG BLEWETT AT HEADINGLEY, BEFORE HIS KNEE 'BLEW' UP ON HIM.

DAY 15 | MAY 24

The Second One-day International, The Oval, London

ENGLAND 4–253 (MA ATHERTON 113*, AJ HOLLIOAKE 53*, AJ STEWART 40) DEFEATED AUSTRALIA 6–249 (MG BEVAN 108*, AC GILCHRIST 53) BY SIX WICKETS, WITH 10 BALLS TO SPARE.

THERE WAS NO CHANGE to Tubby's recent run of bad luck, as the toss once again went England's way and we found ourselves strapping on the pads first for the second time in a row. And when the game began, the wheel of fortune continued to plot against us. First to suffer the dread of any batsman — the run out — was our captain, who was stranded after a succession of disjointed calls. Three balls later, the Waugh boys were at it again when Mark hesitated for a split second and

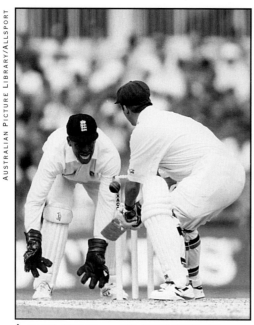

A SLOW DEATH ... MY DISMISSAL AT THE OVAL.

subsequently expired at the hands of an unlikely exponent of the art of direct hits ... Robert Croft. And there were to be a further two calamities of this nature before the innings was complete!

In between these disasters, Michael Bevan produced another masterpiece of mixed dabs and exquisite flourishes, to score an undefeated hundred, while Adam Gilchrist further enhanced his already impressive reputation by scoring 53 at better than a run a ball in a crucial period of the game.

My innings, again, was terminated just when I felt I was about to let the clutch out and accelerate into third gear. Continuing the driving analogies, my dismissal was like being involved in a pile-up on a motorway, where you try to stop hitting the car in front but you can't. I played a perfectly good defensive shot that decided to spin backwards and clip the top of the off stump. In both situations, you do nothing wrong but have to pay the price.

Our final total of 249 looked impressive enough, but we could tell by the English team's body language that they were happy to restrict us to that score. Taking into account the lightning fast outfield and docile wicket, which was getting better to bat on with each ray of sunshine that beamed down from above, you couldn't really blame them. A total of 280 was what we really had in mind, but in One-day Internationals anything over 230 is usually hard to get — especially so if you lose early wickets, which was obviously the key to our chances.

Strike early we did, but our joy was short-lived as Mike Atherton and Alec Stewart slayed our attack at a rate that easily exceeded what they needed for victory. Once again, things weren't going as we had planned, with run out opportunities and tough catches being missed while the bowlers were unable to obtain a consistent line and length. Consequently, we couldn't exert any sort of pressure. By the 20-overs mark, the game and the series had already begun to drift away from us and we couldn't regain any control. In the end, we had succumbed to a player who had been written off as not good enough for One-dayers at the start of the series (Atherton, who answered his critics with a classy century) and a relative unknown (Adam Hollioake, who plundered another 50 before racing off with even more souvenir stumps).

Today's loss was much harder to swallow than our defeat at Headingley. This was because we didn't compete as strongly as we should have. We didn't have enough fight in us, and that is not the way we normally play. Probably the best thing for us was to be present at the handing over of the Texaco Trophy, in front of a crowd cheering for the English and jeering at us. It hit home that this is not how we want the Test series to turn out.

The first task for Swampy, Tubs and I was not to conduct a post-mortem of the game, but to pick a side for tomorrow's 'dead rubber' One-dayer at Lord's. Thankfully, Tubs saved a potentially uncomfortable situation by volunteering not to play. This gives Matty Elliott a chance to gain some touch before the Tests, while Justin Langer will come in for Slats, partly because we feel Lang is a chance to bat No. 3 in the first Test. Slats, I'm afraid to say, now has little chance of making the first Test XI.

The unlucky one at this stage of the tour is Ricky Ponting, who hasn't had many opportunities at all.

But when the touring party has nine batsmen (including Adam Gilchrist), which is one too many, it makes it impossible to accommodate everyone. Fortunately, Punter is a class act and will get his chance at some stage. And knowing his determination and positive mindset, once he gets it, he'll succeed for sure.

For me, the ultimate honour awaited — a chance to captain Australia at Lord's. As soon as I could I rang home to tell Lynette and, of course, to chat to baby Rosalie. I'm missing them so much and wish they could be here for tomorrow's game.

DAY 16 | MAY 25

The Third One-day International, Lord's, London

ENGLAND 4–270 (AJ STEWART 79, BC HOLLIOAKE 63, JP CRAWLEY 52, GP THORPE 45*) DEFEATED AUSTRALIA 269 (ME WAUGH 95, AC GILCHRIST 33; D GOUGH 5–44, MA EALHAM 2–47) BY SIX WICKETS, WITH SIX BALLS TO SPARE.

THE MARYLEBONE CRICKET CLUB (MCC) has some bizarre rules, such as no female members allowed and whites must be worn — even on practice days and during warm-ups on game days. Being an Australian Cricket Board member (in fact, a former ACB chairman), our manager, Alan Crompton, informed us that this second example was to be strictly adhered to, as a courtesy to the MCC. This didn't go down too well with the boys, as we had intended on saving the whites for the real action. Then it was pointed out to Crommo that the English squad had begun their warm-ups with their tracksuits on. Why then shouldn't we? So onto the hallowed turf we went, dressed in the sponsor's product.

I guess these little rules enhance the charm and aura surrounding this venue, and make it what it is. Every time I play here I'm still amazed at its traditions and unique qualities. When you walk out onto the ground you have to go down two flights of stairs, dodging the members chatting happily among themselves, before entering the famous long room. In there you sense something special. Maybe it's the cigar smoke that wafts through the air, or the smartly dressed elderly men adorned with their instantly recognisable 'eggs and bacon' (red and yellow diagonally striped) ties. Perhaps it's the presence of the great WG Grace, immortalised in oils, looking down upon you from the wall.

Whatever it is, you can feel the power. After slicing through the parting crowd, you finally get a glimpse of the fabled turf. Even here, though, all is not what it should be. A slope, from the square boundary on your left to the other, of more than two metres adds still more to the mystique of the arena. To cap it all off, that unique landmark of Father Time, scythe over his shoulder as he removes a bail, remains, although now he is perched atop the new grandstand to the right, having swapped sides of the ground after 70 years in its original location. This is definitely the place to play cricket — you'd only have to ask Justin Langer to confirm this. Lang has visited but never played here before and, judging by his enthusiasm in the warm-ups, he was always going to have the time of his life today.

My two-up skills have always been average at best, so it came as no surprise when my call of heads ended up face down against the batsman-friendly-looking strip. Mike Atherton stayed with his winning formula, electing to have a bowl after including young Ben Hollioake (to make his debut) as well as John Crawley and Chris Silverwood. Two of these guys — Hollioake and Silverwood — were unknown quantities to us and as such posed a threat.

Our batting today was another stop-start affair, with runs coming at a quick rate but, significantly, wickets tumbling at regular intervals. Each time we looked to be gaining the ascendancy, courtesy of a decent partnership, we would lose the initiative through a careless shot or lack of attention to detail. The only exceptions were Mark Waugh, who was excellent, and Adam Gilchrist. Once again, I failed to capitalise on a promising start, falling victim to every batsman's curse — a premeditated stroke, this time an ill-advised cover drive that was caught quite brilliantly by the hot-and-cold Thorpe.

JUSTIN LANGER AT LORD'S ... THE REALISATION OF HIS CHILDHOOD DREAM.

THE ONE-DAY SERIES COMES TO A MERCIFUL END. THE STAND-IN AUSTRALIAN CAPTAIN CONGRATULATES GRAHAM THORPE AFTER ENGLAND'S THIRD STRAIGHT VICTORY BY SIX WICKETS.

Our final tally of 269 looked formidable, but in truth we should have made in excess of 300 on what was the ultimate batsman's paradise. And the outfield was so slick Torvill and Dean would have felt right at home.

Another highlight at Lord's is the lunch. It's little wonder Mike Gatting continues to run around for Middlesex in the County Championship. Each time I play here my admiration for the kitchen staff grows, with today's offering akin to the last supper. Dishes ranged from curried prawns and rice to silverside and hot vegetables, to lamb chops and a variety of salads and pastas. Then, to cap it off, fresh fruit salad or apple pie was on offer for those with any room left. I would love to have been one of those who didn't expect to have to perform deeds of speed or endurance after the interval.

Warney obviously didn't share my sentiments about the quality of the fare on offer. At one point, I saw him tucking excitedly into a roll that had brown stuff oozing out the sides. I soon realised he had helped himself to a makeshift sandwich, complete with a thick coating of butter and topped with a mountain of HP sauce.

Back on the field, things looked to be on the up when Michael Kasprowicz accounted for Atherton early on, and after 10 overs we had restricted them to around four runs per over. But then, rather than increasing the pressure on their batsmen, we went to sleep. Consequently, we drifted out of the game in a rather tame and meek manner. I'm not sure why this happened, but all I know is that it has occurred far too often in One-day International cricket during the past 18 months.

Answers must be found.

I keep coming back to the fact that we aren't aggressive enough and don't seem to have that edge that all hungry teams have. In the end, we only went down with an over to spare, but in reality we were dead in the water from around the 20-overs mark. What is needed in the future is enthusiasm and a ruthless streak, combined with the belief that we have the talent and the courage to express ourselves without fear of reprisals if we fail to come out on top.

As captain, I had to attend the after-series media conference, which was attended by around 50 journalists. It was like being set upon by a firing squad, with questions coming at me like poison arrows. I think I repelled most of them and even had them thinking when I said, 'We are missing five per cent of an indefinable quality that is at present holding us back.'

At the conclusion of any series it's always good to have a beer and a chat with the opposition, so we headed down to the English rooms for a cold one.

It was at this point that we realised how different their situation is to ours. There was no sign of a party.

In fact, their whole team were about to head off in their different directions, to prepare for some domestic one-day quarter-finals. If it were us, we'd have been merry and looking at a worthwhile celebration. It's imperative that you enjoy your success and let some steam off.

The successes are the times that provide lifelong memories. It's what makes playing so enjoyable. For the life of me I can't understand why they don't realise this. I guess it's their loss. In time I'm sure they'll regret it.

After a loss it's always easy to mope around and feel sorry for yourself, or lock yourself in your room and get depressed. We decided to take an alternative approach and go out and have a drink together. As luck would have it, we ran into Allan Border, who is over here commentating as well as performing duties as a supporters' tour group leader. He said that, from the sidelines, it looked as if we lacked our normal aggression. If we were to get back on top, AB reckons, we have to revert back to the way things were. I agree.

AB also told us the story that one of his tour party, who was so disillusioned with our first two losses that he refused to go to Lord's today, as a personal protest against us, even though it was more than likely his lifelong dream to be there. And it had cost him a packet to get to the UK, too. It's more than a game to some people. When you play international cricket you're not only representing yourself, but also millions of supporters. Because of this simple fact, we have a huge obligation to always perform to the best of our ability.

DAY 17 | MAY 26

Bristol

AT A SELECTION MEETING this afternoon, Tubs, Swamp and I had to make a few tough calls so that we can best prepare for the upcoming first Test. We found it nearly impossible to select a starting line-up, especially as the squad has nine specialist batsmen in the ranks. In picking the team for our upcoming match against Gloucestershire we tried to pick as close to what we think will be the first Test team. If we didn't and the next and last match before the Test (against Derbyshire) was washed out, we would go into the Test with one (or maybe more than one) batsman who hadn't played a first-class game on tour. Also of major concern is our mounting injury toll. Bic remains hampered by a lower back problem, Blewey's knee has flared up again and BJ's neck ailment won't improve.

Tubs' lack of form was again discussed, although not at length — it isn't a healthy situation to continually put doubts into someone's mind, which is exactly what happens if we go on about it even if that's not our intention. To his credit, Mark has been very upfront with his situation. He has given himself two county games and one Test match to 'do the business', otherwise he will stand down. I really feel for Tubs at the moment, as he must be continually questioning his self-belief and deep down he must be feeling lousy. However, it's amazing what a few runs can do to turn things right around. Whatever happens, he has acted in a humble and noble fashion. And that, in the long run, is perhaps most important of all.

When we finally completed our deliberations, it was the richly-gifted Ponting and Slater who were unlucky. Our selection strategy means that they will probably not get a chance until after the first Test to show what they have to offer. The one thing we all agreed upon was to inform the guys who miss out exactly why they've been left out, and to try to keep a good solid communication set-up in place. We desperately don't want anyone to become disillusioned.

DAY 18 | MAY 27

Bristol

AUSTRALIANS 249 (SR WAUGH 92, ME WAUGH 66; JJ LEWIS 4–89)
V GLOUCESTERSHIRE.

AS THE TEAM'S NO. 5, I'm normally calmly foraging through my belongings, trying to restore some sort of order to my cricket coffin, when our openers face up to that first ball of the day. However, this morning, during the first day of our match against Gloucestershire, I was forced to speed up this procedure. Sadly, our captain was on his way back to a room which only minutes before had given him best wishes and hopes for a long stay at the crease.

You could almost hear the journos reach for their notepads or begin typing tomorrow's story about how Tubby has once again failed to post the big score needed to extinguish everyone's curiosity on the subject. We, though, had other things to worry about, for both Justin Langer and Matthew Elliott soon succumbed against an attack that, at best, you would call 'honest'.

The wicket was playing as slow as any I've ever seen, which for us was no surprise. It's common knowledge that the local curator was told to produce something along these lines, for two reasons. One, so as to not allow the Australian batsmen to achieve any real form or timing (because the ball won't be coming onto the bat with any pace) and two, so the Australian bowlers can't get any encouraging zip or movement from the pitch. These 'pudding' types of wickets are made for unattractive cricket — they don't do the players or the spectators any favours at all. And to think that the groundstaff only have to roll the pitch for a few more hours to harden it up and make the cricket a much more attractive proposition.

My main concern when I first went in was to fire myself up and not to fall into the complacency trap that is so often associated with these fixtures. Not surprisingly, the lack of atmosphere that results from a relatively small crowd being scattered around a barren-looking ground can make you feel uninspired at times. But this is when you must dig deep and put your professional hat on.

STARTING THE FIRST-CLASS GAMES WITH A BIG SCORE WAS VERY ENCOURAGING.

Despite my best intentions, I did carelessly waft at a few innocuous deliveries early on. I realised I wasn't totally focused on the job, but gradually began to find concentration, and by lunch Mark and I had assumed the ascendancy, to the point that it was some surprise when Junior perished for 66, and then the elder twin for 92. I was a little aggrieved not to make the magical three figures, but my time at the crease augured well for the big matches ahead.

Our total of 249 was, to be truthful, very ordinary and one that must be improved upon in the second innings. Many of our dismissals came from a distinct lack of toughness and discipline — two key areas in the art of batting and things that all genuine top-liners should be accustomed to.

Having scored 92, and with Tubs again under close scrutiny, I obliged the throng of media at the conclusion of the day's play. Once surrounded, I soon realised that my innings was of no real concern. The scribes are totally and utterly obsessed with Mark Taylor. Questions flew thick and fast …

'Will Taylor play in the first Test?'

'Is the team that played today your first Test team side?'

'Will you have to drop him?'

'What's the feeling like in the camp?'

The inquiry seemed to be never ending. It was about halfway through that I realised what it was like for a sheep to stumble into a paddock full of foxes!

Tonight's dinner conversation was much more stimulating than the day's deeds on the field. Justin Langer, Michael Slater, Andy Bichel and I sat down and tried to analyse each other's approach to the game. This is the 'X Files' area of professional sport and, in particular, Test cricket, a game like no other …

Test cricket is an adventure that is long in duration (30 hours over five days), with ample time between each delivery for the mind to wander. Lang, Slats and Bic all gave an insight into their make-up, as did I. We all learnt something and drew inspiration from each other. At one point, Lang suggested that if you want a clear and focused thought, then the obvious way to achieve this state is through meditation. I found his thoughts extremely interesting, because it is common knowledge that when you perform poorly it is almost inevitably due to the fact that you became distracted by previous events or by events you think might happen or you want to happen. The ability to switch on and off when needed is such a tremendous asset to have.

One reason I found Lang's observation so interesting is that, after scoring 170 against Sri Lanka in Adelaide in early 1996, over a post-match beer and chat two of their players asked, 'Do you study yoga and meditate?'

I asked them why they thought this might be possible, to which they replied, 'Because you look like you're in a trance when you were out there batting.'

Concentration is a part of my cricket that I've worked on and my success in this area is, without doubt, the main reason for my success of late. The Sri Lankans' mention of the word 'trance' was interesting, as this is exactly the way I feel when I'm in control and focused. In sport, this situation is known as being 'in the zone'. As far as I understand, it is something that is achieved by very few to a high level.

STEVE WAUGH

It's a state I try to get myself into when I'm out in the middle. And when I manage to get there, I feel as if I'm 'looking in on myself' when I'm batting — almost as if what is occurring at the crease isn't real. But at the same time I'm totally in control.

WHY AM I DRESSED LIKE THIS? THE ANSWER IS ON THE FOLLOWING PAGE …

Bristol

AUSTRALIANS 249 V GLOUCESTERSHIRE 350 (NJ TRAINOR 121, RJ CUNLIFFE 61; SK WARNE 4—97).

PREDICTABLY THE TABLOIDS HAD a field day at Mark Taylor's expense. One tasteless example was a mocking story of Tubs, which had him being presented with a metre-wide bat to help solve his problems. This particularly trashy publication even had the temerity to ask Mark whether he'd be prepared to have a photo taken of him with this cardboard cut-out of a bat. Of course, the answer 'No' didn't stop them pursuing the issue and when we arrived at the ground this morning the cameras began clicking as soon as we hopped off the bus. Surprise, surprise, the guy standing right in front of us was holding up the bat, just at the perfect angle so that Mark appeared to be in possession of the item. I was so unimpressed at this crass piece of work that I confronted the photographer and gave him a gobful, before handing him over to Crommo. I was delighted to learn later that our manager had eventually extracted the offending roll of film from the photographer's camera.

Today, in the south-west of England, had been designated as 'Wrong Trousers Day' — everyone was expected to pull on a pair of inappropriate strides to raise money for charity. We agreed to this request and were duly kitted out in some of the worst threads imaginable. Kasper had the sheepskin daks, while Lang donned a three-legged variety that would have been of more use to at least one West Indian fast bowler I could think of. Tubs chose some 'joker pants', which more than one team member suggested was an improvement on his normal attire. I settled for some 12th-century battle leggings that smelt and felt like they'd not been washed since the day they were created. Never one to miss a photo opportunity, the press boys were immediately licking their lips in anticipation of a good 'mickey take' at our expense. They didn't miss!

This, unfortunately, was as good as the entertainment got. The locals grafted their way to a comfortable first-innings lead, as our bowlers toiled gallantly away on the lifeless track. Here was further confirmation that we had batted very poorly on the first day. No one bowler stood out, but there were encouraging signs from all three quicks (McGrath, Kasprowicz and Gillespie), while Warney enjoyed an extensive bowl that could only help him discover the rhythm he needs.

One ball that stood head and shoulders (if you'll pardon the pun) above all others was an evil bouncer that Dizzy produced out of nowhere. The game was meandering along with none of the quicks really producing anything too lethal when this brute of a delivery reared like a startled cobra and crashed into their opener's helmet. Such was the ferocity of this collision that the ball then cannoned into the advertising boards in the blink of an eyelid. You know a delivery is genuinely quick when your team-mates turn to each other with looks of disbelief that quickly turn into broad grins. Everyone knows it's much better to watch such a ball, rather than face it. This boy will be something special — he's got the quiet composure of an assassin and the steely glinted eyes of a man on a mission.

It's funny how opposites can attract. The close friendship of the Gloucestershire and former England keeper Jack Russell and our own Ian Healy is not unlike the bond between the characters from 'The Odd Couple', Oscar Maddison and Felix Ungar. Heals is of course the meticulous one, fastidious in his neatness and cleanliness of his clothes, whereas Jack Russell comes out to bat in gear that could have been acquired at a garage sale. Jack is a man who some say is eccentric and is somewhat of a recluse. Do you know that his Weet-Bix has to be soaked in milk for exactly 12 minutes? Apart from this meticulously prepared cereal, he exists on baked beans, rice, potatoes, jaffa cakes and digestive biscuits, all washed down daily by at least 20 cups of milky tea. His phone number and home address are known only by immediate family, and he protects his privacy to the extent that a story has been told of a few of his team-mates being blindfolded as they travelled in his car to his home — so that they wouldn't know where they were when they arrived, or how they got there.

The common thread for these two is, of course, wicket keeping. In my opinion, they are the best two custodians in the game today. Whenever their paths cross, they can regularly be seen talking about the game, exchanging ideas and checking out each other's gear. Heals is a keeper who regularly changes his gloves when he thinks they have lost their feel and support. In contrast, Jack at one stage had a pair that had been on the circuit for a full 12 years.

Jack has more than one string to his bow and is, in fact, a well-respected artist specialising in the military and sporting fields. So it was with great enthusiasm that we accepted his offer of dinner at his art gallery. The first thing that struck me when I entered the impressive 'Jack Russell Gallery' was the quality of paintings that hung around the walls. This wasn't a complete surprise to me, as I have half a dozen of his prints proudly hanging in my home (a limited-edition sketch of Sir Donald Bradman being a particular favourite). Many people might think that his work only sells because of his sporting fame, or even through sympathy, but once you've seen how good the final product is, you realise that he is a first-rate artist who plays a bit of cricket on the side. He even suggested that cricket is now almost a 'hobby' for him, that painting has become his main form of work.

His art has become so popular and respected that recently he rejected an offer of £25,000 for one of his cricket works. His sketches, most of which are done during spare moments on overseas cricket tours, start at £750 each.

Inevitably, the talk around the dinner table centred on his paintings and how he became interested in this difficult pastime. The good news for all of us was that it was only 10 years ago that he began as a complete novice. I can accept the argument that if you work hard at something you have some basic talent for, then you can be a success. But then he suggested that it would possible for anyone to reach his standard through simple hard work. I found this statement to be bordering on ludicrous. For a moment I sat there, thinking how I could become the next Picasso, but then I recalled the anguish and embarrassment of many a disastrous performance during family 'Pictionary' games. I quickly and sadly concluded that unless stick figures, cats and houses with chimneys are going to be recognised as strokes of genius on canvas then I was destined to continue as another frustrated would-be-if-I-could-be artist.

Some of the well known, if unbelievable, facts about this intensely shy and introverted man were confirmed during the evening. Dinner for the eight Aussie guests was a buffet of cold meats, salads and quiches. Jack, meanwhile, tucked into a full plate of rice and baked beans, washed down by a couple of cups of milky tea. He also explained that the rumour that he has asked that, upon his death, his hands be embalmed is 100 per cent right. That said, he would also like to continue playing for at least another 10 years on the first-class cricket circuit.

Many say this guy is from way out left field, but I always find him a very interesting and, at times, inspirational character — a man whose personality adds spice and life to the cricket world.

STEVE WAUGH

DINNER AT JACK'S PLACE. LEFT TO RIGHT: BAGGAGE MAN TONY SMITH, JASON GILLESPIE, MYSELF, GLENN MCGRATH, IAN HEALY, JACK RUSSELL, MICHAEL KASPROWICZ, MICHAEL SLATER, SCORER MIKE WALSH AND MANAGER ALAN CROMPTON.

DAY 20 | MAY 29

Bristol

AUSTRALIANS 249 AND 4—354 (DECLARED; JL LANGER 152*,
MTG ELLIOTT 124) DREW WITH GLOUCESTERSHIRE 350.

FOLLOWING TATTOO'S ADVICE, I found myself floundering in the swimming pool first thing this morning. The reason? I was trying to open my puffed-up eyes, which, due to a mixture of the hotel air conditioning and the ever-present high pollen count that inflicts me with nasty bouts of hayfever, had closed during the evening. While I found the swim quite invigorating (eventually!!), the highlight of the morning's activities was undoubtedly the relaxing plunge into the warm spa that followed and then lasted much longer than was originally planned.

Our effort on the playing front today was very encouraging, with Lang and Herb doing a great job in each compiling much needed hundreds. This was not only good for the guys concerned, but also set a tone for all the other batsmen, who until now have been getting starts without going on with the job. Quite often, when someone makes the breakthrough, achieving goals becomes easier for those next in line. It was particularly pleasing for Lang to do well, as he is on the fringe of Test selection — this 'living on the edge' can cause more pressure than being a certain starter. His innings reeked of determination and commitment, and he showed the selectors he's ready and willing to claim a long-term Test batting spot.

The form of Herbie was also very encouraging, especially because he has had little cricket so far on tour. Despite his lack of time in the middle to date, we see him as a vital part of our top-order. He has a technique that is as good as anyone's.

When two players are involved in a lengthy partnership, the rest of the lads tend to relax a little bit more in and around the dressing-room. Recalling last evening's inspirational words from Jack Russell — 'anyone can be an artist, you just have to start somewhere' — the lads decided to give their skills a try. With pencils in hand, Messrs Bichel, Healy and Slater began their sketches of the county ground from high up on the players' balcony, while Kasper attempted a portrait of our long-serving

MATTHEW ELLIOTT, ON HIS WAY TO THE FIRST FIRST-CLASS CENTURY BY AN AUSTRALIAN ON THE 1997 ASHES TOUR.

baggage man, Tony Smith. Within 15 minutes you could have been mistaken for believing a group of pre-school kids had moved in. Slowly, but not so surely, some images did come to life, amid a succession of jibes and hints that rang through the air. The main culprit was Swampy, whose tips were as useful as an ashtray on a motorcycle.

The drawing room (or, as it was formerly known, the players' viewing room) was also the scene of some shenanigans yesterday when the ground announcer fell victim to Gilly, the prankster in the side. It's always good to have a laugh out on the field, and even more so when someone has been set up in the process. Yesterday saw Gilly pass numerous notes to the ground announcer, who eagerly broadcast the messages on the public address. The first announcement came as we began moving to our field positions for the start of a new over …

'Could Harry Dunn please report to the Australian team's dressing-room as soon as possible. Harry Dunn … Could Harry Dunn report to the Australian dressing-room.'

After this call was repeated three times, it became clear that Harry wasn't going to be dragged off the set of 'Dumb and Dumber'. So Gilly, never one to be denied, tried again …

'Could Ray Finkle go to the Australian team's dressing-room urgently.'

Again no reply, and not surprising really. Ray was the ostracised gridiron kicker in 'Ace Ventura'. It would have been a bit of a turn up if he was at the Bristol County Ground.

Another to fall victim to the lads' warped sense of humour was our ever accommodating team manager Alan Crompton, who, at the request of Dizzy, has left tickets for a 'Mr F. Bueller' over each of the past three days. Crommo has no inkling of the joke and has on every day asked Jason for the correct spelling of his friend's name.

Even the cricket action has produced a few laughs, with the unfortunate Richard Davis, formerly of Kent, being the centre of attention. Now here is a man with many lifelong scars. In 1993, Davis became a victim of Mark Taylor's bowling, an event which led to the stinging of a journalist who had backed Tubs not to take two wickets on that year's Ashes tour. Tubby and I both did very well out of that little wager. On the 1989 tour, Davis had to suffer the indignity of having one of his looping left-arm orthodox deliveries fly over the boundary ropes … from a stroke from the sweet caressing blade of Tim May (who had previously never hit a six in any form of cricket, from backyard matches to Tests). Dean Jones had offered 50–1 about this freak event ever occurring. Disastrously for Deano, Ziggy Zoehrer had 10 quid on it, but one had the feeling the embarrassment of the shot caused 'Dicky' Davis even more pain than that suffered by Deano's wallet.

When Davis strode to the crease, we had to let these skeletons of the past out of the cupboard. It was Lang, fielding at short leg, who began loading the bullets. He turned and asked across the pitch to me at silly mid-off, 'Isn't this the guy Tubby got out? And didn't Maysie hit this bloke for six.'

The strain of nursing these catastrophes for four lonely years began to show on his face. I could contain myself no longer, and quipped: 'I wonder what the trilogy of disaster is going to be?' At this point, he finally cracked and began to laugh aloud under his helmet as Warney approached the crease. I think the release of the pressure did him the world of good, and he proceeded to take more than 30 precious runs off our bowling, and helped Nick Trainor to his maiden first-class century.

After the match petered out to a tame draw, largely due to the sluggish nature of the pitch, Jack Russell came into the room to judge the efforts of our debutant artists.

These were his reactions to each masterpiece …

The effort of Andy Bichel — 'What is that?' (Jack was pointing at one of Bic's 'trees' at the time.)

Ian Healy's — 'Is this Heals'? Brilliant … 9½ out of 10.' (It's pathetic the way keepers stick together.)

Michael Slater's — 'Is this abstract?'

Michael Kasprowicz's — 'This is the best — definitely some talent here.'

After these brief appraisals, Slats was the only one who appeared to be disillusioned. 'I was disappointed with his reaction,' he moaned later. 'But everyone's got to start somewhere.'

LEFT: DO YOU THINK THIS IS WORTH 9½ OUT OF 10?

ANDY BICHEL'S FIRST MASTERPIECE … 'GLOUCESTERSHIRE IN THE SUN'.

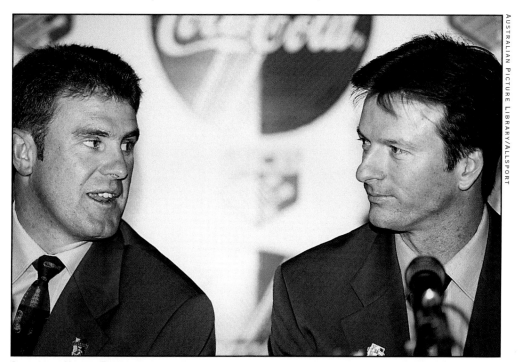

SKIPPER MARK TAYLOR AND ME AT OUR FIRST PUBLIC GRILLING IN ENGLAND —
THE PRESS CONFERENCE AT HEATHROW AIRPORT IMMEDIATELY AFTER WE ARRIVED
IN THE UK.

A BREATHER AT LORD'S, DURING OUR FIRST TRAINING SESSION OF THE TOUR.

THREE OF OUR MOST INFLUENTIAL PLAYERS — IAN HEALY (TOP LEFT), MARK WAUGH (TOP RIGHT) AND SHANE WARNE — AT LORD'S DURING OUR FIRST WEEK IN ENGLAND.

WELCOME TO ENGLAND

GLENN MCGRATH (LEFT), WITH JASON GILLESPIE (CENTRE) AND MARK TAYLOR AT ARUNDEL, WATCHING OUR INNINGS AGAINST THE DUKE OF NORFOLK'S XI.

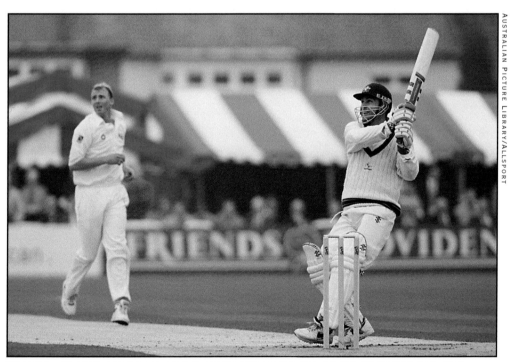

MICHAEL SLATER TAKES TO THE NORTHANTS BOWLERS AS WE PREPARE FOR THE ONE-DAY INTERNATIONALS.

ADAM HOLLIOAKE, ENGLAND'S EXCITING NEW ALL-ROUNDER, DURING HIS MATCH-WINNING EFFORT IN THE FIRST OF THE ONE-DAYERS, AT HEADINGLEY.

MICHAEL BEVAN CONFIRMED HIS REPUTATION AS ONE OF THE ONE-DAY GAME'S MOST EFFECTIVE BATSMEN WITH A BRILLIANT CENTURY AT THE OVAL.

WELCOME TO ENGLAND

RIGHT: ENGLAND'S GRAHAM THORPE AT LORD'S, STEERING ENGLAND TO A THIRD STRAIGHT ONE-DAY VICTORY.

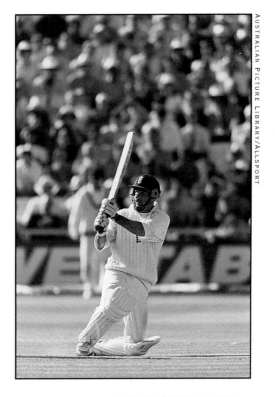

BELOW: ENGLAND'S CAPTAIN MIKE ATHERTON, WHO LED HIS SIDE SUPERBLY THROUGHOUT THE TEXACO TROPHY AND SCORED AN UNBEATEN CENTURY AT THE OVAL.

AUSTRALIAN PICTURE LIBRARY/ALLSPORT

SHANE WARNE (LEFT) AND ADAM GILCHRIST, ON THE LORD'S BALCONY WATCHING THE ENGLISH FANS CELEBRATE AFTER THE THIRD ONE-DAY INTERNATIONAL.

PHILIP BROWN

TED HAYES AT LORD'S. TED IS THE INSPIRING LEADER OF A LOS ANGELES-BASED CRICKET TEAM THAT IS MADE UP OF STREET KIDS POSSESSING HAIRCUTS STRAIGHT OUT OF THE 'MAD MAX' FILMS.

WELCOME TO ENGLAND

RIGHT: JUSTIN LANGER AFTER SCORING
AN UNDEFEATED 154 IN THE SECOND
INNINGS AT GLOUCESTER. BEHIND HIM,
STUCK TO THE WALL, IS THE TEAM
MOTTO . . . 'ENERGY, POSITIVE,
SENSIBLE'.

STEVE WAUGH

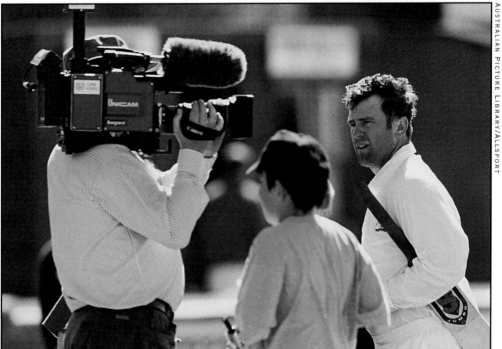

AUSTRALIAN PICTURE LIBRARY/ALLSPORT

MARK TAYLOR AT DERBY, ALWAYS UNDER THE MEDIA SPOTLIGHT.

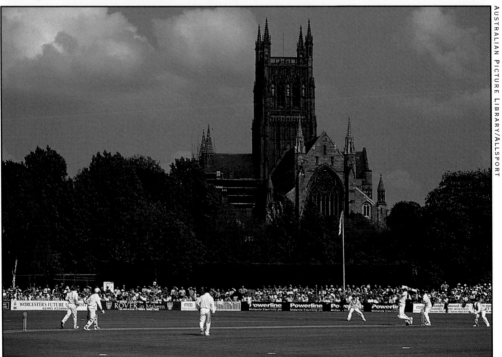

TOP: ARUNDEL, THE TRADITIONAL STARTING POINT FOR ASHES TOURS. **ABOVE:** THE GROUND AT WORCESTER, DOMINATED BY THE CITY'S MAGNIFICENT CATHEDRAL.

WELCOME TO ENGLAND

Derby

I WAS KEEN FOR some sleep on the bus, but was unable to find a comfortable position. So, as a last resort, I decided to venture down onto the floor of the aisle. For a moment I thought I'd found Nirvana, but then a canister full of Jack Russell prints flew across the bus after Huey, the bus driver, slightly misjudged a turn. Consequently, my brow is now sporting a neat little incision over a lump that's increasing in size by the minute.

Our accommodation in Derby was at the Breadsall Priory, a building that had its foundations laid some 700 years ago. Since then, it has been occupied by Monks, Royalty and, some say, ghosts. Well, if it was good enough for them then it will do me, and I settled in for an afternoon of relaxation.

But this only came after another selection meeting had been called, to determine the side to play Derbyshire tomorrow. Our main objective as a squad is to win the Ashes — and we must try and get the Test line-up in good form. The problem of too many batsmen and too few warm-up matches before the first Test has made it tough on a number of players, with everyone feeling the disappointments of those desperate for opportunities. I only hope this situation doesn't lead to any divisions within the squad.

AUSTRALIAN CRICKET BOARD
A.C.N. 006 089 130

MEDIA RELEASE

May 28, 1997

Australian Team Manager Mr Alan Crompton today said he wanted to bring an end to confusion that had arisen in regards to selection of teams for the 1997 Ashes tour.

Mr Crompton said the selection of Australian teams for the tour was consistent with long-standing policy and was entirely the responsibility of the three appointed tour selectors -- captain Mark Taylor, vice-captain Steve Waugh and coach Geoff Marsh.

Mr Crompton said that Taylor, Waugh and Marsh did not need to consult with the Australian Cricket Board or the Australian Selection Panel in regard to any match decision it made on tour.

Issued by:
Alan Crompton
Australian Team Manager

DAY 22 | MAY 31

Derby

AUSTRALIANS 6–362 (DECLARED; MTG ELLIOTT 67, GS BLEWETT 121, MG BEVAN 56) V DERBYSHIRE 1–68.

UNDER NORMAL CIRCUMSTANCES, THE 10-minute drive to the ground would have been a relaxing part of the day — perhaps spent browsing through the papers or having a chat with the boys. But not today. Flicking through the business section of the broadsheet, *The Daily Telegraph*, I noticed a headline featuring my name.

What was in print underneath, I couldn't believe. It had been reported that I had been involved in an argument, in a bar room in Bristol at 4.30am, with a top 'Marks and Spencers' executive.

This was a straight lie. Not only had no such argument ever taken place, but on the night the affair was supposed to have happened, I had gone to bed at 11pm. This report demonstrated, once again, how too many people over here never let the truth get in the way of a good story.

When we arrived at Derbyshire's home track, the Racecourse Ground, we discovered that their fast bowler, Devon Malcolm, who looks certain to be part of the English attack for the first Test, had been ordered to sit this game out by the chairman of England selectors, David Graveney. It is quite clear they didn't want us to have a close look at Big Dev before next Thursday. We all found this a little strange, especially as he's well known to all of us and, now that he's not playing here, he will not have had a bowl in a match for two weeks before the Test begins. I guess only time will tell whether his 'resting' is a smart move!

One thing that is certain is that Derbyshire's captain, the Victorian and former Australian batsman, Dean Jones, was furious when he learnt that his No. 1 strike bowler was out. Deano is desperate to win against us, not least because each county has been offered the incentive of a £9000 cheque if they defeat the Aussies. Our purse for victory is a less impressive £2500, which doesn't go far split between 17 players.

But at this stage we'd be very grateful to receive anything, as the amount of cash in the pool at present is £0.

On yet another slow seaming wicket we elected to bat first. Again, we were in immediate trouble, as the steady local attack accounted for Justin Langer and Mark Taylor before either could reach double figures. Thankfully, though, Greg Blewett and Matthew Elliott steadied the ship to have us nicely placed at the luncheon interval, with both players improving with each minute spent at the crease.

This was a day full of surprises, and the biggest came during the lunch break, when we were served an excellent curried chicken and rice dish. This easily eclipsing the gourmet delights we were offered in 1993 — a baked potato with bolognaise sauce on day one, a slab of pizza on day two, and a spartanly-proportioned cold meat salad on day three. The club was experiencing financial problems at the time.

For most of the afternoon the bat dominated the ball, as most of the lads gained some confidence-boosting form.

Blewey drove with such precision and grace that even the locals rejoiced it its splendour. Matty Elliott continued his important learning process on these wickets, which are so much slower than the ones he's used to at home.

My 43 was compiled in a competent enough manner, but my dismissal was an example of poor shot selection and poor concentration, which disappointed me greatly. My shot was premeditated and speculative, which meant that the outcome was virtually guaranteed.

I guess I should be able to learn from what was going through my mind in the lead-up to the shot … and hopefully not repeat the mistakes again.

It was good to see Bevo and Heals also make worthwhile contributions that completed a pleasing day for most of our batsmen.

Our quick scoring enabled Tubs to declare with a little under an hour left to play, which gave Andy Bichel an opportunity, bowling alongside Brendon Julian, to compete for the third fast bowler's spot in the Test team. However, both bowlers looked underdone, with the very obvious result being quick runs from the Derbyshire blades. Bic appeared to be suffering at the moment of delivery, falling away marginally and not following through with his usual gusto. Perhaps this was because he's a little wary after his problems and doesn't want to incur another setback.

For his sake, I hope this is the case and that his problems today are not indicative of a more serious ailment.

BJ claimed the only wicket we took before stumps, but he wouldn't have been overly happy with the blend of good and bad deliveries he offered. But that mixture can be his strength, as he regularly produces a wicket-taking ball just when a batsman thinks he has his measure. BJ is known in cricketing circles as a 'wicket-taking bowler' and, as such, is a very valuable commodity.

DAY 23 JUNE 1

Derby

AUSTRALIANS 6–362 (DECLARED) AND 2–148 (MA TAYLOR 59*,
MG BEVAN 58*) V DERBYSHIRE 9–257 (DECLARED; MR MAY 67,
BP JULIAN 3–88); AUSTRALIANS 2–148 (TAYLOR 59*, BEVAN 58*).

WE RECEIVED UNFORTUNATE NEWS this morning — Bic has experienced more problems with his lower back and the top of the buttock area, which have ended his role in this match and also destroyed his chances for a spot in our side for the first Test. One thing that did cheer us up a little was the weather. The blue sky and mild conditions were much appreciated, especially here at Derby, where a cold wind on the open ground can make life very uncomfortable.

It has been said that you never know how good someone is until they are given a chance. This theory was confirmed today by the Derbyshire opener Matthew May. During the 1996–97 English off-season, May tried his luck at St Kilda, Warney's district club in Melbourne, where the selectors placed him in their third-grade line-up. Three months later, here he was taking on the Aussie new-ball attack and putting up a formidable display. He split the field with some beautifully timed square drives, albeit among a few flashy play-and-misses, but the bottom line was he was having a go and making a good fist of it. His dismissal, however, was followed by one of the most bizarre incidents I've ever come across in my 13 years as a professional cricketer.

The culprit was the new batsman, Chris Adams, an opener with credentials that clearly warrant monitoring by the English selectors. The incident occurred when Warney pushed through a quicker leg break that skidded onto the batsman, forcing him to hurry an attempted leg glance. The result was a flurry of bat, pads and ball being interwoven into a split second — in fact, Adams probably managed to get the faintest of edges onto the ball, which then raced away to the fine-leg boundary. However, from the bowler's end, it appeared as if the ball may have struck the pad before the bat, hence the confident appeal for lbw from Warney and the decision of the umpire in favour of that appeal.

Adams, who had been running what he thought was a legitimate single, stopped dead in his tracks not far from the umpire. The poor bloke then begged for some sort of

TWO VIEWS OF THE CONTROVERSIAL DISMISSAL OF DERBYSHIRE'S CHRIS ADAMS.
TOP: TUBBY AT THE FIRST SLIP AND HEALS BEHIND THE STUMPS STIFLE THEIR
APPEALS AS THE BALL RUNS DOWN TO FINE LEG. BOTTOM: ADAMS ON HIS WAY FROM
THE FIELD, AFTER BEING GIVEN OUT LBW.

pardon from the ump, continually pointing to his bat. Finally, he began to dawdle backwards towards the pavilion, but not before stopping next to our huddle to ask,

'You're not going to take that are you? Aren't you going to call me back?'

The reply was not the one he was looking for. It went something like this … 'No way, you're out, it's the umpire's decision. See you later.'

Like a little boy scorned he replied with, 'You cheats! You Aussies are all cheats!'

If Adams wasn't sure about his chances of a recall, after that remark we made sure he was quickly made fully aware of our stance towards his dismissal. Finally, he began the lonely walk off the ground, somewhat slowed by the tail between his legs that dragged along the ground. Getting what you think is a bad decision is always hard to

accept, but the way you accept the umpire's verdict generally says a lot about your character. Although we all have our moments, common sense says that once you've been given out you may as well go quickly, because the decision will not be reversed. Any objection makes you not only look ridiculous, it also damages your reputation.

To Adams' credit, once he had some time to think about his behaviour, he did apologise to Mark Taylor during the luncheon interval, and in doing so won back some admiration from all concerned.

This wasn't the only notable incident of the morning session, with the other belonging to Greg Blewett. For a man blessed with abundant natural talent, Blewey has of late been catching with a style similar to that of a blind beggar asking for cash on the streets of Bombay. His attempt today to reel in a top edge left him with nothing more than a handful of high pollen count and an ego that may not be able to take much more ridicule from the boys. Needless to say, Blewey was pretty timid and decidedly quiet for the remainder of the session; no doubt he was deep in thought, trying to come up with some excuse for when we probed him over the luncheon table.

However, he had nothing inventive to say while we tucked into a pasta dish of moderate quality. The best he could do was that oldest of all excuses, 'The sun was in my eyes.'

The afternoon session was another reasonable one for us. All the bowlers snared a couple of 'poles', but, as it had been in the morning, it was not the actual cricket that provided the entertainment. This time we found ourselves closely observing the unusual mannerisms of Derbyshire's keeper, Karl Krikken, while he was at the batting crease. I've never seen a guy fidget with his gear more than this guy, so Warney and I decided to put a count on his touches between deliveries. His best effort was an extremely impressive 23, with his protector and helmet coming in for the harshest of treatment.

Our second innings began somewhat shakily, with Herb and Lang barely troubling the scorers. However, the most notable incident came when Dean Jones dropped a straightforward catch at first slip … from the blade of Mark Taylor when Tubs had only a single to his name.

This missed catch may well prove to be the most crucial single moment of the entire tour. Mark finished the day unbeaten on 59, and it appeared that his confidence and strokeplay were improving as each ball passed. Another failure here would have seen our captain go into the Test under enormous pressure to succeed, without him having enjoyed any reasonable recent time in the middle.

During the day, the English side for the first Test was announced. There are no real surprises, perhaps with the exception of uncapped Mark Butcher instead of Nick Knight at the top of their batting order. In my opinion, it looks a well-balanced and in-form squad. The full side is:

Mike Atherton (captain), Mark Butcher, Andy Caddick, John Crawley, Robert Croft, Mark Ealham, Darren Gough, Adam Hollioake, Nasser Hussain, Devon Malcolm, Alec Stewart, Graham Thorpe and Phil Tufnell.

DAY 24 | JUNE 2

Derby

AUSTRALIANS 6–362 (DECLARED) AND 4–265 (DECLARED; MA TAYLOR 63, MG BEVAN 104*, BP JULIAN 62) LOST TO DERBYSHIRE 9–257 (DECLARED) AND 9–371 (AS ROLLINS 66, CJ ADAMS 91, DM JONES 56; SK WARNE 7–103) BY ONE WICKET.

IN AN EFFORT TO make a result possible, we raised the tempo during the morning session. Michael Bevan effortlessly compiled another hundred, while Brendon Julian gave all present a demonstration of his prodigious ability by slamming 62 from only 49 balls. The result was an equation that left the locals chasing 371 off 66 overs, on a batting-friendly wicket and with a slick outfield to help them.

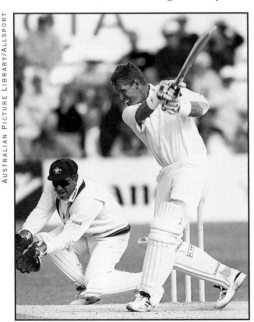

AUSTRALIAN PICTURE LIBRARY/ALLSPORT

DEAN JONES HITS OUT, AS HE LEADS DERBYSHIRE TO A RARE VICTORY BY THE COUNTY OVER AN AUSTRALIAN TOURING TEAM.

We were confident of gaining our first first-class win of the tour, even though we were without the services of Bic. However, after just a couple of overs we were missing Dizzy as well, after he complained about a sore foot. But though these guys were absent, we should have played much better than we did. From very early on we appeared in trouble, as shoddy fielding, undisciplined bowling and poor body language strangled our cricket.

To me, it feels as if the team is operating like a car being driven around with its hand brake on. The result was a history-making win for the home side and a soul-searching loss for us, with the only good news to come out of our display being Warney's seven wickets. Strangely, in the end, despite our numerous lapses, we still had many opportunities to grab a victory.

But although only one wicket separated the teams at the end, we know we have to re-assess our approach to our cricket, or else it's going to be a long tour.

The atmosphere in the change rooms at stumps wasn't exactly the way brother Mark and I had intended to celebrate our 32nd birthdays, but our mood was cheered up a little by the cakes presented to us by our tour sponsors, Coke. Later on, during what was a fairly subdued evening journey down to Birmingham, Swamp and I had a bit of a chat about the current state of affairs. We agreed that the squad lacked a bit of hunger and, crucially, that the team's spirit seemed to be lacking that little bit of something that, when it's there, you don't try to think about what it is.

Later in the trip there was some hilarity, though, when Herb relived the catch in the outfield he took off a no ball during today's play. Unaware that he had taken an 'illegal' catch, Herb began to celebrate by mockingly raising the ball in triumph towards the commentary box. He was aiming specifically at the former England fast bowler and now commentator, Bob Willis, who had earlier made reference to Herb's fielding by remarking that 'Elliott's been to the Phil Tufnell's school of fielding'. Rather embarrassingly for 'Bill Lawry's love child', his animated celebrations gave the Derbyshire's batsman an opportunity to scamper through for a second run before the 'pill' was finally returned to the keeper. At the time we all found it quite amusing, retold again it was doubly enjoyable!

THIS IS BIRTHDAY NO. 32 FOR MARK AND ME.

DAY 25 JUNE 3

Birmingham

BY THE TIME WE assembled in the lunch room at Edgbaston, the time had finally come for a few home truths to be explained to the squad. Swampy left us in no doubt as to what was expected from each of us. His major theme was that it is fatal to wait for someone else to do 'it'; we all have to put our hands up. More discipline is needed from everyone, combined with greater attention to detail and a desire to have fun. It really all comes back to a commitment — do we really want to be here and help Australia to win.

The coach's comments must have hit home, because the intensity and enjoyment at training afterwards was a dramatic improvement on what we have being doing lately. I, for one, felt much more positive, and much more confident afterwards that I had gained something from the session.

It was time to relax this afternoon, so quite a few of us headed for the highly-regarded Belfry golf course. Unfortunately, though, the round turned nasty, and later in the clubhouse the foursome of Bevan, McGrath, Gilchrist and S. Waugh were seen squabbling over a series of incidents.

The ground rules had been laid down early … no 'gimme' putts and unlimited sledging. The wager was £10 for the first nine holes, another £10 for the second and a further £10 overall. Two teams — Bevan and McGrath versus Gilchrist and Waugh, with Gilly getting a shot on each of the four toughest holes on the course.

The early pace was set by the bad guys, who bolted to a two-hole advantage before my grip began to resemble anything like that suggested in the coaching manuals. To compound matters, Gilly was having serious problems with his rhythm, no doubt the result of the fact that he only plays a couple of rounds each year.

So it came as a major shock to our opponents when 'Happy Gilchrist' (as in 'Happy Gilmore') suddenly sank a monster putt from the uncut rough surrounding the green without even checking the speed and undulations of the putting surface or before anyone had time to man the flag. It was a spectacular effort, and proved to be the catalyst for a much improved showing by Gilly and I in the holes leading up to a brief half-time break (and a much needed calorie injection, courtesy of a couple of Classic Magnum ice creams).

However before the Magnums could be unwrapped, Gilly nearly managed to assassinate a group of corporate clients having a quiet drink well away from the ninth green. What was supposed to be a delicate, lofted approach instead became a 'scud' missile — those guys will never know just how close they came to tragedy.

Perhaps my partner was shaken by all this (I certainly was) and the 10-minute breather after the ninth did nothing for our games, to the point where we found ourselves four holes down with seven to play, against a duo that had demonstrated many times that they would stop at nothing to gain victory. More than once, we suspected that they had resorted to ball swapping, illegal drops, even dubious mathematics at the conclusion of holes. At the 12th, though, came a turning point. McGrath, in trying to run over Gilly's ball with his motorised buggy, actually knocked it back out onto the fairway. We made the most of our luck from here and came storming back to claim successive holes.

At the crucial 17th, McGrath carelessly back-handed a half-metre 'tiddler', and saw it trickle past the hole. Quick as he could, he snatched at the offending ball, hoping, no doubt, that no-one had seen his miss. No such luck, Pigeon! Then he tried the 'what no-gimme rule?' line. Then he argued that his marker had been moved while he helped Bevo look for his ball in the deep rough at the back of the green. This heated debate continued as we marched, all square, to the all-important 18th tee.

Even now, as I write the story of this unsavoury affair, I can't quite piece together everything that went on. Suffice to say, it was a complete shambles.

Lost balls were miraculously found, balls flew into the water traps, shots were re-taken for the most absurd and bizarre reasons. The arithmetic at the end was flawed, to say the least. And then, after all the scores had somehow been agreed upon, 'Happy Gilchrist' revealed to our devastated rivals that the 18th was one of the four toughest holes on the course. What had looked like a deadlock was, in fact, a victory for the good guys. The arguments continued long into the night, and in the end our vanquished opponents had no choice but to ask for a re-match at St Andrews, later in the tour.

While we were having dinner at the club, Swampy showed us a motivational video-tape, which featured some golden moments from our cricket during the past 18 months. The jewel in the crown, however, had nothing to do with cricket but everything to do with glory and achieving your goals. It was footage of Kieren Perkins winning the 1500 metres freestyle at the Atlanta Olympics, and included Kieren's inspirational words during his post-race interview.

Watching that great swim … it felt good to be an Aussie!

DAY 26 | JUNE 4

Birmingham

ALL 22 OF US — players and support staff — assembled in the 'gers' room at 8.30am. The purpose of the meeting was to spend time thoroughly assessing our opponents, via a highlights tape that our management had acquired for quite a hefty sum. We also witnessed one of the best motivational speeches I've heard, from Ian Healy. It turned out to be one of the longest team meetings I've ever been a part of, but it was also one of the most searching and probing, as we attempted to dismantle the opposition, exposing their weaknesses and recognising their strengths. Only time will tell whether we tried to cram too much information into our skulls or whether such a process will prove to be a masterstroke. All I know is that, in Test cricket, it takes discipline and patience to come out on top. Combine that with a thorough knowledge of what the other side can and cannot do, and you can't go too far wrong.

Training sessions the day before a Test match tend to take on extra significance, as the players involved try to duplicate what will be expected of them come match day. This is part of the process of trying to peak at the right time, which isn't as easy as one might think. You want to feel as physically fit as possible — perhaps by taking it a little easier at practice or by making sure you get exactly the right treatment for a niggling injury. Cutting down on alcohol and making a big effort to eat correctly can also give you that little extra edge that could make the difference.

For a batsman, this is time to switch on, to get those feet moving a fraction of a second quicker. In the nets, you might think about where the fieldsmen are likely to be, and then try to hit the ball into or through the gaps. For a bowler, the day before a Test is when you want to be slotting into a nice rhythm, and pitching the ball into the 'danger areas' on a regular basis. Finding the right length is the key for most bowlers.

Sometimes, for various reasons these objectives are impossible to achieve — a batsman might be hindered by poor practice wickets, for example. Unfortunately, this

SHANE WARNE (AT BACK) TAKES A BREATHER DURING OUR PREPARATIONS FOR THE FIRST TEST.

is exactly what we encountered at the nets this morning, with balls deviating in unplayable fashion, complemented by every batsman's nemesis. Uneven bounce. All such conditions do is deflate a batsman's confidence and also give the bowlers an unrealistic view of how they're performing. But, despite the lousy conditions, I was happy with my form and, most importantly, came out of the nets feeling more positive than when I went in.

One player who did turn in an unusually poor net session was brother Mark, who got out a number of times and seemed ill at ease with the whole situation. To be fair to him, his turn came late in the practice, by which time the wickets had deteriorated to a very poor standard. It will be interesting to see how he fares after such a negative experience the day before such a big match, and whether he can just turn it on when he has to.

The press from home has once again been very negative and extremely hurtful. Both Ian and Greg Chappell and, to a lesser extent, Bob Simpson have written less than favourable articles about the situation Mark Taylor is currently facing.

Tubs is not quite his usual positive self, although he remains very determined and anxious to turn in an inspiring performance. During a brief breakfast conversation, I suggested to him, 'Don't worry too much about the outcome and remember whatever happens, it is meant to be!'

Tubs agreed and replied, 'I'll just try to really enjoy the game, and not put too much pressure on myself.'

First Test — Day One
Edgbaston, Birmingham

AUSTRALIA 118 (SK WARNE 47, AR CADDICK 5–50, D GOUGH 3–43)
v ENGLAND 3–200 (N HUSSAIN 80*, GP THORPE 83*)

THIS IS WHAT IT'S all about. The first day of the first Test of an Ashes series — something the average cricket fan would die to be a part of.

As always, the bus trip to the opening day was a subdued affair, as players ponder what lies ahead for them. Many questions will be answered here ...

Can Mark Taylor regain the form that saw him at the forefront of the world's opening batsmen?

Will Matthew Elliott have the big series everyone expects of him?

Can Michael Bevan confirm his place in the Australian middle order, batting in a country he knows well and has succeeded in during the past couple of county seasons?

Will Mark Waugh's recent comments about England being 'soft' ring true?

Can Shane Warne take more Test wickets this time than the 34 he took in 1993?

These and many more puzzles will be solved in the next three months. Everyone has expectations and aspirations — some will be fulfilled, others won't. To get us in the mood, coach Geoff Marsh played a motivational tape which featured some of our recent Ashes triumphs, and also showed a video of The Don and some other greats who've worn the baggy green.

We always get to the ground on the first day of a Test 15 minutes earlier than on the later days, mainly so we can get our gear and our places in the dressing-room sorted out. This also gives us a chance to soak up the first-day atmosphere and all the activity that's going on around us. The ground is always a hive of activity on the opening morning, with television crews everywhere, commentators, match referees and cricket officials scurrying about, and the state of the centre wicket the focal point of most conversations.

I felt our warm-ups were a fraction flat. Perhaps it was because the crowd was well below the expected full house at this point — there were still thousands queued up outside, waiting to get through the turnstiles. A closer inspection of the pitch revealed it wasn't as flat as it could have been. Here was a mixture of grassy and bare patches, with the green bits soft and the brown areas much harder. This suggested a wicket with uneven bounce. It appears the mower and the roller have both bypassed the 'lower' parts of the wicket, which therefore remain soft and encourage grass growth while the 'higher' parts are rolled and cut, and firm up as a result. On this type of wicket, you are generally better off batting first, as the unevenness becomes more noticeable as the impact of the pre-game rolling begins to diminish during the game's latter stages.

The first battle was won by us when Mark Taylor called correctly at the toss. He elected to bat first, to see what England might throw at us.

The first ball of the Test was a sign of things to come, with our captain being comprehensively beaten outside the off stump by a Darren Gough delivery. A huge, collective sigh of disappointment filtered through the home crowd. From this moment on, the cricket was like a nightmare for us, except we couldn't wake up and pretend it wasn't happening.

If anyone had said that after 18 overs we would be 8–54 they would have been sent straight to a shrink. Mind you, the way we played we certainly needed help of some kind, and it was only due to a fightback from Shane Warne that we managed to scramble past the 100 mark. Six overs after lunch and the embarrassment was complete. All out 118.

It was a highly professional display by the English attack, backed by a hunger in the field that I have rarely seen from our Ashes adversaries in recent times. Capping off

SHANE WARNE IS ABOUT TO BE CAUGHT AT THIRD MAN TO END AUSTRALIA'S FIRST INNINGS. IN THE BACKGROUND, THE SCOREBOARD TELLS THE STORY OF THE DREADFUL COLLAPSE.

their inspired performance was the execution of what appeared to be an overall strategy that involved different game plans for different individuals.

Taylor went to a ball of full length, angled across him. Matthew Elliott was bowled between bat and pad as he overbalanced. Michael Bevan fell to a short ball, aimed at his armpit, Mark Waugh bowled as he remained anchored to the crease. I was tested out with bowling of a much fuller length than I've faced in the past couple of years — it was obvious they were trying to catch me out playing back early on. Eventually I edged an excellent Caddick delivery to the wicketkeeper.

We'd been caught offguard, at a time when we haven't been playing well. Looking ill-prepared, we failed to pay sufficient attention to detail and didn't appear fully switched on or ready for our confrontation with the enemy.

For England, Caddick walked away with a 'five-for'. He bowled intelligently, swinging the ball away from the right-handers and also took advantage of the extra bounce that his height allows him to generate. However, the bowler who really fired things up was Gough, who charged in, hit the wicket hard and varied his pace cleverly. Perhaps most importantly of all, he revved the home supporters up with his theatrical appeals and animated celebrations. This created the most impassioned support for an English cricket team I've ever heard on English turf.

We needed some inspiration from our new-ball attack, and for a while things looked to be turning our way, as Atherton, Mark Butcher and Alec Stewart all fell. Then came what might easily be seen as the turning point of the Test.

From the first ball he received, the left-handed Graham Thorpe tried to fend off a rising delivery, only to see it fly off a thickish edge through the gap between third slip and gully — a spot that had been filled when the right-handers were on strike. For Thorpe, that fieldsman had been shifted to a leg-gully position, to wait for an 'evasive' jab off the ribs. The score then was 3–50. Our only other sniff of a wicket before stumps came when Bevan spilt a difficult chance behind square leg, when Thorpe mistimed a flick off his legs, but apart from these two opportunities, Thorpe and Nasser Hussain played superbly. Their aggressive outlook continued on from their team's performance in the field earlier in the day, and a lead of 112 to the Englishmen, with seven wickets still in hand, was a fair indication at the end of the day of the difference between the teams.

Sitting in the change rooms after play, it felt as if we'd been had by a pickpocket. In all my years in the Australian side I couldn't remember a worse day, or one where we had been so comprehensively outplayed. Geoff Marsh brought some sanity back to proceedings when he commented, 'Today's over. Let's concentrate on having a better day tomorrow. Let's get back into the game then.'

There was one bloke even more dejected than the rest of us. Sitting in the corner, icing his damaged hamstring which he had pulled chasing a ball around the boundary, was Jason Gillespie. His injury is a real blow to us, not only leaving us a bowler short for the remainder of this match, but leaving him in serious doubt for the second Test. A muscle strain of this kind takes a minimum of 10 days to recover from.

DAY 28 | JUNE 6

First Test — Day Two
Edgbaston, Birmingham

AUSTRALIA 118 V ENGLAND 6–449 (N HUSSAIN 207, GP THORPE 138).

TODAY WAS ANOTHER DAY, and it was with this in mind that we went about our warm-ups with renewed enthusiasm and an upbeat tempo that had been sadly lacking yesterday. The game plan for the morning was simple in theory but much harder to put into practice. It required a discipline that few sides can constantly produce. Being in such a poor position, we had no option but to try to keep things as tight as possible and give away as little as we could afford.

Don't you hate it when a plan goes horribly wrong? Well, this one certainly did, although we thought Hussain was fortunate to survive an lbw appeal before he had added to his overnight tally. The rest of the session, however, was carnage, with 135 runs being added for the loss of no wickets, which put us completely out of the hunt. Shane Warne bowled as poorly as I've ever seen him bowl in a Test match, although he wasn't helped by the sluggish nature of the pitch, which gave the batsmen the liberty of playing him off the pitch rather than through the air.

I didn't have to look at the scoreboard to know we were in deep trouble. That news came in the form of a cricket ball tossed my way, with the accompanying words from captain Taylor, 'Have a bowl, Tugga.' I was grateful for the opportunity, and pleased I was able to get through 12 overs without any niggles. And I found the edge a couple of times, even though the ball went safely through the slip region.

Both Thorpe and Hussain reached well-deserved centuries, on a wicket that still offered something to the pacemen because of the sometimes unpredictable bounce. The breakthrough was finally achieved, shortly after lunch, when the left-hander mistimed a pull shot to end a partnership worth 288 runs.

As so often happens, the man who has been waiting for a long time (in this case John Crawley) failed to post a score. This, a faint edge to the keeper, was Michael Kasprowicz's first Test wicket and came during a spell where the big Queenslander gave it everything he had. Hussain then went to his double century, hitting Warne for three consecutive fours and receiving a deserved standing ovation from the Edgbaston crowd. Soon after, however, Warne turned one with enough vigour to catch the double centurion's outside edge. Thus ended one of the best knocks I've seen for clean hitting and astute placement.

Mercifully, rain put an end to our suffering about an hour before the scheduled close, at which point we were 331 behind and still four wickets away from bowling England out.

After another poor day, it was nice to see a friendly face from home tonight, in Mum and her fiance Daryl. They're over here for a holiday and to catch a couple of the Tests. During our conversation, the former British Prime Minister, John Major, who only the previous month had been voted out of office, bumped into me and said hello. Pleasantries were exchanged, and then I commented to him, 'Your blokes have had a good couple of days.' Brother Mark then added, 'Yeah, you even won the soccer the other day.' (England had recently won a four-nation football tournament in France, which featured world champions Brazil, as well as Italy and the Frenchmen.)

Proving he has a good sense of humour, Mr Major shot back, 'It must be the change of government that's done the trick!'

AUSTRALIAN PICTURE LIBRARY/ALLSPORT

NASSER HUSSAIN HAS JUST REACHED HIS CENTURY, AS HE AND GRAHAM THORPE (RIGHT) BAT ENGLAND INTO A SEEMINGLY IMPREGNABLE POSITION.

DAY 29 JUNE 7

First Test — Day Three
Edgbaston, Birmingham

AUSTRALIA 118 AND 1—256 (MTG ELLIOTT 66, MA TAYLOR 108*, GS BLEWETT 61*) V ENGLAND 9—478 (DECLARED; MA EALHAM 53*, MS KASPROWICZ 4—113).

MY BROTHER HAS BEEN feeling off-colour for the past few days, and this morning he finally got a doctor's opinion. The diagnosis wasn't what we were looking for. Suspected appendicitis was the verdict and immediate hospitalisation the treatment, at least until exactly what is wrong with him is determined.

Not before time, we finally achieved a winning session, as we claimed three wickets this morning and then kept England wicketless until the lunch break. Michael Kasprowicz picked up four wickets, after earlier playing two Tests without achieving a breakthrough, and was probably our best bowler. But in truth that status wouldn't have been too hard to achieve, as we had put in one of our worst efforts in a number of years, perhaps even on par with our batting effort on the opening day.

Taylor and Elliott continued on after the lunch break until the score reached 133, which was more than our first innings total, when the Victorian was deceived by a ball from Robert Croft that didn't turn. Taylor, though, continued on — it was great to see our skipper back to something like his best, in what would have been, in all honesty, his last Test innings if he'd failed. His first Test 50 since December 1995 was reached, and such was the look of determination and commitment etched on his face at this point, it seemed a century was a distinct possibility, rather than the remote hope so many of the press contingent had dismissed in the days before the game.

Together with Greg Blewett, Taylor brought us back into the game. Both players looked much more assertive and in command than any of us had in our first dig. It was as if we had woken up today and realised we actually were playing in a Test match, and not just in a warm-up. When Mark reached 99, every Australian player was standing in anticipation, while the Channel 7 and Channel 9 television crews had their cameras hard up against the windows in our rooms, ready for the team's reaction. A quick single

STEVE WAUGH

was taken, and the boys erupted with genuine pleasure at seeing a comrade come through the toughest struggle of his career. This was a courageous display of inner strength. It was goosebumps all round, but thankfully Tubs settled himself down quicker than the rest of us — he batted through to the close — we were still pumped up some overs after he reached his hundred.

At stumps, the Taylor/Blewett stand had realised 123 runs, leaving us only 104 runs behind with nine wickets still in hand. From a seemingly lost cause, we are now in a position to not just save the game but perhaps even force an unlikely victory. We need to bat all day tomorrow to have a chance.

It was interesting to see how Tubby reacted when he returned to the dressing-room after not so much getting the monkey off his back as shaking King Kong clear. After discarding his protective gear, he simply sat in his chair and then, probably for the first time, realised exactly what he had just achieved. He was very subdued as he accepted the congratulations from his team-mates, not once showing any emotion. It was more of a relief than anything — that seemed to be his feeling.

His performance proved that it is possible to achieve anything if you dig deep enough. There was no way Mark Taylor could have gone into today's innings with any degree of confidence, but he showed that inner strength and mental toughness are the two key ingredients if you want to be a successful run-scorer.

First Test — Day Four
Edgbaston, Birmingham

AUSTRALIA 118 AND 477 (MA TAYLOR 129, GS BLEWETT 125)
LOST TO ENGLAND 9—478 (DECLARED) AND 1—119 (MA ATHERTON 57*,
AJ STEWART 40*) BY NINE WICKETS.

FOR A WHILE IT was all going smoothly. We were decreasing the deficit with increasing momentum, thanks particularly to Greg Blewett, whose century was one of the best displays of strokemaking anyone could ever wish to see. But just when we were looking at further deepening Mike Atherton's anguish, the stand was broken after 194 runs had been added. Taylor played a tired drive at Croft and was caught and bowled. At this point we were just 33 runs behind, with eight wickets still in hand.

Unfortunately for Australia, Blewett followed soon after, bat-padding to silly mid-off, and the balance of the game had been completely turned around once more. Michael Bevan again fell to the short ball, a fact that will be preying on his mind from now on. His struggles in this area must be sorted out quickly, or else they will be ruthlessly exposed — Test cricket is all about sensing a weakness in the opposition and then exploiting it. Mark Waugh, still not feeling well but out of hospital, managed to get an edge to a virtually unplayable lifting delivery from a recharged Darren Gough and was out for 1. We were 5–399 at this point, and back in very serious trouble.

Watching this collapse from the other end was very hard to take, but I knew we needed just one more good partnership to be in a position to make a victory bid. I was beginning to feel at ease at the crease, as I settled in (hopefully) for the long haul. My timing and placement weren't as good as I would have liked, but I could feel myself getting stronger by the minute. With Ian Healy, I took our second-innings score towards 450.

A severe afternoon storm halted proceedings for a short period. Immediately upon the resumption of play, I lost my wicket, playing across the line of a Gough delivery which did little and I was trapped lbw. Just when things seemed as if they were falling into place, I drifted into the 'comfort zone' and paid the price. This game will bite you if you don't give it your utmost respect. A similar fate befell Ian Healy, who appeared to be travelling smoothly until Mark Ealham took a leaf out of Ian Botham's book and lured our keeper into a false stroke at a long hop. The Kent all-rounder then took a further two wickets for no runs, and left his side needing 118 for a morale-boosting victory.

Chasing a target such as this can sometimes present difficulties, if you let potential problems dominate your every move, but England didn't appear ruffled or wary at any stage, even though they lost Mark Butcher early on.

The experience of Stewart and Atherton shone through, with glorious shot-making sending the raucous crowd into delirium as the runs-required figure came down rapidly. Significantly, the winning runs came from a spanking cover drive from Stewart off Shane Warne that epitomised the Englishmen's domination of the game.

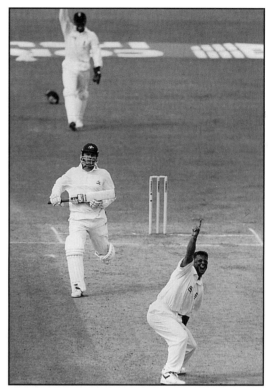

ABOVE: THE END OF MY SECOND INNINGS AT EDGBASTON — LBW TO DARREN GOUGH FOR 33.
OVER PAGE: THE VIEW FROM THE PLAYERS' BALCONY AFTER ENGLAND'S VICTORY.

Getting off the ground after a home-town victory is always a difficult and dangerous assignment, as Matthew Elliott discovered when he was wrestled to the ground by a spectator looking for any type of souvenir.

It's only a matter of time, while the level of security remains amateurish, before a serious incident occurs and a player or supporter is injured. Once we reached the safety of the pavilion, we were obliged to observe the delighted home team accept their winner's cheque and spray the crowd with champagne, which I guess isn't a completely bad thing — this sight should make everyone extremely determined not to have to see it happen again.

A losing dressing-room is always a very sombre place. But the gloom did lift eventually and the post-mortems began in earnest. For us to come back from what has been a disastrous first month to this Ashes campaign, each player will need to make an honest assessment of their own game and attitude and come up with a plan to turn things around. It has to come from within. Words are cheap unless they are backed up with self-belief and desire.

AUSTRALIAN PICTURE LIBRARY/ALLSPORT

A TALE OF TWO TEAMS. THE EXCITED CELEBRATIONS OF THE ENGLISHMEN ON THE
EDGBASTON PAVILION'S BALCONY (ABOVE) CONTRASTS SHARPLY WITH THE ABJECT
DISAPPOINTMENT IN THE AUSTRALIAN DRESSING-ROOM.

STEVE WAUGH

DAY 31 JUNE 9

Birmingham

THERE WAS NOTHING UNUSUAL about us arriving at the ground and changing into our Australian gear — except that today's scheduled fifth day of the first Test was now a training day, courtesy of the fact that we had lost inside the allotted time. Disappointing as our loss was, we must go forward, learn from our mistakes and build on the positives to come out of the match.

This morning's agenda involved a team discussion on our performance (without going into too much detail) before we broke off into three groups for a 'think tank' session. I found this type of small-group 'practice' enlightening, and a welcome break from the usual routine.

The quick bowlers went out to the outfield, where they had a chat about what happened during the match and came out of their discussion conceding that they strayed away from the basic fundamentals of line and length. The best way of rectifying this situation is quite simple — it involves the use of two cones that are put on a place on the wicket deemed to be the good line and length the bowlers should be aiming for.

The batsmen opted to go to the practice nets where we had a chat about what had transpired during the match and in particular during the disastrous first morning. We came to the conclusion that we were a little underdone in our preparation and, more significantly, that we didn't tough it out enough. It was also noted that it was perhaps also 'just one of those mornings' when we nicked everything. And the Englishmen bowled exceptionally well.

We focused on the positives to come from the Test, especially our much-improved second-innings effort, where we applied ourselves so much better. We now believe that the key to the English attack is to nullify their strike bowler which, if accomplished, leaves them 'flatter' and can therefore alter the tempo of the game. Their 'main man', the bowler Atherton turns to when they need a wicket, is Darren Gough, essentially

AUSTRALIAN PICTURE LIBRARY/ALLSPORT

THE AUSTRALIAN BATSMEN GET TOGETHER, TO TRY TO IDENTIFY EXACTLY WHAT WENT WRONG IN THE FIRST TEST.

because he has the ability to 'fire up' the whole side with his enthusiasm and spirit. He is similar to the West Indian quicks in that he 'plays dead' during spells — you think you've got him covered after he delivers a couple of innocuous deliveries. But that is when he is at his most dangerous, and his 'effort' ball (delivered with an extra yard of pace) will often catch you off guard. The way to counteract this is to be aware of his methods and to make sure you play each ball on its merits.

The third group comprised the two wicketkeepers and the two spinners. They talked in more general terms about what had transpired during the match and also discussed ways to try to personally improve for the Lord's Test.

This is a tour almost bereft of a day away from either practice or a game, so time away from the everyday pressure and concerns of being a professional cricketer is vital to staying fresh. On such days or (as today) afternoons, it is important to break free and have some fun. So, while a foursome took to the golf course with great enthusiasm, another group went for a look around the local shops and to catch a 'flick', and a third, larger contingent took the go-kart racing option.

Among the 10 who attacked the karts was the highly-rated (by himself) Mike Slater, a well-known petrol head and lover of fast cars.

The boasts and taunts began as soon as we boarded the coach, to venture to what was supposedly 'the fastest, longest and biggest go-kart track in the midlands'. This claim in the yellow pages was what lured me into making the phone call and subsequent booking for the boys. On our arrival at the track, we were outfitted in our racing overalls — to make us feel 'like the real thing'. We were quickly realising that this was no 'two bit' operation we had stumbled upon, especially when the course marshall escorted us around the track, explaining the correct line and speed into each corner (which, of course, no-one took any notice of) as he went.

By the time the safety procedures and rules had been explained, we were desperate to burn some rubber. Each player had been given a separate number to attach to their karts, in order to keep tabs on their respective points after the completion of each heat.

It was the very first heat nearly trimmed our squad back by two, when a wayward piece of driving from Kasper resulted in his kart becoming closely acquainted with the rubber-tyre safety barriers. What happened was that his kart became an uncontrollable missile after I snuck under his guard on a sharp left hander. His efforts to stay ahead caused him to slide sideways at good speed, before crashing into used Michelins. From there he rebounded back onto the track and straight into the path of a driver who refuses to acknowledge the existence of brake pads — our fitness freak, Steve Smith.

The end result was a nasty bingle that left one kart being hauled off to the workshop and Kasper walking as if he'd had a steel girder inserted into his backbone. Next to wrestle with the safety tyres was the 'smiling road-hog', Matty Elliott, who, to everyone's enjoyment, outmanoeuvred himself and lost control on a tight section of the course.

The early pacesetters were the suicidal Slater, whose eyes had suddenly become glazed the moment his helmet was slipped on, and Blewey, whose light frame gave him a distinct advantage as he tore round the circuit in near record time. I wasn't too far behind these two, alongside Warney, who seemed to delight in causing mayhem at every opportunity. Dizzy, however, was a complete disaster — driving like a 'mother-in-law'. But even he was marginally better than the conservative Heals, who seemed preoccupied with holding up traffic. Swamp was a model of consistency, obviously

KASPER SETS THE PACE, EVER FEARFUL THAT SLATS 'THE SPEED DEMON' COULD BE ON HIS TAIL AT ANY MOMENT.

with an eye to the trophies on offer at the end of the day, while Pigeon's large frame didn't allow him to cause the carnage he would so dearly have loved to create.

After a series of elimination heats and semi-finals, the afternoon's entertainment came to a grand finale in the form of a six-man, 15-lap final. The quest for top spot on the victory dais proved to be the undoing of the pre-race favourite, Slats, who in the eyes of the race marshalls put personal glory in front of the welfare of his fellow competitors. He was deemed to have used a number of illegal moves, including not backing off into a corner when he had the incorrect line into it and generally harassing any driver that stood in his way to victory. This news came as a cruel blow to Slats, who learnt of his disqualification just as he was preparing himself to be crowned 'king of the track'. The word 'disqualified' had the same effect on Slats as a hot dagger through the heart — his expression changed from that of a man who had just won the lottery to a man who had all the winning numbers but forgot to put his ticket in.

Taking third place on the podium was that 'model of consistency', Swampy, who dispelled the popular theory that only ratbags can succeed at this sport. The runners-up trophy was mine, something I'll keep to show Slats every time he comes around to my house for a cuppa. The top honour for the day went to Blewey, who then proceeded to spray the two other placegetters with the traditional celebratory bottle of champagne (in this case a £1.99 concoction from Marks and Spencers).

Being in a relaxed mode, quite a few of the lads caught Clint Eastwood's new flick *Absolute Power* in the evening, to cap off an enjoyable day that did plenty for the team spirit among the boys.

STEVE WAUGH

TO THE WINNERS GO THE SPOILS. LEFT TO RIGHT: MARSH (THIRD), BLEWETT (FIRST), S WAUGH (SECOND).

DAY 32 | JUNE 10

Nottingham

IT WAS A CASE of the blind leading the blind, with Warney in the driving seat and me trying to come to grips with some shoddy street signs and illegible photocopied directions to our proposed exit out of Birmingham, intended destination, Nottingham. It was only after seeing the prominent landmarks of this unspectacular city at close quarters on more than one occasion that we finally extracted ourselves from the spaghetti-like road system and were on our way.

The two of us had left before the rest of the team so we could spend some time at the Nottingham headquarters of our gear sponsor, Gunn and Moore, to have a couple of new bats made up for the remainder of the tour. Players at the top level generally have their own specifications for things such as bat weight and shape, handle length and shape, and so on. My bats are usually around the 2lb 10oz mark, with an oval-shaped handle (conventional shape is round). If possible, I prefer a slight bow-shape for the face of the blade, too.

Our new hotel proved to be a major disappointment, with the rooms being nothing short of abysmal. My particular 'kennel' had only enough room for one piece of luggage before the 'house full' sign needed to be put up, but this was only a minor irritation compared to the 'one temperature for all' air-conditioning system that left us Aussies sweltering while the locals soaked up the warmth. I guess the heat wouldn't have been so intolerable, if only I could have prised the windows apart.

With Tubs sitting out tomorrow's fixture, the game against Notts will be my first opportunity to captain Australia in a first-class match. Training this afternoon was a non-compulsory one for the guys playing tomorrow, but compulsory for the reserve players. I went along, and the session proved to be a blessing in disguise for me, because it gave me the opportunity to have two hits — Warney wanted an extra bowl, Stuart MacGill (the NSW Shield leggie) had come along and was happy to keep going, and Ricky Ponting was keen to continue his experimentation with the art of off-spin bowling. This second net went for over 45 minutes and by the time I walked away, I felt like a new player, with my timing, footwork and confidence restored to something that approached what I considered acceptable.

The good thing about a long net session when you're not overly happy with your game, is that it gives you an opportunity to work on a few things and occasionally try something different. I now believe my ordinary early-tour form has been affected by a lack of alertness and sharpness at the crease, which can easily be rectified as long as you recognise it. I picked up the tell-tale signs during this second net, when I became frustrated at being late on the ball on a regular basis and constantly felt rushed in my movements. I tried picking my bat up a little earlier and to put more weight through the front part of my feet instead of through my heels. It's amazing what a split second of extra time can make, by the end of the net I was hitting the ball sweetly. The difference in my batting and confidence between when I went in and when I finally came out was both a relief and a reward for the extra work.

Phoning home is always something to look forward to, but at the same time it can be enormously frustrating because one minute you feel reunited, but the next you're back to being separated. Luckily this separation will end next week, as Rosalie and Lynette, in tandem with the in-laws, Phil and Ethel Doughty, will travel to the UK to join up with the squad. Without doubt, the hardest thing for me at the moment is listening to Rosalie either laughing, crying or playing in the background when I'm talking to Lynette, but this is somewhat compensated when I get a chance to talk to her on the

phone. Lynette tells me she recognises the voice and looks around, not knowing where the familiar sound is coming from — for me it's reassuring she hasn't completely forgotten who her dad is.

While I've been away Rosie has started eating a variety of different foods, including broccoli, porridge and tomatoes. And she's sporting two new front teeth. Her crawling has improved too, to the point where she is tearing across the floor in search of any mischief she can find. In a way I feel I'm being cheated of something special, but as always, sacrifices have to be made if you are to achieve the ultimate in your chosen profession.

THE GUNN & MOORE BAT FACTORY AT NOTTINGHAM.

DAY 33 JUNE 11

Nottingham

AUSTRALIANS V NOTTINGHAMSHIRE, PLAY ABANDONED DUE TO RAIN.

JUST WHAT THE TEAM didn't need greeted our arrival at Trent Bridge — an ashen sky coupled with consistent drizzly rain that looked to be here for some duration. Consequently, an early lunch was taken, which proved to be the highlight of a very dismal day. After tearing into the baked spuds and grilled salmon main, the apple pie, ice cream and custard went down a treat, especially so as the chances of any exercise being required from me today appeared to be diminishing by the minute.

When the captain and vice captain are summoned to an impromptu meeting with an injured player and the team physio it generally isn't good news. True to form, the meeting was a difficult one for all involved — the news on Bic's troubled lower back is all bad. After a series of extensive tests and injections, it was revealed that the L4–5 level in his lower back are on the verge of developing a stress fracture which would put him out of cricket for between six and 12 months. That area of his back, as it is now, is a potential time bomb. Rest, apparently, is the only cure, which means three months of no bowling, not even strenuous exercise.

To see the anguish and hurt in Bic's eyes as he faced this painful end to his problems is definitely the lowlight of the tour. And it's a real shame for a player who not only has a lot of talent, but is also very influential in helping bond the side and enhance team spirit. It has been decided by everyone concerned that it would be better if Bic left the squad immediately, because for him to keep hanging around the team would be like a slow form of torture for him. Inevitably, he would keep thinking about what could have been.

His imminent departure also leaves a hole in the footy-tipping competition, as he was the man responsible for organising the whole event. But he's probably relieved to be going, as he won't have to cop any more sledging about tipping NSW against Queensland in the rugby league State of Origin series. Heals did, too! These boys are supposed to be staunchly parochial towards their birthplace.

In a dire situation such as Bic's, you have to make a positive come out of the negative. It seems things could have been much worse if the back problems hadn't been diagnosed this early. Now, Bic has the opportunity to be fit and strong for our upcoming domestic and international home season.

It's funny how quickly things can turn around in cricket. Take the examples of Paul Reiffel and Andy Bichel. Just six weeks ago, 'Pistol' received the shock of his life when he wasn't part of the touring squad, and in the heat of the moment he contemplated retirement. Now he's here, having arrived last night after being called over to cover for the injury problems of Bic and Brendon Julian. Bic, on the other hand, has been on the crest of a wave — he made his Test debut and had a prominent role during our One-day success in South Africa.. Pistol is in today's team and is also a big chance to play in the Lord's Test, Bic is now considering a holiday in Scotland with his wife before departing back to Oz.

Not only is it frustrating not to be playing due to the weather, it also means that Smithy, our fitness adviser, comes into his own. In seasons gone by, a wet cricket day

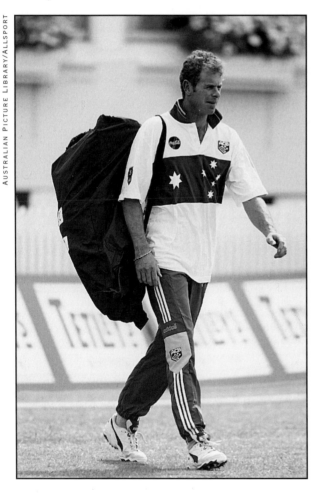

was seen as a bit of a godsend, as it allowed you the luxury of putting your feet up and relaxing until the captains and umpires deemed it appropriate to start again.

Now it is the signal for hard work, usually via the exercise bikes and a mix of gym-circuit exercises such as sit-ups, push-ups and strength work using light weights.

By the time we were scheduled to have the tea interval, both the Notts captain and I agreed it was time to leave the game until tomorrow, much to the relief of both sides who had been frustrated enough for one day.

NONE OF US WERE DISAPPOINTED TO SEE THE FAMILIAR FACE OF PAUL REIFFEL ARRIVE FOR HIS FIRST PRACTICE SESSION.

BUT FOR SHANE WARNE'S CAVALIER 47, BELTED AFTER WE HAD SLUMPED TO 8–54, OUR FIRST INNINGS OF THE FIRST TEST, AT EDGBASTON, WOULD HAVE BEEN FAR WORSE THAN OUR EVENTUAL MEAGRE TOTAL OF 118.

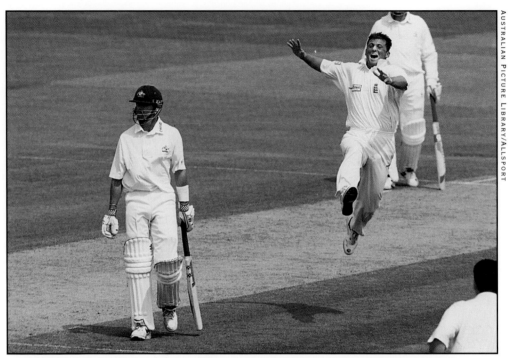

ENGLAND'S BEST BOWLER, DARREN GOUGH, CELEBRATES THE DISMISSAL OF GREG BLEWETT ON THE OPENING MORNING OF THE FIRST TEST.

BLEWETT GOT HIS REVENGE IN THE SECOND DIG, BECOMING THE FIRST MAN TO SCORE CENTURIES IN EACH OF HIS FIRST THREE ASHES TESTS.

THE FIRST AND SECOND TESTS

AUSTRALIAN PICTURE LIBRARY/ALLSPORT

GRAHAM THORPE, HITTING ENGLAND INTO A COMMANDING POSITION ON THE FIRST
DAY AT EDGBASTON.

AUSTRALIAN PICTURE LIBRARY/ALLSPORT

WITH THORPE (WHO SCORED 138), NASSER HUSSAIN ADDED 288 FOR THE FOURTH
WICKET. HUSSAIN WENT ON TO SCORE 207, THE FIRST DOUBLE CENTURY BY AN
ENGLISHMAN IN ASHES CRICKET SINCE 1985.

THE FIRST AND SECOND TESTS

MARK TAYLOR SQUARE CUTS ROBERT CROFT DURING HIS HEROIC CENTURY IN OUR SECOND INNINGS AT EDGBASTON.

OUR CAPTAIN PROUDLY STRIDES INTO THE DRESSING-ROOM AFTER BATTING THROUGH TO STUMPS ON DAY 3. AT THIS POINT MARK WAS 108 NOT OUT. THIS RATES AS ONE OF THE MOST COURAGEOUS KNOCKS I HAVE EVER SEEN.

THE FIRST AND SECOND TESTS

ABOVE: ENGLAND'S ALEC STEWART HAS JUST STRUCK THE WINNING BLOW IN THE FIRST TEST.

RIGHT: IAN HEALY CONGRATULATES MIKE ATHERTON, WHILE MARK TAYLOR SHAKES STEWART'S HAND AFTER ENGLAND WENT ONE-UP IN THE TEST SERIES.

GLENN MCGRATH AT LORD'S, WHERE HE TOOK 8–38 IN ENGLAND'S FIRST INNINGS
OF THE RAIN-RUINED SECOND TEST. THESE WERE THE BEST BOWLING FIGURES IN
AN INNINGS BY AN AUSTRALIAN AT LORD'S (THE ONLY BETTER EFFORT BY A BOWLER
FROM ANY COUNTRY AT LORD'S IS IAN BOTHAM'S 8–34 AGAINST PAKISTAN IN 1978).
THEY WERE ALSO THE BEST BY AN AUSTRALIAN IN ENGLAND BESIDES FRANK LAVER'S
8–31 AT MANCHESTER IN 1909, AND THE THIRD BEST EVER BY AN AUSTRALIAN IN
TEST CRICKET (AFTER ARTHUR MAILEY'S 9–121 AGAINST ENGLAND AT THE MCG
IN 1920–21 AND LAVER).

THE FIRST AND SECOND TESTS

TWO VIEWS OF THE STORMY SKIES OF LORD'S, 1997. **TOP:** A SNAPSHOT OF THE FAMOUS PAVILION (FAR LEFT), AS ANGRY CLOUDS CLOSE IN. **BOTTOM:** THE SCENE FROM THE VISITORS' DRESSING-ROOM, WITH COVERS ACROSS THE SQUARE AND A SATURATED FATHER TIME WATCHING FROM HIS NEW LOCATION TO THE FAR RIGHT OF OUR VANTAGE POINT.

THE FIRST AND SECOND TESTS

ABOVE: GLENN MCGRATH (STANDING, FAR LEFT) WATCHES SHANE WARNE, MICHAEL BEVAN, MARK TAYLOR AND MATTHEW ELLIOTT PLAY YET ANOTHER GAME OF 500 IN THE LORD'S DRESSING-ROOM. IN THE BACKGROUND ARE JASON GILLESPIE AND A WEARY GREG BLEWETT.

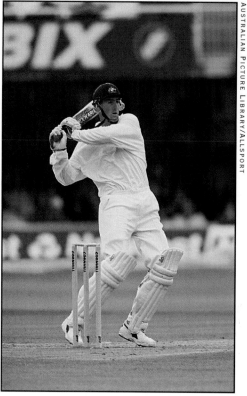

LEFT: MATTHEW ELLIOTT, DURING HIS FIRST TEST CENTURY, COMPLETED ON THE FOURTH DAY OF THE SECOND TEST.

THE FIRST AND SECOND TESTS

DAY 34 JUNE 12

Nottingham

NOTTINGHAMSHIRE 239 (NJ ASTLE 99; GD MCGRATH 4—63)
V AUSTRALIANS 1—51.

AS I WANTED TO fire things up a bit and get us going, I decided to have a bowl upon winning the toss. Not that I needed any firing up myself, after what I heard from the groundsman this morning. When Swampy and I inspected the wicket well before the start of play, we asked the head groundsman. 'Are you going to cut any more grass off the wicket?' His reply was one that you wouldn't normally associate with fair play ...

'I'll wait and see who's playing in the home team's side before I make a decision.'

In other words, if we (Notts) include our quicks I'll leave the grass on and if we don't I'll cut the grass off!

Bowling first seemed to have the desired effect on our four-pronged speed attack of McGrath, Kasprowicz, Reiffel and Julian. All bowled with good pace, even if the greenish-looking wicket failed to live up to its devilish appearance. It was, in fact, quite placid and slow-paced. I thought the pick of our bowlers was the ever-improving Kasprowicz, who looks as if he believes he should be here, rather than just being happy to be here. Reiffel, as always, found an immaculate length and troubled all the Notts batsmen as a result, but Julian was again a little inconsistent, with too many 'boundary' balls (as in balls that get hit for four) to go with his customary splattering of unplayable deliveries. McGrath looked a little disjointed in his run-up. It appears to me that he needs a good workout to sort out some minor problems in his action and approach to the crease before he gets back to his best.

The keeping of Adam Gilchrist was the biggest plus for the day. Considering the lack of opportunities and match practice his was a polished display behind the stumps, only further enhancing his reputation as a player who looks well-suited to the additional pressures that a Test-match situation throws up. If he had been born anywhere except in Australia, I believe he would already be a success at the top level.

Overall the team's performance was a big improvement on our recent form. The general lift in our energy output and an increase in intensity combined with a few good laughs to make it an enjoyable day all around.

By virtue of a ridiculously small boundary on one side of the ground, the local fans gained a rare insight into what was happening on the field. This led to Pigeon giving not only the lads some funny moments, but most of the crowd, too. This highly comical turn of events began when a prying spectator, who had perched himself on the top tier of an open-aired seating facility at a point exactly opposite the bowling crease at which Pigeon happened to be bowling, began shouting advice. From his vantage point, this keen student of the game believed that Glenn was continually overstepping the front line without being brought to justice by the umpire. And he let everyone know. As soon as this loudmouth realised he was now the centre of attention, he began screaming out 'No ball' each time a delivery was bowled.

This didn't go unnoticed by Pigeon, who made his own thoughts known by way of a couple of well-known gestures.

The umpire, being only human, was now uncertain as to whether or not he had been caught out by the spectator. So he began studying the crease with renewed interest and indeed found a transgression shortly afterwards. Needless to say our illustrious quick from Narromine began to show some signs of frustration, which was shortly to be compounded when a boundary was struck off the last ball of one of his overs. This shot certainly livened up the small band of spectators who were now giving Pigeon a real going over.

The ensuing conversation between player and spectator had all at the ground thoroughly engaged.

Pigeon was fuming and in the process of pulling on his Aussie sweater in a real huff he was left standing in front of his animated audience with an item of clothing that was on back to front. Not only had all his fellow players spotted this act of folly and begun to laugh hysterically, but so had his tormentors in the crowd. Sensing something was not as it should be, the big tearaway looked down in dismay and instantly ripped the sweater off his body as if it was full of funnelwebs. Down it went to the turf, then up and over the advertising boards seconds later, thanks to a strong looking right-foot place kick.

After such an enjoyable episode, we couldn't let the whole affair die a quick or quiet death. So it was decided to relive the nightmare one more time before the end of play. The opportunity arose shortly after tea, after Glenn had bowled the first ball of an over. As he walked back to his bowling mark, the entire slip cordon quickly turned their jumpers around so that each fieldsman's look mirrored the one Pigeon had modelled earlier. Because he is such a competitor, totally focused on his job, this stunt had to be continued for three balls before it was noticed by our spearhead, who immediately saw the humorous side of the prank and had a good laugh before simply saying, 'Very funny guys.'

DAY 35 JUNE 13

Nottingham

NOTTINGHAMSHIRE 239 DREW WITH AUSTRALIANS 5–398
(MTG ELLIOTT 127, SR WAUGH 115, MG BEVAN 75*).

WITH ANY HOPE OF a result gone after the loss of the first day, we decided to try to bat out the day. And against yet another sub-standard pace attack which was without the county's top-notch bowlers (who generally rest in games against touring sides), this task wasn't too hard to achieve.

Matthew Elliott once again confirmed he is a class act with an effortless century, displaying all the hallmarks of a man destined for prolonged success at the top level. On the other hand, I felt very disappointed and sorry for Slats and Punter, who both got starts and looked impressive before perishing to their only blemishes at the crease. With so little cricket under their belts, it was a rare chance on tour to impress and push for a Test berth. But the lack of opportunities means they aren't match hardened at the moment and the pressure on them is pretty intense.

They must be thinking, 'I'll never get a chance right now.' The key for them is to be ready and expect the unexpected.

After a scratchy start, I played reasonably well, rediscovering my sense of timing and placement enough to reach my 42nd first-class century and give me a boost in the confidence department.

Bevo cruised into the seventies before rain curtailed his century aspirations, while Gilly made his initial first-class appearance at the crease during this tour, batting for a full 14 minutes in scoring an unbeaten 9. However difficult this situation has been for him to handle, Gilly has remained a positive influence around the side, which doesn't go unnoticed by the team's hierarchy.

Even though we didn't get the victory we were after, the team certainly looks on the way back to something approaching good form. Not surprisingly then, we were able to take a little confidence onto the bus with us, as we headed down the motorway to Leicester for our next fixture, which starts tomorrow.

DAY 36 | JUNE 14

London

AUSTRALIANS 8–220 (RT PONTING 64, DJ ORMOND 6–54)
V LEICESTERSHIRE.

AFTER THE FIRST TEST, only 13 players are required to attend each county fixture. Our game against Leicestershire thus represents my first chance to have three days off. However, before setting off for London I decided to head down to the ground to catch the first session, and to get some 'brownie points' with Tattoo by way of half an hour's walking around the oval.

Not surprisingly, the dull lifeless sky made play impossible in the morning, for much of which a persistent drizzle tumbled down to add to our frustrations. Being in a poorly-equipped dressing room made for only 12 people is certainly not the place to be when your touring squad has 22 members and no play is possible, so, quicker than I had intended, off I went down the M1 to the always exciting city of London.

My reasons for going there are twofold. Lynette, baby Rosalie and in-laws Phil and Ethel are due in at Heathrow tomorrow morning. And an overdue piece of dentistry, in the form of a crown fitting, is to be performed the morning after.

Driving down the motorway in far from ideal conditions I couldn't help but notice how much worse my hayfever is in England compared to what it's like in Australia. It may sound as if it's a minor irritation, but when you go out to bat and your eyes are cloudy and itchy it can have an impact on your game. This was definitely the case for me during the first Test, and no matter what eye drops were inserted the end result was still the same. Even the usually safe option of tablets didn't stop the running nose, sneezing and eye soreness. I only hope I can locate a suitable remedy for the remainder of the tour.

Upon checking in at the Westbury Hotel it was obvious that my earlier request for one of the larger rooms to accommodate my family had been forgotten by the staff. The room I was given barely accommodated my luggage. This was particularly annoying,

RICKY PONTING AT LEICESTER, STAKING HIS CLAIM FOR A TEST BERTH. CIRCUMSTANCES HAD MEANT THAT THIS WAS HIS MAIDEN FIRST-CLASS INNINGS OF THE TOUR.

especially so as this request had been confirmed more than a week ago, and now 24 hours before my family was to arrive the head of bookings at the hotel curtly informed me the previous arrangement is null and void.

Being single for the night I decided to wander into the happening part of town, Leicester Square, to check out the buskers on the streets and to catch a movie. While waiting in the queue to see *The Fifth Element*, I was confronted by six drunken louts who had just been to the cricket at The Oval to watch Surrey play a County Championship match. They spotted me immediately and, of course, reminded me of the current situation in the Test series and the Texaco Trophy scoreline. Not content with that, they began to angle for some sort of confrontation. The cretin who headed this 'brain-dead cast' eventually said, 'Hey, you know what you Aussies are going to win this summer?' To which I replied in great expectation, 'What?' The answer was in keeping with his intellect, '%@#$ all, you Aussie bastard.'

The whole episode left me with a sour taste in my mouth. I wondered what sort of sporting fans had suddenly become attracted to cricket in England. On previous tours nothing like this had ever even remotely looked like happening.

DAY 37 JUNE 15

London

AUSTRALIANS 8–220 (DECLARED) V LEICESTERSHIRE 4–62 (PR REIFFEL 3–12).

DUE TO MIXTURE OF excitement and apprehension, my sleep pattern during the night was spasmodic, which was a blessing in disguise as it meant I was well awake when a 7.30am tap on the door signalled the arrival of my family.

It was great to see both my girls, but at the same time their arrival once again underlined the downside to touring life. I have to get to know my daughter again after every period away from home that extends over more than a couple of weeks, which is so disheartening. On this occasion, Rosalie thought she recognised something familiar about me — enough to smile at me — but at the same time I sensed she had some reservations and doubts as to my exact link to her. It was some hours later before I felt we had bonded again, after we'd played some familiar games and mimicked sounds that she knew I had made for her before.

My instant family hadn't travelled all that well, with Lynette and both her parents sporting pretty severe bouts of the flu. And this after the 'bub' had exhibited signs of a nasty virus days before leaving Australia. Today's atrocious weather certainly won't help their cause, so it was early to bed for all in the hope of a change in fortunes tomorrow.

DAY 38 | JUNE 16

London

AUSTRALIANS 8–220 (DECLARED) AND 3–105 (DECLARED; MA TAYLOR 57) DEFEATED LEICESTERSHIRE 4–62 (DECLARED) AND 179 (SK WARNE 5–42, PR REIFFEL 3–49) BY 84 RUNS.

HAVING NEEDLES, FINGERS, INSTRUMENTS and all sorts of chemicals shoved into your mouth for two-and-a-half hours is, by anyone's standards, a poor way to start the day. But the dentist's chair was my calling and it was here I contemplated what I would like to achieve at Lord's over the next week. To cap off a rather painful stint, the final blow came with the presentation of the bill, which came to a tidy sum of £675.

STEVE WAUGH

MY DAUGHTER ROSALIE AT LONDON'S HYDE PARK — HER FIRST DAY OF SIGHTSEEING.

Back at the hotel, the staff had agreed to let us swap our room for a somewhat larger one, although still some way short of what had been promised. As we were keen to get out of the claustrophobic atmosphere, we ventured down to Hyde Park for a couple of hours of relaxation watching all the events going on around us, in weather that was so much better than yesterday's gloom. There were the paddle boats, families on roller blades, desperate sun seekers topless on the 20-pence-a-session deckchairs and, in the distance, a substantial crowd listening to anyone game enough to mount a soapbox at the famous speaker's corner. This park is such a treasure, as it allows you to feel relaxed and free of the pressures and hassles of life in such a hectic city.

When we returned to the hotel, there was good news on the teletext, which revealed that the guys had just defeated the defending county champions, Leicestershire, thanks to a couple of sporting declarations. It is great to get a victory on board and hopefully it will be the catalyst we've been looking for.

Our new room does provide Rosie with some much needed crawling space. She responded accordingly, scouring the floor in Hoover-like fashion. Hopefully, she'll sleep much sounder tonight than she did last night, when she woke me many times. I guess her time clock is in disarray, a reaction to the long flight from Sydney via Hong Kong.

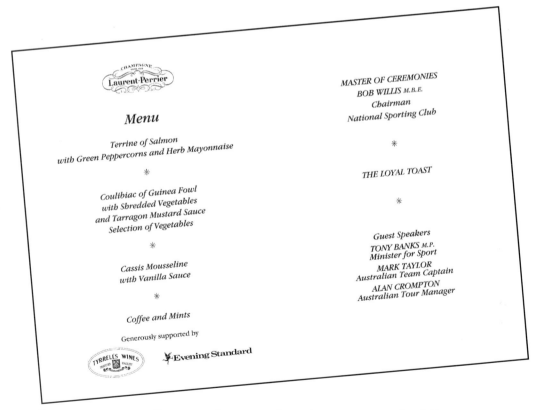

THE MENU FOR THE NATIONAL SPORTING CLUB LUNCHEON, AT CAFÉ ROYAL.

London

CRICKETERS ARE BY NATURE a superstitious lot. If you are returning to a ground, you generally want to have the same piece of dressing-room that you have occupied the previous time.

Of course, most of the guys have played at Lord's many times, so we have a number of players who not only know where they will be putting their bags, but where others will be located as well. The newcomers are then left to fill out the remaining spaces. My position, first claimed in 1989, is to the right of the dressing-room balcony, when we are seated looking out towards the wicket. It is a lounge-style seat, big enough to handle two players and stretches the width of two viewing windows. Parked next to me in 1997 is Glenn McGrath, who will no doubt help make this section of the room a messy affair.

When we realised we were to be neighbours for this Test, I said to Glenn, 'Okay Pigeon, you take five wickets and I'll make a hundred.' These feats are, of course, significant milestones for players, but at Lord's they take on a special importance. For it is here that you can be forever immortalised on the honour boards that hang at opposite sides of the dressing-room walls. A century for a batsman means you join the likes of Sir Donald Bradman, while a five-wicket haul places you alongside names such as Dennis Lillee, Malcolm Marshall and Sir Richard Hadlee.

Practice at Lord's is always a well-organised affair, with the local MCC groundstaff providing both teams with a plentiful supply of net bowlers, which has the double bonus of making sure everyone gets a decent hit out while also relieving the workload on the teams' frontline bowlers. The downside to today's practice session was the nature of the practice wickets, which due to persistent rain during the past week had not been prepared adequately. The outcome of all this was that the wickets were extremely slow in pace and low in bounce and bore no resemblance whatsoever to the match wicket that will confront us in two days time.

Under these conditions, every player must make the most of what's available. I concentrated on trying to tighten up my defensive technique and getting on to the front foot in a more positive manner. Because of the nature of the wickets, however, by the conclusion of my net, I felt as if nothing much had been achieved. But there was always tomorrow to sharpen up for the Test, even though I'd rather be peaking around now.

On a more positive note, it was great to see so many Aussie faces at the nets today. The influx of tour groups into London has boosted our support noticeably. It's always good to hear that Aussie accent, to see the flags being flung about and to know that you are going to get some rowdy, but good-natured backing.

Lunch today for the team was at the 'Cafe Royal', where we were the guests of the National Sporting Club. Recalling past tours, this was one of the better luncheons, but the downside for the lads is that we were split up again and had to face the music by ourselves. Luckily my table partners were both friendly and interesting, and fortunately for me they thought I wasn't a bad guy either, especially so after they told me that in 1993 'Billy' McDermott had refused to talk to them all through lunch.

Gilly, after assessing all his fellow table guests, decided that a particular Irish lady, who admitted she knew next to nothing about cricket, was 'ripe for the picking'. The opening Gilly was looking for came after the sweets trolley had cleared. First came the innocent question, 'Where do you guys stay whilst you're in England?'

'We're all billeted, and I'm with an Indian family who eat curries three times a day and speak very little English,' Gilly responded.

Lang, located nearby, joined in the fun. 'I'm staying with a family who have eight children and I've got to share a double bunk with a five-year-old who wants stories read to him each night before he goes to bed and then wants to play games when he wakes at 6.30 in the morning,' he explained.

The lady from the Emerald Isle was horrified. She immediately offered her house to the boys, adding, 'I don't even care what my husband thinks.'

Some time later in the evening, she must have realised she'd been had, but she was about to have the last laugh.

Not unusually, the conversation at the table turned to sledging and our alleged expertise at this part of the game. Before either Lang or Gilly could muster any sort of counter attack their Irish friend chimed in with, 'Sledging, these boys don't sledge, they don't even get snow in Australia!'

This was a long day for the team. This evening we had function No. 2, an event sponsored by Carlton and United Breweries. Disappointingly, what was supposed to be a private event, with little or no media, turned out to be an invasion of privacy — there were cameras, television crews and tabloid journos crawling all over the joint.

The *Mirror* newspaper was again the major culprit, trying to talk Tubs into giving them a story just weeks after they had tried that 'three-foot-wide bat' prank. The same tired old line — that they were only trying to have a little fun — didn't ring true with the boys, who all declined requests for interviews.

DAY 40 JUNE 18

London

THE PRE-MATCH TEAM BREAKFAST and meeting was a fairly subdued affair. We've placed the onus on each individual to adhere to the basics and improve on their first Test performance.

The only change to the side from Edgbaston is that Paul Reiffel will come in to replace the injured Jason Gillespie. The inclusion of Pistol will add not only experience but also solidarity to our attack, for he will make it hard for the Poms to score as quickly as they often did in the first Test. This should allow us to build up pressure.

Training was again not as one would have hoped for the day before a Test match, again largely due to the under-prepared practice wickets. But we gained strength from an excellent, intense fielding session — usually a fairly good guide to a confident mood in the camp.

An amusing tale was played out last night, which had as its punchline the back page of this morning's *Sun* newspaper. Ronnie Wood, of Rolling Stones fame, was the host of a private function at the Café de Paris, at which some expensive art was to be displayed. Not surprisingly, Warney received an invitation and as that invitation was for two, he decided to take one of his team-mates with him. BJ was the lucky man.

When they arrived there was a large number of 'hangers-on' lingering around and a long queue to get in. Warney didn't like the idea of waiting in line, so he and BJ marched to front. You're okay,' said the bloke on the door to Shane. 'But who's your mate?'

'I'm his bodyguard,' BJ shot back, as he stood tall, shoulders straight, chest expanded. And in they went.

So where was BJ in the photo that appeared on the back page of the *Sun*? Well, actually he was standing on the other side of Ronnie Wood. But the people at the paper had cropped him out of the shot.

He was only Warney's minder, after all!

AN INTERVIEW
WITH BILL BROWN

MY LINK WITH THE Seven TV Network in Australia has opened up many new and exciting opportunities for me over the past few months, but without doubt the highlight came today. I was given the chance to interview Bill Brown, the former Australian opening bat of the 1930s and 1940s, and a former Australian captain (against New Zealand in 1946). Bill not only played with The Don, he also managed to score a Test century here at Lord's in 1934 and achieved the distinction of reaching 206 here during the second Test of the 1938 tour. Of all the many great past players I have been fortunate enough to meet, I can honestly say Bill is the most modern thinking of all, as well as being a thorough gentleman and a decent bloke with a humility and modesty that matches his renowned integrity. If the term 'Australian cricketer' was ever to be defined in a dictionary, they should look no further than Bill Brown.

I began our conversation, which took place just outside the famous Long Room, by asking him how much this famous ground had changed over the past 50 years ...

BILL BROWN: There has been a few changes, yes, but basically it looks much the same. It still has a beautiful outfield. You know there was no real excuse for missing the ball like I used to do.

STEVE WAUGH: Like we've done so far ...

BB: Do you feel any atmosphere here, Steve?

SW: Well, the first time I came here I played for Somerset, and I immediately thought there was something special about this game. In fact, when I walked out here, I walked out the wrong door, I didn't know where to go, thought I was lost. I walked down there and came out beside the crowd. And they're all thinking, 'What's this bloke doing?' So the first time I played here I got that nervous I didn't even walk out the right gate. For me it was something special.

BB: I can remember when I first came over here, back in 1934, we played the MCC side. They had 10 amateurs and one professional, and the professional was dear old Patsy Hendren. There was a big 'to do' about the fact that Percy Chapman (the MCC captain) came down and walked out of the professional gate with Patsy Hendren. In those days they had the professionals downstairs and the amateurs upstairs, and we were goggle-eyed at this. You know, we'd never seen anything like it before!

SW: So who did you have opening the batting with you in the Test here in 1934, who did you walk down these stairs with?

BB: Bill Woodfull. He was a wonderful man, Steve, a great captain and the sort of fellow you really admired and respected.

SW: He must have been a great player.

BB: Yes. I think I got my chance because, if I remember rightly, (Bill) Ponsford wasn't well, and they put me in.

SW: You certainly took your chance, getting a hundred here.

BB: Yes, very nice memories. We all like to get a few runs. I found the wicket suited me. They banged them down and from this end they used to angle in to me and I was able to poke them around.

SW: So was your strength on the leg side, working off the hip?

BB: I had nothing on the off side, so it would have to be. You've bowled here haven't you?

SW: Yeah, but not with much success.

BB: No, but did you find that one end suited you more than the other?

SW: Yeah, the far end did. You've still got to put them in the right spot, of course.

BB: Of course. It helps, too, if the wicket does a bit. It staggered us to learn that the ground here was on a slight slope.

SW: So you didn't realise it, though you'd heard the stories about it sloping a long way. It's always different when you first come here, you still can't quite believe how much it slopes.

BB: The slope doesn't make a great deal of difference to your batting, I don't think. It gives the bowler a slight advantage, do you think? Having bowled on it you would have a far better idea than I.

SW: It didn't give me much of an advantage, but they tell me it does.

BB: I didn't get a bowl, of course. I remember the 1938 Test at The Oval when they scored 900 and something — now there were only two fellows who didn't get a bowl. One was the wicket keeper and the other one was another fellow.

SW: They must have thought a lot about your bowling!

BB: I think they'd seen it at the nets and that was sufficient.

SW: Can you remember the shot you got the 200 with (in 1938, when Bill scored 206 not out)? How did you get the 200?

BB: Can't remember. Probably a push on the on side somewhere.

SW: A quick single?

BB: When you get to 199 you get a bit keen, a bit quick on the next one. You were asking me about Sir Donald before — I think he was probably one of the best runners between the wickets I had the pleasure of playing with. He was so very quick and a very good judge of a run, and always after that extra one, turn a one into two.

SW: In the footage I've seen he looks hungrier than the other players, keener to get those singles, turn the twos into threes and keep scoring those runs.

BB: That's right. Of course, he was always very fit, never carried any excess weight, a very fast runner. He was a great man. I played with him in Sydney once, a grade match and he came in — the first time I'd ever played with him. He had the ability to lift your game when you were in there. I remember I was hitting and running and having a wonderful time. He called me down the wicket and I thought, 'Oh, this is tremendous, a conference with the great man.' When I got down there, he said, 'Bill, I haven't had the pleasure of running with you before. Do you think you could call when you are going to run.' I was committing the cardinal sin.

SW: A bit nervous?

BB: Oh yes, running without calling. How the devil he ever ran any runs with me at all I'll never know.

SW: Was it a nerve-racking experience batting with Sir Donald Bradman at the other end?

BB: Well to a certain extent you were in awe, but it was a tremendous thing to bat with him because there was an air of excitement round the ground when he came in. I remember in those days I used to open with Jack Fingleton for New South Wales and if we had a good day we'd bat till lunchtime, but after lunch the crowd would give us about half an hour and then they'd start to get restless. If you got out, you got tremendous applause, not because you'd been playing well, but because you were getting out of the way. Then he'd come in and away he would go. He would provide wonderful entertainment for them and very seldom let them down.

SW: Did he build an innings or did he get straight into it?

BB: First of all, he liked to get that single. Bowler, fieldsmen, crowd, everyone knew he was looking for that single off the first ball. It would come down and he would tuck it away somewhere. And away he would go.

SW: So he didn't worry about leaving the first ball, he'd always try to score first ball?

BB: That single, first ball. Depending on the situation of the match, he would gradually get his first 50 in 60 or 70 minutes, something like that, and then he would progressively get faster and faster. It was amazing really.

SW: You were saying he was fitter. Did he do anything extra off the field?

BB: I don't think so.

SW: He just batted longer.

BB: I think he obtained fitness running up and down the wicket. He enjoyed making runs, he always had a smile on his face. It was hard work for us, but it didn't look hard work for him.

SW: I guess one thing that is different on tour these days is that we fly to England. You took the boat. How long did it take to get to England?

BB: Five to six weeks. Oh, it was dreadful. You were waited on hand and foot, cocktail parties with the captain and ship's officers. It was a wonderful trip. You stopped in those days in Colombo and played a match, and you could, if you liked, get off the ship in the South of France and go to Monte Carlo and Paris and those places and then pick up the rest of the team in London. It was a wonderful initiation into cricket. We would dress for dinner every night — you became accustomed to that. The girls in their evening frocks. Black tie. We wore these little white jackets with a cummerbund in the tropics. It was a wonderful way to go from Australia to England, and by the time you finished the trip the side had got to know one another.

SW: A perfect way to get team spirit going. We do it on the bus. We travel around on the bus and that's a good way to get the team spirit going. But six weeks together must have been fantastic. What sort of stuff did you get up to on the boat — did you play any cricket? Any practice on there? A bit of fitness work?

BB: Not if we could help it.

SW: I've seen a bit of footage with guys playing cricket with people on the boat. But that was just for photographs?

BB: Just for fun, yeah. There were deck games. They'd stretch a net across and you would throw the quoit over and that was very active and very good. We had the Davis Cup team with us the first time I came over. There was Harry Hopman and Jack Crawford and Vivian McGrath, Vivian was my mate in the tennis, we had a lot of fun together. Jack Crawford was a delightful fellow and, of course, a wonderful player. We saw him play in the Wimbledon final.

SW: Who were the players you most remember out of the English sides?

BB: In 1934 and 1938 there was Walter Hammond, he was one of the really great players. I had the pleasure of playing against Sir Jack Hobbs in a festival match. And there was Patsy Hendren, Maurice Leyland and a chap named Cyril Walters who used to open for Worcestershire. Now he was a fine player. He carved the new ball about, but got in a little bit of a tangle a few times with Bill O'Reilly.

SW: A lot of players did, didn't they? O'Reilly didn't turn the ball a lot, just a couple of inches at a quicker pace than Shane Warne, almost at medium pace?

BB: Yes. Bill was a big tall fellow, who came right down at them and bowled a very good length. I can't remember him bowling a full toss. Neville Cardus (the great cricket writer) said that one of Bill O'Reilly's chief assets was the fact that he was preceded down the wicket by waves of hostility. That's pretty true.

SW: His body language was pretty important to his bowling?

BB: Oh yes. As a partnership they (O'Reilly and Clarrie Grimmett) were superb, you see, because Grimmett had such wonderful control that runs were extremely difficult to get from either of them.

SW: Grimmett was more of a turner of the ball wasn't he, slower through the air?

BB: Slower than Shane.

SW: Slower through the air than Shane?

BB: Yes, and a bit higher. He had a straight ball which didn't come out of the back of his hand so much. He squeezed it out. He also bowled a wrong'un — it is generally conceded that that is the particular ball that got Bradman out.

SW: Yeah, such as in his last innings (in Test cricket, at The Oval in 1948, facing England's Eric Hollies), that was a wrong'un wasn't it?

BB: Yes, it might have been more of a straight one than a wrong'un, but whatever it was, Don finished with a Test batting average below 100 (Bradman needed four runs from that innings for a century Test average). If anyone deserved to finish with an average of 100 he did.

SW: That was cricket having its say — that no-one could average 100.

BB: Probably, yes.

SW: What about sponsors. Did you have sponsors in your day for all your gear? Were you all looked after with batting equipment and shoes?

BB: Oh yes. We were given bats, anyway, I'm not sure whether we were given anything else, but certainly bats and probably batting gloves and things like that.

SW: What do you think of today's bats. This is my bat — it's probably a little bit heavier than what you used. How would this compare with the bats of your day?

BB: Well it is more spectacular for a start. The willow look is fairly similar, although it is a little bit heavier than we used. I think we followed in the footsteps of Sir Donald and used bats weighing about 2lb 3oz. What would this weigh, Steve?

SW: This is about 2lb 10. I need all the help I can get! That's pretty much an average weight these days, though some players use over 3lb.

BB: Well, how do you play those shots off the back foot with this?

SW: I'm struggling at the moment, Bill. Maybe that's the problem, the bat's too heavy.

BB: To me, it looks like quite a nice bit of willow, nice and sweet.

SW: Gunn & Moore will be happy.

BB: You must have very good strong wrists, because you seem to be able to hit off the back foot tremendously hard.

SW: I guess back foot is probably what I prefer in my batting. What about your batting, were you a back foot or front foot player?

BB: I was back foot.

SW: Was that the same with most of the players in your day?

BB: I think they seemed to favour back foot a little bit, but that's not to say they didn't go for the half volley. But in the main, they didn't play forward quite as much …

SW: Bill, it is a real honour for me to talk to someone from the past era, to a great player and a great man. Thank you.

BB: Steve, my wife wouldn't know who you were talking about when you say that!

THE 1938 AUSTRALIANS.
STANDING (LEFT TO RIGHT): CL BADCOCK, WA BROWN, JH FINGLETON, EL McCORMICK, WJ O'REILLY, WH JEANES (MANAGER), ECS WHITE, LO'B FLEETWOOD-SMITH, FA WARD, CW WALKER.
SEATED (LEFT TO RIGHT): AL HASSETT, AG CHIPPERFIELD, SJ McCABE, DG BRADMAN (CAPTAIN), BA BARNETT, SG BARNES, MG WAITE.

DAY 41 | JUNE 19

Second Test — Day One Lord's

PLAY ABANDONED.

For every Australian cricketer, the chance to play in a Test match at Lord's represents a dream come true. Unfortunately, today it was not to be for any of us, as constant rain tumbled down all day and gave groundstaff their worst nightmare — every time they mopped up some water off the covers, more rain would fall minutes later. By 5pm it was obvious to all that enough was enough and play was called off for the day.

Having arrived at the ground at around 9.15am, this meant that we had hung around the dressing-rooms for nearly eight hours. Believe me, it felt twice that long. Thankfully, the Lord's rooms are probably the roomiest of all, otherwise we would have gone stir crazy. To help pass the time away, Tattoo set up a 'circuit-type' fitness workout around our room, with different stations featuring sit-ups, push-ups, stomach work, step-ups and weights. A boxing routine also kept us active, and away from the abundant food supplies that seemed to be topped up every half hour or so.

A surprise visitor to our humble abode was the Australian Prime Minister, John Howard, who popped in for a chat and a couple of photo opportunities. As Mr Howard strolled around the room, I noted what each player was doing ...

- Warney and Tubs were playing Herb and Bevo at 500 (again!).
- BJ was lying on his back, reading a book.
- Dizzy was reading a cricket magazine.
- Punter and Blewey were working out an order for some new golf clubs.
- Gilly was 'juggling' a soccer ball.
- Slats was strumming his guitar and singing to himself (thankfully).
- Lang was writing his report for the ACB internet site.
- Pistol was signing the official team autograph sheets.
- Junior was watching the races on the television.

- Heals was sorting out his gear, making sure everything was nice and neat.
- Hooter was treating Kasper on the bench.
- Crommo was sorting out the hospitality and ticket requests for tomorrow.
- And Smithy and Swampy were doing an extra boxing routine together. These guys just hate doing nothing!

Where Pigeon was at this moment was anyone's guess.

It was a rain-soaked group of spectators who hovered around the team bus afterwards, trying to salvage something from the washout. Near this lot stood Tim Farriss of INXS fame, waiting patiently for a cab that was never going to come. Tim is a cricket nut and well known to many of the lads, so he was immediately offered a ride back into central London on the team bus. Each time I've met Tim, his knowledge of and enthusiasm for the game is infectious. He's such a fanatic that when he needs to use an alias, checking into hotels, to protect his privacy he signs as 'WG Grace'. (Sorry Tim, I hope I haven't blown your cover in Australia. My guess is your alias in your home country might be 'DG Bradman'.)

From all reports, the guests in the private boxes (3100 people in all) didn't let the lousy weather get them down. They decided instead to make the most of the situation by downing 1800 bottles of champagne — an impressive effort which must surely be a new Test record.

STEVE WAUGH

THE VISITORS' DRESSING-ROOM AT LORD'S — THE BEST IN WORLD CRICKET AND OUR HOME FOR ALL OF THE ABORTED FIRST DAY OF THE SECOND TEST.

Second Test — Day Two
Lord's

ENGLAND 3–38 (GD McGRATH 3–21).

TODAY'S FORECAST WASN'T PROMISING, but it was good enough for play to begin on time, 24 hours after the original proposed starting point. We realised, because the weather was going to play a significant part in the Test (the forecast for the coming days is not flash), that we had to be aggressive if we wanted more than a draw and concluded that our best chance of victory was to send England in on what looked to be an under-prepared pitch. Mike Atherton, captaining England for the first time since being awarded an OBE and breaking Peter May's record for the most appearances by an England captain by leading his country for the 42nd time, duly lost the toss to Mark Taylor and we put our game plan into action.

Without doubt, the most lasting memory for me today was the complete hush that swept over Lord's before the first ball of the match. It was one of those special moments that one can only appreciate when you're actually at the ground. Within minutes of that first delivery, Glenn McGrath had their top-order backpeddling with

IAN HEALY SPORTINGLY INFORMS UMPIRES SHEPHERD AND VENKAT THAT HE DOESN'T KNOW WHETHER HE CAUGHT GRAHAM THORPE.

DARREN GOUGH ON THE LORD'S BALCONY, DOING HIS BEST 'GAZZA' IMPERSONATION. TO GOUGH'S LEFT IS DAVID GRAVENEY.

some quality pace bowling. Glenn's displays nowadays are highlighted by his ability to pinpoint a batsman's weakness and then go in after that failing like an anteater attacks a termite mound.

The most talked about incident of the day came immediately after Graham Thorpe came to the crease with the score at 3–13. He played tentatively at his first ball and edged what at first seemed to be a regulation low catch to Ian Healy. But such was the uneven bounce, the ball 'died' on its way through to the keeper and barely carried. Healy dived forward and came up with the ball in his gloves, together with a quizzical look that suggested he didn't know whether he'd caught the ball before it hit the turf.

I was fielding in the gully and had my doubts as to whether it had carried, as did Greg Blewett at short leg. However, the guys in the slip cordon — Mark Taylor, Mark Waugh and Shane Warne — all thought it was a fair catch.

Heals, to his credit, went to umpire David Shepherd and said, 'I'm not sure, Shep.' The umpires then conferred and gave Thorpe the benefit of the doubt. This incident just proves that at full speed it is often impossible to know exactly what goes on, that things can look very different from different perspectives and vantage points, and that the use of the third TV umpire in these situations is essential.

Making the most of this shaky start, Thorpe, with Nasser Hussain (who seems to be enjoying something of a golden trot as far as playing and missing goes), kept us at bay until even more rain put an end to our aspirations. Even though it was another day of frustration, we have at least set the tone for the Test and let England know we are back and ready for the battles ahead.

Second Test — Day Three
Lord's

ENGLAND 77 (GD MCGRATH 8–38, PR REIFFEL 2–17) V AUSTRALIA 2–131
(ELLIOTT 55*, GS BLEWETT, 45, ME WAUGH 26*)

GLENN McGRATH AND PAUL Reiffel worked beautifully as a combination when play began this morning, building on our great start of yesterday. McGrath came tearing down the slope, angling the ball into the right-handers and away from the lefties, while Reiffel diligently worked on each batsman, like a dental surgeon would on decaying teeth. These two bowled unchanged through the morning session, the only break coming through a 15-minute rain delay, as they cut a swathe through the English batting order.

Hussain probably battled the hardest of the Englishmen, lasting 108 minutes for 19 runs, stats which underline the quality of our bowling. It was like playing back in the under–10s again, with figures you'd normally associate with that level of cricket being returned. McGrath 8–38, Reiffel 2–17, England all out 77.

The mood in our room was buoyant, as there is definitely now the distinct possibility of an Australian win. When we entered the rooms, the 'benchies' and our support staff gave us a huge ovation, and also updated the honour board to include Glenn's amazing figures. They are the best-ever by an Australian in Test cricket at Lord's, and we can count ourselves lucky to have been here to see it. A huge credit must also go to Reiffel, who kept up the constant pressure at the other end and conceded little more than one run per over.

When we batted, the rain again made the game a stop-start affair, refusing to allow anyone to settle into a rhythm or to dominate proceedings. Mark Taylor reverted to his most common form of dismissal, immediately chopping a ball back onto his stumps, which gave England a ray of hope that their tiny total might be competitive after all. But at the other end, Matthew Elliott rapidly gained confidence, stealing quick singles at every opportunity. Greg Blewett, meanwhile, produced a mixed bag of streaky shots combined with his trademark cover drive with that extra flourish.

The scoreboard would have looked a lot better for the home side if chances offered by both batsmen had been accepted. The miss that allowed Greg to escape was a blunder you wouldn't expect from a schoolboy side. He was beaten for pace while attempting a pull shot, and the ball ballooned off his gloves into the area near second slip Mark Butcher. For some reason Butcher didn't move until it was too late, leaving the ball to lob gently between himself and Graham Thorpe at first slip. The bowler, Andy Caddick, was left to tear his hair out.

Then, after Blewett was eventually dismissed, Mark Waugh should have followed him immediately, but the usually safe hands of Nasser Hussain let England down when Mark teased him with a difficult chance off Robert Croft. The stumps scoreline of 2–131 was reasonably flattering to us, considering the loose nature of our play, but England failed to convert their chances and may come to rue their slackness come the final day of this Test match.

Shane, Mark and I had a rather unique dinner appointment tonight, courtesy of our chaperone for the evening, Ian Botham. We were guests of the son of the Sultan of Brunei, at the Prince's London mansion. 'Beefy' is a part-time employee of the Prince, along with Viv Richards, Javed Miandad, the squash champion Jahangir Khan and a number of other sports stars, who are occasionally invited to Brunei and are feted as celebrities by the royal family of Brunei all around the world. It was an enjoyable experience to talk to some great cricketers and learn how the Prince operates. As he's only 22, it was a little strange calling him 'Your Highness', but he didn't make us feel uncomfortable. In fact, he was extremely humble and polite, preferring to listen to, rather than initiate, conversations.

There were, of course, plenty of security people patrolling outside, and no shortage of staff inside catering for our every need. The Prince's father is, after all, reputedly the richest man in the world.

GLENN MCGRATH IN THE AUSTRALIAN DRESSING-ROOM AT LORD'S AFTER TAKING 8–38 IN ENGLAND'S FIRST INNINGS. THIS IS WHERE GLENN PARKED HIMSELF THROUGHOUT THE TEST, WHEN I WAS HIS 'NEXT-DOOR NEIGHBOUR'.

DAY 44 JUNE 22

Second Test — Day Four
Lord's

ENGLAND 77 V AUSTRALIA 7–213 (MTG ELLIOTT 112).

JUST WHEN WE THOUGHT we would get another early mark, after another day that again left the groundstaff cursing the Gods, the umpires decided that play would get under way at 5.40pm, with the rule that an extra hour can be added to make up for lost time being brought into play. The dedicated few who had braved (many without cover) the chilly, wet conditions were rewarded with 17.4 overs of action-packed drama.

A chase for quick runs was our only option and it was with these instructions that Mark Waugh and Matthew Elliott returned to the centre. Shane Warne had been promoted to No. 5, with a licence to play shots from ball one, and it wasn't long before he was at the crease, after Mark was caught by Devon Malcolm at third man. This was a grab the bookies would have offered about 20–1 about Big Dev taking, such is his reputation as a fieldsman.

The use of a pitch hitter such as Shane is a move that rarely comes off, probably because the guy involved suddenly has expectations of himself, whereas when he swings away late in the order he has no such responsibility. Straightaway, Warne went for a big six but only managed to sky a catch. My stay was even shorter — the shortest possible time, in fact — as I was trapped in front by Andy Caddick as I played across the line.

Michael Bevan became the fourth part of the procession, when he was unluckily caught behind, trying to pull, off a bottom edge. Elliott, however, was playing like a genius at the other end, gorging himself on a series of short-pitched offerings from Darren Gough and company, who were trying to either bounce him out or knock him out. That glorious moment for any cricketer finally came for Matty at around 6.50pm, when he pushed Croft into the covers and took off like Donovan Bailey to register his initial Test century.

This is a special moment for any cricketer, but to achieve it at the Home of cricket is as good as the script gets. He finally perished, just before stumps, to the hook shot that he had reaped such rewards from throughout his superb knock. Surely many more hundreds are to follow for this technically gifted batsman.

After the helter-skelter of this 'mini-session', that saw 82 runs scored and five wickets fall, we are still in with an outside chance of victory, though much will depend on our efforts with the new ball after we declare in the morning.

Getting into the Lord's showers is always something to look forward to, with their fire hydrant pressure and heads the size of dinner plates. There are also a couple of extra-long bath tubs available if that's what you desire.

Once showered, we shared a couple of relaxing, congratulatory beers with Herb, before I headed off for the Westbury to grab some Chinese takeaway and contemplate my dismissal.

MATTHEW ELLIOTT HAS JUST COMPLETED HIS FIRST TEST CENTURY, HAVING PICKED THE PERFECT PLACE AND AN IMPORTANT TIME TO DO IT.

I've been in a negative frame of mind since the first scheduled day of this Test. I think this can sometimes happen in rain-marred matches, where you can tend to drift a bit and lose focus. When I arrived at the crease today, I felt rushed and not ready for the ball that was about to be bowled to me. This explains my lateness on the delivery. I hope I can use my mistakes here as a lesson for next time. I must begin to work harder, stop whingeing at little things and get stuck into my net practice with renewed vigour and enthusiasm.

DAY 45 JUNE 23

Second Test — Day Five
Lord's

ENGLAND 77 AND 4–266 (MA BUTCHER 87, MA ATHERTON 77) DREW WITH
AUSTRALIA 7–213 (DECLARED).

THERE WAS A MUCH smaller crowd at Lord's today than there had been for even the washed-out days, and it was made up predominantly of Aussie supporters. They were there, I presume, in the hope of a stirring victory. Unfortunately, they were denied, primarily by a solid 162-run opening partnership between a dour Mike Atherton and an increasingly confident Mark Butcher. Following in the footsteps of Taylor and Elliott in our second innings at Edgbaston, Atherton and Butcher put together an opening partnership here that surpassed their team's complete total in the first innings.

It might have been different, however, had Mark Taylor at first slip accepted an early chance from Butcher, off Paul Reiffel, that our captain would normally have held blindfolded. But it wasn't to be. Instead the day developed into an exercise in psychological warfare, to see who could milk something positive out of the remaining hours of play.

Both Englishmen were denied centuries. Atherton stepped rather carelessly onto his stumps when a hundred looked a good thing, while Butcher had his defences invaded by a sharply-turning leg break that spun out of the bowlers' footmarks.

Nasser Hussain's dismissal represented many bonus points for us, as he was lured into a big drive by a dipping Warne leg break. The warning here was that if Hussain doesn't treat our leggie with the utmost respect in future he will suffer the consequences — the dismissal must leave negative thoughts in the batsman's mind. Alec Stewart, too, now has plenty of food for thought, after being caught off a wayward hook shot once again. He loves that shot, but it is one that is fraught with danger unless you are in great form and seeing the ball well.

John Crawley and Graham Thorpe played out the remaining time, which was especially important for Crawley, who has scored only two runs in two innings to date in the series. It's amazing what a score such as 29 not out can do for one's confidence and self-belief in such circumstances, and I'm sure the man from Lancashire will sleep a lot more soundly tonight for having scored these precious runs.

The moral victory, if there is such a thing, was ours. Glenn McGrath, deservedly, collected the man-of-the-match award, but only just ahead of Matthew Elliott, who will come away from this match as a Test player who not only believes in himself but who expects to succeed at this level.

After such a mixed-up week, the team decided it should get together for a drink and a chat at one of London's trendier restaurants and bars, 'Quaglinos'. As lady luck would have it, behind the bar was an Aussie on a working holiday. He had a lot of trouble locating the cash register throughout the evening, which ended up saving us quite a few pounds before the night was through.

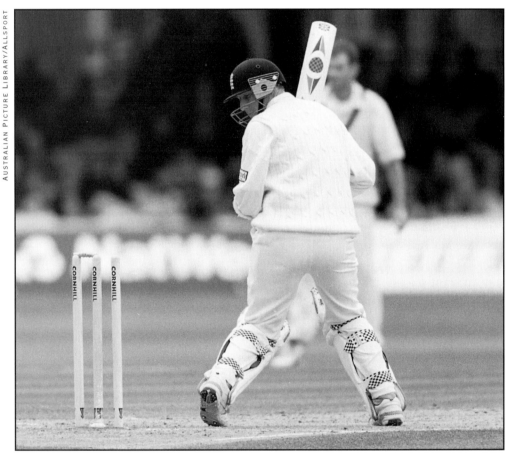

ENGLAND'S CAPTAIN MIKE ATHERTON TREADS ON HIS WICKET DURING THE FINAL DAY OF THE SECOND TEST. HE MADE 77.

DAY 46 JUNE 24

London

HAVING A BENEFIT YEAR on the county circuit is always beneficial from a financial point of view, but often the beneficiary's form on the field suffers because of the increased commitments and responsibilities the benefit involves. However, because Devon Malcolm's benefit year coincides with this year's Ashes tour, it has been our turn to do the suffering. This is particularly true of Gilly, who has been targeted by Dev as the man he should approach if he wants anything not nailed down to be signed by the Australian team. It has reached the stage where, whenever Dev knocks on our doors, Gilly sprints for the safety of the toilet. Considering our benevolence, you would have thought Dev might have thrown the odd half-volley our way, especially after we reached the thousand signature mark, but there is about as much chance of that happening as there is of no more autograph requests coming our way from Test cricket's most unorthodox but entertaining batsman.

Thankfully, the event we attended today was to be one of the last of our official functions on the tour. The venue was Australia House, with the purpose being to promote an Ashes exhibition that is being conducted in the building throughout our 1997 tour. Also at the function was the Australian Prime Minister, and the boys who had not been introduced to him at Lord's now took advantage of the opportunity.

During our visit, I was lucky enough to be presented by Mr Howard with the Variety Club of Australia's award for the cricket personality of the year. This is quite an honour.

As usual, the function went on far too long and to make matters worse the food trays were too hard to track down for our liking. After two hours of small talk, we dashed to the bus, the mood of the team best summed up by a comment that was heard more than once ...

'We're outta here!!'

DAY 47 JUNE 25

Oxford

AUSTRALIANS V BRITISH UNIVERSITIES, PLAY ABANDONED.

ON MOST OCCASIONS WHEN you play a team like the Combined Universities during a long and arduous tour, the sight of rain tumbling down, together with grey leaden skies, would be a time to rejoice for all. Not so today, as all the squad are keen for some cricket and many are still searching for that elusive good form. Even more of an incentive to get out there and play is the thought that Smithy is forever hovering around, looking to put into action some fiendish routine sure to leave us praying for the next fine day. That's exactly what happened this morning after Swampy and Tubs returned from the picturesque but rain-sodden ground appropriately named 'The Parks' to inform us that no play looked likely on day one.

At precisely the time the first ball was scheduled to be bowled, we were strewn all over the hotel gym and squash court complex, beginning a circuit of activity that would last for well over 90 minutes.

Each player had to complete at least 20 minutes on a bike or treadmill, followed by a light weights circuit and capped off by some sprints coupled with a tortuous boxing routine. The way things are going with the inclement weather we will soon be stale cricket-wise, but the potential for unearthing a triathlon or boxing star from among the squad appears very promising.

If I had to choose a way to stay fit, I'd definitely choose a boxing routine, as it sharpens up your footwork and co-ordination as well as aiding stamina and enhancing strength. And it's also enjoyable.

The title for the team's worst boxers sits with either Junior, who refuses to don the gloves at all, claiming some sort of previous wrist ailment, or Heals, who it must be said can't really pack a decent punch because of his deformed-looking arthritic fingers that refuse to bend when asked. At the other end of the scale, we have the fast-emerging heavyweight contender, Kasper, whose right hook is assuming Tyson-like proportions (although his lack of nimbleness around the ring appears to be an obvious weakness). Lang, of course, is more than useful, with speed, agility and eyes that glaze over when he starts jabbing those explosive left and rights. But, for mine, the title of best pound-for-pound pugilist goes to Punter. Here is a man who is deceptively powerful and strong — he isn't one to back down and has already had dressing-room dust-ups with the likes of McGrath and come away with the points.

I didn't want to be hotel bound, particularly as the rooms are once again cramped, so I opted for a bit of sightseeing with the family in the city of Oxford. This is certainly one of the most lively places in the UK, with numerous colleges and thousands of students all accommodated in and around the town centre. Some of the other lads went for a round of golf, while others chose the old saviour on a wet day, the haircut.

The most interest however, surrounded the impending birth of the Warnes' first baby, which happened to be due today. Or at least Warney thinks so! The odds are it will be a boy with red hair and a toasted cheese sandwich held in its right hand. Seriously, though, I think Shane is very disappointed he won't be there for the birth and feels a bit helpless as a result. I'm sure it must be a difficult period for him right now, especially so as we've been inactive for the past week or so. This has given him more opportunities to think about what he's missing out on.

Thankfully, Swampy tracked down some indoor nets for those wishing to have a practice session. Under normal circumstances most players prefer not to use the synthetic wickets as they play nothing like a turf pitch and are onerous on the body. For a batsman, they can cause bad habits, largely due to the predictable pace and bounce which leads to poor footwork and technique — you can get away with murder by just using your eyes only. Bowlers dread indoor nets, primarily because they can't go back to their normal run-ups and the stress caused by running on concrete often leads to sore shins and backs. My session was one of getting back to basics, with the main aim to start playing in the 'V' between mid-on and mid-off. I want to use the full face of the bat, combined with a forward movement and a bent front knee, to enable me to keep the ball on the ground. After an extensive session, where Swampy threw balls until his shoulder begged for mercy followed by a full net in which Kasper, Lang and Gilly toiled away, I came away feeling as if I had achieved something. This last point — achieving something positive — is what all players should be looking to get out of a practice session.

We were totally unaware (until we were informed by the local caretaker of this sporting facility) that it was on the adjoining athletic track that Roger Bannister ran the first sub-four-minute mile, back in 1954. When I turned my mind back to that famous footage, I indeed saw the similarities in front of me.

DAY 48 JUNE 26

Oxford

AUSTRALIANS V BRITISH UNIVERSITIES, PLAY ABANDONED.

IT'S BEGINNING TO FEEL like Groundhog Day again. We woke to yet another bleak, ashen coloured sky, which was accompanied by steady drizzling rain and an icy cold breeze. This inclement weather meant we found ourselves once again in the hands of our increasingly unpopular fitness adviser.

Smithy must have sensed we were after his blood, because he toned down today's workout to include a racquetball competition ... with the losers going straight to the gym for some extra fitness. The draw for today's play was posted on the notice board and, of course, a competitive edge was quickly added, including prizes for first, second and third.

The prize list read as follows:

First — no gym work for the rest of the tour; Second — no gym work for the rest of the week; Third — no conversation with Alan Crompton for the rest of the tour.

The only problem with these incentives was that it seemed inevitable that all the semi-finalists would be trying to lose. Crommo is a man who has a deep-seated love for cricket and this, together with a background in law, makes for a deadly conversation to anyone who crosses his path. Perhaps it was better that the competition never reached its latter stages, and the 'prizes' were left unclaimed.

Looking around the shops with Lynette and baby Rosalie proved to be a foolhardy way to spend a few hours. The air temperature dipped appreciably and the pelting rain stung our bodies as we tried to scurry back to our car minus an umbrella. Making matters worse, I began to suspect the symptoms of flu were about to strike me down, especially as my throat was beginning to burn and the body ache.

And there was still no news for Warney, who is permanently attached to his mobile phone. I don't think I've ever seen Shane quite this nervous. He tells us the names they have picked out are Duke for a boy and Jordan for a girl.

Hopefully it will be a girl!

DAY 49 JUNE 27

Southampton

AUSTRALIANS V BRITISH UNIVERSITIES, MATCH ABANDONED.

IT WAS CERTAINLY NO surprise to once again find the sky lifeless and crying when I drew back the dark brown curtains that must have been fashionable at one point in time. Consequently, the talk over the breakfast table was of an early departure to our next destination, Southampton, rather than us hanging around all day in the hope of a session of play. There was, though, much more encouraging news on the baby front, as Warney nervously informed everyone that his wife, Simone, was having a Caesarean section.

Our bowling champion subsequently spent the next couple of hours sitting in the leisure centre, waiting, phone in hand, for the final verdict, like a man condemned to the death chair. As time went on, a crowd began to build as most of the boys, plus Shane's parents, anxiously added their support. Finally, the phone rang and off scurried Warney to receive the news in private while we settled on our last-minute selections. Minutes later it was announced: 'It's a girl! Brooke! She weighs 9lb 6oz and is 56cm long.'

'And she looks like me!!'

It wasn't long before we were choking on our cigars and throwing back the champers, even though it was 10.30am. It's a special moment when one of your team-mates becomes a Dad for the first time.

As is always the case with Warney, the media seemed to know his every move. Within no time at all, the 'snappers' wanted that exclusive photo and the TV cameras wanted that priceless footage. I'm not sure if Warney fully realises what has happened and how much his life will change from now on. No doubt he'll make a good father, and I bet he can't wait to get home to see what his daughter looks like.

After the game against the Combined Universities was officially abandoned, we did set off early to prepare for tomorrow's fixture against Hampshire, a team which contains a good friend of all the squad in Matthew Hayden. When we reached Southampton, I went

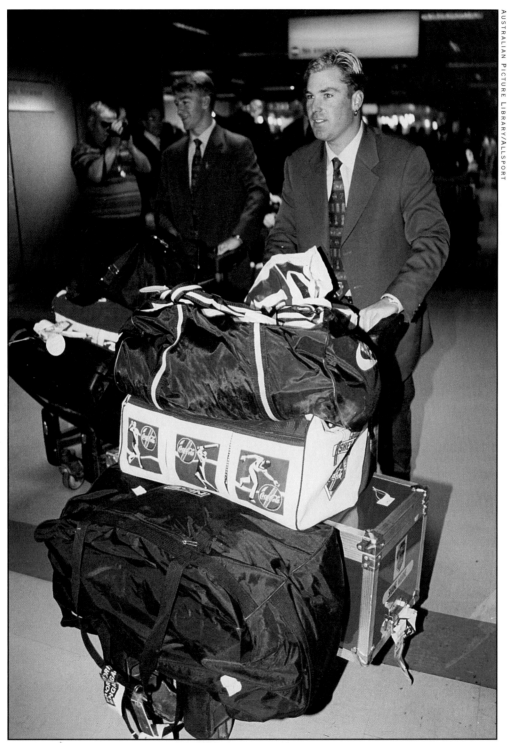

SHANE WARNE ARRIVES AT HEATHROW, AND WALKS STRAIGHT INTO THE MEDIA
SPOTLIGHT. ANDY BICHEL IS IN THE BACKGROUND.

AUSTRALIAN PICTURE LIBRARY/ALLSPORT

LEFT: GLENN MCGRATH AND ME AT THE BRANDS HATCH MOTOR RACING CIRCUIT, ABOUT TO FIND OUT JUST HOW FAST THOSE CARS CAN GO.

BELOW: THE LADS AT BRISTOL, SUPPORTING THE LOCAL CHARITY EVENT . . . 'WRONG TROUSERS DAY'.

OPPOSITE PAGE

TOP LEFT: JUSTIN LANGER AND ME AT THE REMARKABLE LANDMARK, THE 'GIANT'S CAUSEWAY', ON THE OFTEN SPECTACULAR COAST OF NORTHERN IRELAND.

TOP RIGHT: LEADING THE AUSTRALIANS ONTO THE FIELD FOR OUR GAME AGAINST SCOTLAND IN EDINBURGH.

BOTTOM: MATTHEW ELLIOTT WETS A LINE IN THE COOL, CLEAR, APPARENTLY FISH-FREE WATERS OF NORTHERN IRELAND.

PHILIP BROWN

BOYS ON TOUR

STEVE WAUGH

AUSTRALIAN PICTURE LIBRARY/ALLSPORT

AUSTRALIAN PICTURE LIBRARY/ALLSPORT

BOYS ON TOUR

AUSTRALIAN PICTURE LIBRARY/ALLSPORT

THE TWO BEST GOLFERS IN THE AUSTRALIAN SQUAD, GREG BLEWETT (LEFT)
AND RICKY PONTING.

BOYS ON TOUR

SOME MORE OF THE CRICKET GROUNDS OF BRITAIN. **TOP:** JOHN PAUL GETTY'S PRIVATE GROUND AT IBSTONE. **MIDDLE:** EGLINTON CC IN NORTHERN IRELAND. **BOTTOM:** THE OVAL IN SOUTH LONDON.

CLAY TARGET SHOOTING ON THE OUTSKIRTS OF NOTTINGHAM.

DRIVING TOWARDS THE 18TH GREEN, AND THE FAMOUS CLUB HOUSE,
AT ST ANDREWS.

THE GUYS AT NOTTINGHAM, DRESSED IN THE COLOURS OF THEIR FAVOURITE AFL
TEAMS. BACK ROW (LEFT TO RIGHT): PAUL REIFFEL (RICHMOND), MATTHEW ELLIOTT
(COLLINGWOOD), MICHAEL BEVAN (HAWTHORN), MICHAEL KASPROWICZ (BRISBANE),
BRENDON JULIAN (WEST COAST), JASON GILLESPIE (ADELAIDE), MARK WAUGH,
GLENN MCGRATH, MANAGER ALAN CROMPTON AND STEVE WAUGH (ALL SYDNEY).
FRONT ROW: SHANE WARNE (ST KILDA), SPONSORS' LIAISON OFFICER RAY PHILLIPS
(COLLINGWOOD), JUSTIN LANGER (WEST COAST), IAN HEALY (BRISBANE), RICKY
PONTING (NORTH MELBOURNE), GREG BLEWETT (ADELAIDE), MARK TAYLOR
(HAWTHORN), MICHAEL SLATER (SYDNEY), DARREN BERRY (ST KILDA), SCORER
MIKE WALSH (ESSENDON).

PHYSIO ERROL ALCOTT (LEFT) AND COACH GEOFF MARSH IN FRONT OF
LONDON'S TOWER BRIDGE.

STEVE WAUGH

STEVE WAUGH

TOP: WITH DAUGHTER ROSALIE IN THE HISTORIC CITY OF BATH.
BOTTOM: IN MY TAUNTON HOTEL ROOM, AT ROSIE'S FIRST BIRTHDAY PARTY.
MY IN-LAWS, PHIL (AT BACK) AND ETHEL, ARE AT THE FAR LEFT. WIFE LYNETTE
HAS ROSIE ON HER KNEE.

in search of a haircut, only to be told the earliest anyone could squeeze me in was next Monday. Either there aren't enough hairdressers in town or they all recognised my accent. Whatever, the bonus was that I was able to hit the sheets half an hour earlier than expected and it was there that I stayed for the whole afternoon and into the early evening.

When I did venture downstairs, I found all the lads gathered around the bar area (very unusual, that!). Not only was everyone still toasting Warney's new arrival, they were also celebrating the announcement of Blewey's engagement to Jodie, his girlfriend of 12 months. And Bevo is to become a Dad! The gossip columnists would have given anything to be privy to all this information.

Meanwhile, Lynette, Rosie and the in-laws had headed off to stay with some good friends of ours who we know from my days as a professional in the Lancashire League for Nelson, and who live on the outskirts of Manchester. The team rules demand that during the Tests the wives and girlfriends can stay with the players, but during the county fixtures the team must exist without the family. This gives the team every opportunity to develop a strong team spirit and allows us to get to know each other better.

For me, this line of thought is much harder to accept now that I've become a father. It seems ridiculous that my wife and daughter have to find alternative accommodation, which is often hard to find, when I have a room all to myself. However, in the interest of team unity I'm willing to go along with the rule, especially because, unlike on previous tours, on this trip there has been a concerted effort by management to encourage the families to be part of our Ashes experience.

STEVE WAUGH

CIGARS ALL ROUND, AFTER WARNEY CONFIRMED HE HAD BECOME A DAD FOR THE FIRST TIME. LEFT TO RIGHT: STEVE SMITH, MICHAEL KASPROWICZ, JUSTIN LANGER, IAN HEALY, ERROL ALCOTT, MARK TAYLOR, SHANE, JASON GILLESPIE, STEVE WAUGH, GEOFF MARSH, GLENN MCGRATH AND MARK WAUGH.

DAY 50 | JUNE 28

Southampton

HAMPSHIRE 156 (MS KASPROWICZ 3–33, SK WARNE 3–30) V AUSTRALIANS 2–157 (MTG ELLIOTT 61, MA TAYLOR 61*).

STILL NO SIGN OF the sun, only a dull and menacing sky. However, play began on time and, quite amazingly, the home county won the toss and chose to bat. This is a strategy that means that they'll have to make all the running in the game if they want to win. Normally, a county captain will bowl first and hope that we will eventually give them a total to chase in the fourth innings. This is easier than having to bowl us out to win a game. Such an approach reflects the poor attitude that prevails among many of the counties, as does the fact that most of these teams don't put up their strongest team against us. Playing a touring side should be seen as a challenge for the local team, and a chance for the players to impress the England selectors. Even the incentive of a £9000 cheque for beating us (compared to our meagre £2500 pay-out for a victory) doesn't seem to inspire our opponents.

So the Hampshire captain, John Stephenson, should be congratulated for his initiative. Unfortunately, his poor judgment of the pitch's condition led to his team's disastrous lunchtime score of 8–93. Given that precarious situation, their final tally of 156 was more than we wished for, but the encouraging form of Kasprowicz, Warne, Reiffel and Gillespie was exactly what we needed in the lead-up to the Manchester Test.

Against yet another sub-standard bowling attack, the lads enjoyed an extended 'net session' which left us nicely placed at 2–157 at stumps. Matthew Elliott again showed his invaluable ability to accumulate runs against any opposition, at any time. This is a trait all the great players have — the desire to keep churning out the runs. It's called 'hunger'.

I had another early night, as I tried to speed up my recovery — what was a nasty cold in Oxford has now developed into the flu. However, the room service menu didn't really offer any culinary delights. I settled for the 'vegetarian bake', which in reality was a bowl of mashed potato and raw onions that came with the outrageous price tag of £9.75 (more than $20.00 in Australia).

Southampton

HAMPSHIRE 156 AND 2—71 V AUSTRALIANS 8—465 (DECLARED;
MA TAYLOR 109, ME WAUGH 173).

THE RUN FEAST THAT had begun the previous afternoon continued at a pleasing rate for the sizeable crowd, who saw Mark Taylor score his 36th first-class century and Mark Waugh his 63rd. Both centuries were morale boosters for the guys involved, particularly Junior, who in recent weeks had been surprisingly quiet in the runs department. The ease with which my brother scored his big century will no doubt be a chilling reminder to the English team of his credentials. So far he has looked threatening without going on with the job. I believe his problems have been caused by him going at the ball too hard in his defensive prods, which, because he is already committed, has not allowed him to counter any movement or bounce. Going at the ball with soft hands allows you to adjust and improvise to get out of difficult circumstances — you are more relaxed and in control.

Tubby's hundred was a typically hard-nosed effort, which eventually drained the opposing bowlers to a point where our captain was completely on top of the situation. His long stay at the crease was exactly what he needed before the next Third Test. Batsmen will often say they need more time at the crease to get themselves back into form. There is nothing like batting in a game situation to restore your confidence, and practise your concentration and technique. Net practice is good, but it has its limitations, because the intensity isn't the same as in a match situation.

My brief stay at the crease (for a score of 11) sounds like a failure, but for me it was more of a minor triumph. During the past week or so I've been working on playing straight and making sure I'm looking to get forward at every opportunity, especially early in my innings. For me this is vital, because I know the English bowlers, because of my tendency to play off the back foot, fancy trapping me lbw or bowled early on. If I'm to be successful during the remainder of the tour, I have to find a solution to this challenge that has been thrust upon me.

Of the first six balls faced, I drove confidently at three of them, collecting two runs for each shot. Immediately, I felt reassured and confident.

It's amazing how 'fragile' cricketers can be — even after 12 years at the highest level, doubts which can spread like a cancer still enter my mind. You have to back your own ability, work hard on fine-tuning your technique, and enjoy the challenges that come your way. Easily said, sure, but sometimes hard to achieve, as it is always easier to take the soft option and look for excuses rather than do a hard, honest appraisal. Even though I squandered an ideal chance to get a big score, my gut feeling as I walked back to the pavilion was, 'I'm, back.' I'm looking forward to the next Test.

I must admit to feeling a little sorry for Matt Hayden, who let the second ball he faced from Dizzy go, only to see his off stump cartwheel out of the turf. This was exactly the mode of dismissal that led to Matt losing his way during the recent South African tour. His problems in this area will be another test for him to overcome, and how he recovers will be a good indicator of his mental fibre. I'm confident Matt will be back to play a vital role for Australia in the future, as he has a hunger and desire that very few others possess.

By the end of the day's play, the only thing that stood between us and an early start to our journey to Manchester was the former Test star, Robin Smith, still one of the best players of pace bowling in the world. Smith looked ominous in reaching 31 in a hurry.

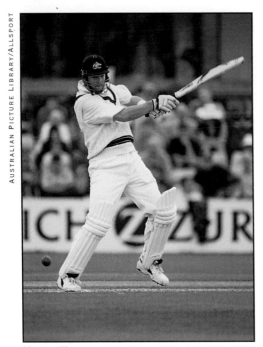

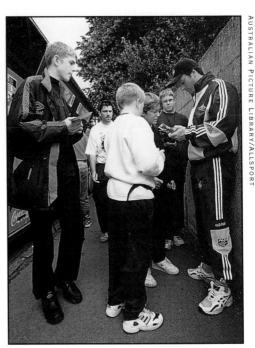

MARK WAUGH SQUARE CUTS DURING HIS BIG HUNDRED.

I'M TRYING TO KEEP THE AUTOGRAPH HUNTERS HAPPY.

DAY 52 JUNE 30

Manchester

HAMPSHIRE 156 AND 176 (RA SMITH 44, JN GILLESPIE 5–33,
MS KASPROWICZ 3–69) LOST TO AUSTRALIANS 8–465 (DECLARED)
BY AN INNINGS AND 133 RUNS.

AS EXPECTED, THE LOCALS crumbled after the departure of Robin Smith, as Jason Gillespie collected 5–33 off 13 highly impressive overs of pace and swing.

I believe this lad will, by the end of his career, go down as a 'great', alongside his new-ball partner Glenn McGrath. Australia is indeed fortunate to have both these guys at their disposal. My tip for Gillespie is 250-plus Test-match wickets. And while I'm making predictions, on the batting side of things I'll back Ricky Ponting to score 5000-plus Test runs. These two are players of rare calibre and temperament, who both possess a deep desire to not only play at the top level, but also to enjoy it. And, perhaps most important of all, they believe in themselves.

We hit the asphalt just after lunch and arrived in the soccer-mad city of Manchester in the late afternoon, to a typically wet welcome. Lynette and family arrived late in the evening, after spending the day touring the beautiful Lake District, which is located to the north of here.

As always, Rosie appears to have grown up overnight. If there's one thing, above all others, that I miss on tour it has to be her cheeky smile. Just seeing it again made me feel that I'm the luckiest man alive.

DAY 53 | JULY 1

Manchester

OLD TRAFFORD IS A ground that has been kind to us on our previous two Ashes tours. In 1989, there was that memorable series-clinching win that led to a team singalong in the showers that lasted well over an hour. In 1993, we started the series with another hard-fought victory which ignited some more frenzied celebrations. It was with these cherished memories that we assumed our positions in the change rooms, secure in the knowledge that this was 'our' turf. It may sound a little strange, but such feelings can make a huge difference to the way a side thinks. The tempo becomes more upbeat and the vibes are noticeably positive.

This morning's net session was much better than we had envisaged, particularly considering the moist nature of the wickets. Fortunately, the groundsman had prepared the practice wickets well beforehand, making sure they were rolled adequately to ensure a solid surface, which meant that the ball skidded on instead of digging into the pitch and jumping off a length, which would have happened if they were softer. Even so, the tracks were hard work for the batsmen. But they weren't impossible, especially if you applied yourself.

My 15 minutes were the best I'd turned in for the tour. I played straight, bent my front knee, watched the ball, and left the dangerous ones alone. Later on, because of my recent lack of time in the middle, I opted for a second net session against the Lancashire second XI bowlers which left me feeling full of confidence. My fielding workout was also of a higher standard than I'd put in recently, which I put down to increased energy and enjoyment levels — sometimes you become lazy on tour, a bad habit that gradually creeps up on you.

These days, there doesn't seem to be any spare time on tour. However, a lot of that is my own doing, especially the work I am doing for Channel 7 and Triple M. Both are new, exciting challenges, but they can occasionally be a little hard to squeeze into the schedule.

OUR CAPTAIN DISCOVERS JUST HOW COLD MANCHESTER CAN BE.

I was required to interview Herb and Pigeon, as part of my Test preview for Seven. Whenever you try to be sensible with a fellow player, chaos is the outcome and today it was Glenn's turn to take the mickey. He chose to offer no more than one-word answers to my questions, which left us standing there, staring at each other like imbeciles. This disaster doesn't compare to a comical Gillespie–Waugh effort in Johannesburg earlier this year, however, which required 10 'takes' for one simple question, including three efforts where at least one of us was left on the ground in fits of laughter. A 30-second preview for Seven's main news bulletin involves me asking the questions, doing a 'stand up' straight to the camera (normally the finishing two or three sentences at the end of the story) and a 'voice over' (where I say my lines that are overlaid with footage), which is usually completed back in the quiet of a hotel room.

Sticking to my tried and trusted formula, I indulged in a haircut and a massage, and then set about organising tonight's team dinner at Bill Wyman's fast food restaurant chain, 'Sticky Fingers'. Wyman, of course, is a former member of the Rolling Stones.

We all realised that a long team meeting wasn't required, especially as the England team hadn't changed a lot (except for the omission of Devon Malcolm, replaced by Test debutant Dean Headley). So we kept the talk to a minimum. But we did decide to target a few opponents for special significance — those who we feel hold the key to England's chances. On the batting side of things, we believe Mike Atherton is the 'stabilising' batsman in their side, the player they look to build their innings around. Taking Atherton's wicket early will give us a significant psychological advantage. Our plan is to bowl six inches outside his off stump on a good length, to try to induce him to spar at the ball in the hope of an edge to the keeper or slips. And we'll occasionally attempt to flick his glove with a short ball down the legside, or even a wider fuller-length ball down the legside which we've seen him glance through to the keeper more than once.

Graham Thorpe is the other batsman we'll target, largely because he can take control of an innings and set the tempo for the rest to follow. We see him as being a bit loose early on, so a concerted effort at immediately bowling in 'the corridor of uncertainty' might lead to his downfall. Thorpe is also a player who must be denied any loose balls, because hitting boundaries is for him a great pressure reliever and something he needs to do. Thorpe isn't a player who likes to slowly build an innings, he likes to get to 20 in a hurry.

Bowling-wise, we have singled out Darren Gough as the focal point. He is the bowler Atherton relies on to get that crucial wicket. If we repel him, however, the spirit in the English side drops noticeably. Gough is a bowler who runs in hard during his first spell, as he desperately tries to take wickets. This, of course, is what England needs. However, he doesn't seem to adapt to situations that need him to tighten up and keep things under control. He lacks a little bit of patience. In such circumstances we can score quickly off him. He remains, though, a bowler to respect, for he can produce a wicket-taking ball and can swing the old ball significantly.

These three players are the dangermen. If they can be kept under wraps, I believe we'll win and win comfortably.

DAY 54 | JULY 2

Manchester

THE GOOD THING ABOUT having a new person such as fitness guru Steve Smith in and around the team is the fresh ideas and enthusiasm that get brought into the equation.

For example, instead of the regulation 'one-lap followed by a stretch' warm-up, day after day, we have found ourselves playing volleyball, touch football, even badminton, which has been combined with a variety of skill work and running. The only downer with Smithy is his love of the dreaded yellow plastic cones, which when placed strategically on the turf mean only one thing … a combined fitness and 'sharpening-up' session.

Without fail, Pigeon boots these cones as far as he can whenever he gets within striking distance. The downside to this ploy is they always get put back where they'd been and Smithy 'gets off' on the attention we pay to him. He seems to think our complaints mean we are keen and ready to go.

I don't think I've ever done a fitness routine without hearing deep moaning noises from the lads. The loudest gripes usually belong to the Waugh brothers and Warney, but Smithy just keeps telling us that the work will extend our careers, and who are we to doubt their value.

Today's practice featured a 'fielding soccer' game, designed to sharpen our reflexes, which involves members of two teams trying to throw the ball to their team-mates at knee height or under until they reach the goal without dropping the ball. Unfortunately, during the game Gilly suffered a serious injury. He was attempting to take an awkward catch, just as Punter was making a last-ditch diving effort at an interception. Our reserve keeper was left in a vulnerable position, with his top half twisting in the opposite direction to his bottom half, so when Punter landed on Gilly's knee something had to give.

No-one likes to see a fellow player injured, so it was no surprise that we began our pre-Test net session in a subdued mood.

For the second day in a row, I completed training feeling that I had prepared as best I could for the upcoming match. This is something Swampy has constantly stressed that we should be aiming for at every practice during the tour, and an objective I always try to achieve. It's an attitude that I think caught a journalist by surprise afterwards, too. He asked me, somewhat casually, 'Is this Test match a vital one?'

I don't think he was ready for my reply, which was without hesitation, 'This Test is the most important one of our careers.'

I believe if we have this attitude then we will be hungry and ready to seize the initiative when the moment presents itself. And anyway, you never know which Test is going to be your last, so you owe it to yourself to play as if you mightn't get another opportunity.

WARNEY WITH THE MAN HE CALLS 'THE SPIN DOCTOR' — FORMER AUSTRALIAN LEG-SPINNER AND NOW COMMENTATOR TERRY JENNER.

DAY 55 JULY 3

Third Test — Day One
Old Trafford, Manchester

AUSTRALIA 7–224, (MTG ELLIOTT 40, SR WAUGH 102*, PR REIFFEL 26*).

AS I WAS WALKING up the steps to our dressing-rooms on arriving at the ground this morning, I had mixed feelings about the day ahead. One moment, I was full of doubts. I didn't want to fail again, as I had at Lord's, and I kept thinking about the poor state of this Test wicket. But then I was telling myself to see our situation as just another challenge, to be positive, confront the situation head on, back my technique and mental strength. I thought about Bob Simpson scoring his epic 311 here in 1964 and realised that anything is possible if you really want it. Fortunately, it was the idea of creating a small piece of history that was my lasting thought as I settled into our cramped home for the next five days.

It was a cold, overcast morning, further encouraging the abundant grass cover on the moist-looking Test wicket. Losing here will virtually guarantee England the series. Having said that, part of our game plan is not to worry about long-term objectives such as the series result, but rather concentrating on winning the next session of cricket we play and then each subsequent one. That approach will ensure that our overall objective will be achieved.

At about 10.25am, 35 minutes before the scheduled starting time, Mark Taylor, as usual, returned to the dressing-room to put on his playing gear and don the Australian blazer in preparation for the 10.30 toss. It was at this point that he turned to me and dropped a bombshell. 'Tugga,' he said, 'I think I'm gonna have a bat if we win the toss today.'

I couldn't believe it. However, there was a method to his madness. Tubs believed the wicket looked similar to the pitch of 1993, which turned out to be hard work for batsmen on the first day but after that got even more difficult as it turned quite appreciably. The only problem I could see with his strategy was that we needed to survive the first day to be in a position to let our spinners take control of the game.

Mark's was a gutsy decision that very few would have agreed with. But it is a move that confirms that we are playing for a win and encourages our opponents to be more aggressive in their attitude. Soon after, the toss was once again ours and we were getting ready to take on the under-prepared track.

Following in the footsteps of his famous grandfather, the legendary West Indian batsman of the 1930s and '40s, George Headley, and father, a West Indian Test batsman in the early 1970s, Ron Headley, Kent's opening bowler Dean Headley became the first example of three generations from the same family all playing Test cricket. He certainly wasn't out of place, settling into a nice rhythm from the start as he moved the ball off the wicket at good pace and created enormous problems for our left-handed opening combination. In tandem with Darren Gough, Andy Caddick and Mark Ealham, Headley gave us the fight of our lives as he we struggled to reach the lunch break without losing a grip on the Test.

Taylor, Greg Blewett and Mark Waugh all fell early on to edges, as the ball darted about alarmingly. On such a wicket, where the sideways movement is often extravagant, the ball that gets results is more than likely the one that doesn't deviate much. This is because you start to look for 'gremlins' in the wicket, which leads to a loss of concentration and focus on the next delivery. A tentative prod at the ball, with your feet going nowhere, is the usual end result and that's exactly how our top three perished.

Watching the ball constantly dominate the bat can be very unsettling from the pavilion. I found myself again having to fight hard to exorcise the demons that wanted to take control. When the moment of truth arrived, I took a deep breath and heard the boys wish me well. Out the door I went.

I think it's important to get out in the middle as quickly as possible, to let your opposition know they're in for a battle. Positive body language definitely helps. It was a bonus to get off the mark first ball — there is something significant about seeing runs next to your name and not that big '0'. But it was a real battle early on, with the ball beating the bat a few times and a close lbw appeal going in my favour. Ever gradually, though, I managed to find the middle a few times and began to relax.

Making matters even worse for the batsmen was the fact that one of the sightscreens wasn't big enough to cover the full height of Andy Caddick's arm when he delivered the ball, which, of course, gave him a significant advantage. A lunchtime score of 3–78 was, in the conditions, a pretty even opening session and it left the next two hours as potentially the most important session of the whole Test, perhaps even the series.

As the afternoon wore on I began to grow in confidence. I realised that the English attack had 'lost' their game plan and had got carried away with the extra bounce at their disposal. The short stuff came thick and fast, but from my perspective it was a godsend as it meant the bowlers were exerting a lot of energy but not putting the ball in the danger zone on a good length.

With the score on 85, Matthew Elliott went to a faint edge that, after studying the super-slow-motion replay, probably wasn't an edge at all (but in 'real-life' speed the ump's decision did appear to be the correct one). Michael Bevan copped a real going over with the short stuff, before obliging Alec Stewart, and when Ian Healy (after a stand of 37) and Shane Warne fell we were in dire straits at 7–160.

By now, though, I felt in control of the situation. I had benefited from time I'd spent in the middle and from the attack that was feeding me plenty of half volleys in between the bouncers, which allowed me to not get stagnated but rather to keep the score rolling along at a good pace. We badly needed a partnership, and our saviour was found in Paul Reiffel, a guy whose batting has often been underrated. He is a sweet timer of the ball and his placement is generally very good, but at times he can be a shaky starter. Today, however, he looked the goods from ball one and together we clawed our way towards a reasonable position. But it wasn't all smooth sailing and had Stewart held onto a steepling Headley delivery that found the edge of Reiffel's blade we would most probably have been all out for under 200.

In the last hour of play we turned down three offers from the umpires to go off for bad light, mainly because we felt the runs were coming as easily as they had at any time during the day. The final opportunity to take the light presented the toughest dilemma. There were three overs left in the day, the quicks were still bowling and I was well into the nineties. On the scoreboard there are five lights which are used to help the umpires judge the quality of the light. If no lights are on the batting conditions are perfect. If three lights are on, the umps will confer. Now, all five lights were shining brightly.

I took the unusual step of asking Mike Atherton who was going to bowl. Realising the quicks would mean an end to the day and being hungry for an eighth wicket the England captain replied, 'Croft and Ealham will see out the day.' Knowing this, Pistol and I elected to bat on.

With one over remaining I was within four runs of a century. Croft prepared to run in. In this situation, it is difficult not to premeditate any shots, as you want your 100. Of much greater importance, of course, was that I had to be there at the close of play, so I put the hundred to the back of my mind. Croft moved into bowl ...

I have never been more appreciative to see a short ball come my way. I rocked back and clouted it through cover point to bring up one of my proudest moments as a cricketer.

In the dressing-room, a great reception awaited me, with plenty of backslapping and handshaking. But the first thing I needed to do was get some ice on my right hand, which had taken a beating today from all the deliveries that hit the splice of my bat. Then it was off to do the rounds of the media — three separate TV interviews on top of the media conference.

It was a huge relief for me to score a century today — it was a crucial innings in difficult circumstances and I had successfully fought some self-doubts that had crept into my mind, almost to the point where I doubted my ability. You can imagine what a relief it was to be finally able to venture back to the hotel to see my immediate family. They, like me, are ecstatic with the outcome of today's events.

Third Test — Day Two
Old Trafford, Manchester

AUSTRALIA 235 (SR WAUGH 108, PR REIFFEL 31, DW HEADLEY 4–72)
V ENGLAND 8–161 (MA BUTCHER 51, SK WARNE 5–48).

REACHING A TOTAL IN excess of 250 proved too tough an ask for us this morning. I was first to go, managing to chop an inswinging half volley from Darren Gough onto my stumps. It was a lazy shot, and disappointing considering how hard I'd fought yesterday to survive and prosper. Still, the partnership of 70 between Paul Reiffel and myself was an invaluable one for the team and one that I believe could be the difference between winning and losing.

Reiffel and Jason Gillepsie went shortly after, leaving Glenn McGrath to dwell on yet another century nipped in the bud. We thought our total of 235 was at least very competitive and this was further confirmed when Mike Atherton gave himself every opportunity to cash in on the lunchtime fare by perishing just before the interval.

The remainder of the day was dominated by the genius of Shane Warne, who visibly grew in confidence as he saw the ball gripping and ripping on a surface that was ideally suited to his skill. From a comfortable 1–74, England capitulated to a disastrous 8–123 before an unlikely alliance of Andy Caddick and Mark Ealham came together to add 38 runs by the close of play.

Watching Shane bowl was immensely enjoyable for us all, but without doubt the highlight of the day was the freakish leg-side stumping Ian Healy produced off Michael Bevan's bowling to rid us of Mark Butcher. Bevan is a spinner who bowls the ball at almost medium pace, which obviously makes life difficult for the keeper, who hasn't much time to move around while he's standing up to the stumps. Healy, who had his vision impaired by the batsman in front of him, took a wide half volley that had been speared down the leg-side, and swung round and dislodged the bails in one motion. It was quite extraordinary. To glove such a delivery and at the same time know instinctively that the batsman has overbalanced requires a skill very few possess.

Butcher's dismissal provided the impetus that got us on a roll, to a point where the

The Guardian Friday July 4 1997

6 | Sport97

Cricket

England v Australia: third Test, first day

Gunslinger Waugh leads the fight-back

Mike Selvey sees resolute Steve save his side after an ambush by England's seamers

CHEWING the fat on Wednesday after a golf match in aid of his left fund, Mike Atherton glanced at the Wimbledon coverage on television and remarked that the tennis players and the Lions in South Africa were stealing his team's thunder. There is something to be said for British sports bouncing their successes off another.

Yesterday, though, it began to go belly-up Rusedski and Henman are now history, with parts of their demise viewed by the Old Trafford crowd on the giant screen, and an untidy final session of 14 overs, when the England bowlers lost their discipline, undid much of their earlier good work.

Scoreboard

AUSTRALIA
First Innings

M A Taylor c Thorpe b Headley		2
M T G Elliott c Ea'wa b Headley		40
G S Blewett b Gough		40
S R Waugh c Stewart b Ealham		12
S R Waugh not out		102
M A Healy c Stewart b Caddick		7
S R Waugh c Stewart b Ealham		5
P R Reiffel not out		9
Extras (b 2, lb 4)		11

Total (for 7, 89 overs) 224
Fall of wickets: 1, 72, 42, 95, 113, 155

To bowl: J N Gillespie, G D McGrath
Bowling: Gough 17-6-48-1, Headley 25-4-37-3, Caddick 14-2-53-1, Ealham 11-0-34-2, Croft 4-0-15-0

ENGLAND: M A Butcher, M A Atherton, N Hussain, G P Thorpe, J P Crawley, M A Ealham, R D R Croft, D Gough, A R Caddick, D W Headley
Umpires: G Sharp and S Venkataraghavan

Cricket

The Ashes
0891 22 88 +

Live commentary	28
Match reports	29

Counties News & Scores

Derbyshire	31	Middlesex	40
Durham	32	Northants	41
Essex	33	Nottingham	42
Glamorgan	34	Somerset	43
Gloucs	35	Surrey	44
Hampshire	36	Sussex	45
Kent	37	Warwicks	46
Lancs	38	Worcester	47
Leics	39	Yorkshire	48

Complete county scores
0891 22 88 30

The **Guardian**
INTERACTIVE

By the close of a day shortened by 21 overs because of rain and bad light, Australia had reached 224 for seven, a substantial recovery from 113 for five, the innings held together by a century of the highest class from Steve Waugh. His unbeaten 102 gave his side an edge that ought not to have b en allowed.

With Iunt at the close on 26 was Paul Reiffel who held his end up with some panache, survived a couple of chances and has helped add 64 for the eighth wicket, the highest part nership of the innings.

It could be the difference between winning and losing said Waugh. 'The last hour was really important for us. If England had taken three wickets they would have won the day. But the way it turned out, we won the day.'

Before Waugh's riposte the damage had been done by England's seamers, led on his debut by Dean Headley, who sounds like he might be the first churchman to represent England since the recently retired Bishop of Liverpool.

The man of Kent removed all three left-handers in the top order — Mark Taylor, Matthew Elliott (unlucky to be given out caught behind off his sleeve) and Michael Bevan, to finish with three for 37. There were also two wickets for his county team-mate Mark Ealham, and one each for Darren Gough and Andy Caddick.

Alec Stewart held five catches. Had he accepted a fast but not overtaxing chance from Reiffel when Headley was bowling, or had his the umpire George Sharp agreed that the same batsman had edged Croft in the last over of the day, Stewart would have equalled the Ashes record for an innings, held jointly by Rodney Marsh and Jack Russell.

The bowling, however, had been only competent on a pitch that lacked the snap and spit of Edgbaston and the early part of Lord's, but was sufficiently grassed and clammy to offer extravagant help at times. The ball moved off the seam for Headley, Gough and, occasionally, Caddick, and swung nicely for Ealham; the conditions England promised themselves would beat Australia.

Having won the toss for the third time in the series, Taylor chose to bat first, mindful, no doubt, of the pitch's capacity to iron out. Warne's increasing potential as the game wears on and, perhaps, of the unnerving fact that no captain has asked the opposition to bat first on this ground and won the Test.

Atherton, on the other hand, may well have mulled over the merits of taking first knock and then risked bowling in any case. They had cut their coat according to the cloth by omitting Devon Malcolm, saying thanks but no thanks to Mike Smith, and bringing in Headley.

Waugh's last innings against England had been brief, leg before first ball to Caddick at Lord's. Earlier this week, gunslinger eyes glinting, he announced his intention to rectify the situation. Waugh means what he says and he responded magnificently.

He went to the crease after Headley, Gough and Ealham had disposed of Taylor, Greg Blewett and Mark Waugh respectively. In the next 3½ hours, he made no discernible mistake, defended resolutely and was absolutely certain of his shot selection.

His driving was emphatic and brought him the bulk of his 12 boundaries. But in the gloom of the day's last over, it was a typical square cut, as Croft dropped short, that brought him to his 13th, and in his estimation, the best, hundred of his Test career. It was his fourth against England, all in this country. Somehow it seems a lot more.

Slogger's
side-on glance

Most Excited Man in M6 Traffic Jam: Ron Headley, jumping up and down with excitement around Sandbach Services when his son, Dean, took his first Test wicket.
Reluctant Coach Award: Ron Headley, again. 'I never taught Dean how to bowl against lefthanders or I never taught him how to bowl at all.' 'Good job really. You might have been a fine batsman, Ron, but we've seen your bowling record.'
Most Stylish Accessory Award: Dean Headley's earstud.

Quick off the mark . . . England's Dean Headley made an early impact on his Test debut

English batsmen didn't know how they were going to survive, let alone score runs. We're now in the 'driving seat', with every chance to square the series. Warney's haul of five wickets puts him equal with Richie Benaud on 248 Test wickets for his career, while Heals' great stumping was his 100th victim in 25 Tests against England.

Tonight presented the opportunity to have dinner with Mum, Beverley and Daryl, brother Mark and his fiancee, Sue, and good friends Peter and Iris, who looked after Mark and me some 13 years ago when we first came to England to play league cricket.

It was pleasing for me to get that first-innings hundred, while Mum was in the crowd. She, along with my father, Rodger, played a huge part in where Mark and I are at now. Hopefully, Mark can get a few in the second dig, before she goes back home to Oz.

Third Test — Day Three
Old Trafford, Manchester

AUSTRALIA 235 AND 6-262 (ME WAUGH 55, SR WAUGH 82*, IA HEALY 47,
SK WARNE 33*) V ENGLAND 162 (SK WARNE 6-48, GD MCGRATH 3-40).

THE LAST TWO ENGLISH wickets fell for the addition of only one run, which left us with the opportunity for the batsmen to go out and win the Test match. By making England chase anything over 300, we will set up a position where they would have to defy history for us to lose — few teams manage more than 300 to win a Test match. Because of the nature of the wicket, and the way it's going to turn, getting anything more than 150 batting last will be very, very difficult.

Unfortunately, our second innings began poorly when Taylor was out for half his first-innings score, and Blewett fell in highly-controversial circumstances. Judging from the replays, Greg has every right to question whether or not Nasser Hussain caught him cleanly at first slip off Robert Croft. It appeared to most people that some turf preceded contact between flesh and leather, but the England vice-captain came up from the ground claiming a vital wicket. This certainly left a nasty taste in our mouths, especially after Ian Healy's sporting gesture at Lord's when no-one, including the umpires, knew for sure whether the ball had carried or not. The debate after stumps had been drawn over this dismissal focused on whether the third umpire should be used to rule on catches that even the fieldsman involved can't be 100 per cent certain about.

Dean Headley, meanwhile, continued his love affair with our left-handers, disposing of Elliott with a ball that left the batsman off the wicket. We were 3–39 and the match was wide open once more.

Elliott's was a dreaded dismissal for me, as I was in the cubicle having a 'nervous one' when I heard the roar of the crowd and knew I was required out in the middle. Fortunately, I got off to a dream start, finding the gaps and timing the ball nicely from the jump, a legacy of my time in the middle in the first innings.

At lunch, Mark Waugh and I were set to produce a big partnership. We were both in the twenties and had enjoyed the benefit of playing ourselves in on a wicket that was never going to get any better for batting. But after putting on 92, Mark was deceived by a fine change of pace from the always thinking Ealham. In the meantime, I had been struggling with my hand problem at the other end. By now it was restricting my shot making and the power I was able to get on the ball. At the fall of Mark's wicket, I called for an ice pack to ease the swelling and to relieve the soreness a little. However, the pain gradually worsened to a point where I couldn't force

THE MUCH-TALKED-ABOUT DISMISSAL OF GREG BLEWETT.

the ball through the field at all. I was basically defending one-handed, as I tried to minimise the pain that was going through my thumb joint and the space between thumb and forefinger.

When Michael Bevan came to the crease, it looked as if his mind was tortured. He failed to come to terms with a barrage of short balls aimed at his body, before popping up a catch to the gully. I really did feel sorry for him, as he looked like he'd hit rock bottom as he walked away. The only consolation is that now there's only one way to go and that is up, but in between a lot of hard work and soul-searching must transpire.

I needed a partner to keep things moving, as I wasn't about to set the game alight with dashing strokeplay. This time it was Ian Healy and then Shane Warne who put their hand ups. Healy hit a crucial 47, while Warne played his shots from the very first ball he faced. But he was a little fortunate. If Blewett had been unlucky earlier in the innings, then Warne probably made up for this when he was given not out to an appeal for a catch close in. The umpire thought the ball had been jammed into the ground, but that super-slow-motion replay revealed the umpire had erred (from my vantage point at the bowler's end, however, it was virtually impossible to tell what the correct answer was).

By the conclusion of play, I had battled to an unbeaten 82, while Warne had made it look easy on his way to 33 not out. Our lead was 335. For England, Headley was again the pick of the bowlers. Croft claimed a couple of poles, but didn't turn the ball as one would have expected him to have done in the conditions.

My hand wasn't a pretty sight when I pulled it from the glove to give Errol a closer look after play. It was nearly twice its normal size, with a deep bruise dominating the area in distress. After ice treatment, the joint was wrapped and bound to try to stop any further bleeding and to reduce the existing inflammation.

Third Test — Day Four
Old Trafford, Manchester

AUSTRALIA 235 AND 8–395 (DECLARED: SR WAUGH 116, SK WARNE 53, PR REIFFEL 45*, DW HEADLEY 4–104) V ENGLAND 162 AND 5–130 (JP CRAWLEY 53*).

I WASN'T FEELING TOO nervous as I tucked into a bowl of honey snacks this morning … until I read in the paper that if I managed to score another 18 more runs today I would become only the third Australian in Ashes history to score two hundreds in the same match. The two Australians to achieve this feat were both left-handers, Warren Bardsley and Arthur Morris, with the last double being achieved by Morris back in 1946–47. Now I was a fraction nervous about the prospect of becoming part of such an elite group. The hand had pulled up reasonably well, with a distinct reduction in the swelling, but the sharp pain in the joints remained, as I stretched out in the hotel's indoor swimming pool.

Warne and I got off to the perfect start, hitting 20 runs from the first three overs to set the tone for the day, and to further put England out of the game. Shane completed his second Test half-century, but just when a 100 seemed a possibility, the way he was striking the ball, he fell 47 short of that landmark.

Whenever a player gets to 99 he immediately tenses up — you're so close to that elusive milestone that you don't want to stuff it up now. On this occasion, going from 97 to 98 to 99 was torturous, especially as I kept recalling how I'd been robbed of three runs earlier in the innings when the umpire had given leg byes instead of runs. My second hundred was finally secured with a push through mid-wicket off Robert Croft. The elation was not as intense as in the first innings, but the satisfaction was the same, especially considering the handicap I'd played through.

Headley put paid to my aspirations of a big hundred when he produced a near unplayable lifter that steepled off a good length and 'gloved' me through to the keeper. The good news to come out of this event was that it confirmed that the wicket was still playing a few tricks. But Reiffel and Gillespie made the pitch look benign, scoring freely in an unbeaten ninth-wicket stand of 62 before Mark Taylor declared 20 minutes after

WITH PAUL REIFFEL AFTER BECOMING THE FIRST AUSTRALIAN RIGHT-HANDED
BATSMAN TO SCORE A CENTURY IN EACH INNINGS OF AN ASHES TEST.

lunch, leaving England the option of surviving a minimum of 141 overs for a draw or scoring an imposing 469 runs to win.

England got off to a solid start before Gillespie started the rot, sending back Atherton with one that beat him for pace and trapped him in front, not long after the English captain had sent a hook shot into the full-house crowd. Stewart became Warne's 250th Test scalp shortly after, and he was closely followed by Hussain and Butcher.

Butcher was again beaten for pace, top-edging a hook to Glenn McGrath at fine leg, who came sprinting in to take a fine one-handed catch (even though he attempted to gather it in both hands). Glenn's fielding has improved out of sight on this tour with his ground fielding being exceptional. There was, though, one notable exception to this earlier on our trip — an 'air swing' off a top-edged sweep that, to everyone's amusement, spun wickedly past his outstretched arm at deep backward square.

The prize scalp of Thorpe went to Warne, who out-thought him with a wrong'un that claimed the edge and plunged the home side further into the abyss at 5–84. Restoring some local pride was John Crawley, who feasted himself on Bevan's mixed bag of goodies. Generally, it was the gift full tosses that the batsman hit to the advertising boards, but in between Crawley had to be watchful of that unplayable ball Bevan has the ability to produce.

The afternoon session was marred by spectator interference, which seemed to be some sort of protest against the home side's poor showing. The pitch invasions were numerous and tiresome, with play continually held up while the intruders frolicked around the outfield. One notable exception was the 'kamikaze kid' who raced out and dived full length into the stumps, in an imaginary tackle that may well have even stopped the All Blacks' Jonah Lomu. When play was possible, Ealham and Crawley added 46 before we

AUSTRALIAN PICTURE LIBRARY/ALLSPORT

left the field in search of a cold one and to have a chat about the day. Once more, my post-match time was taken up by the media, to whom I offered pretty much the same spiel that I'd given them two days before.

IAN HEALY NEEDED A HELMET TO KEEP TO SHANE WARNE AND MICHAEL BEVAN.

DAY 59 JULY 7

Third Test — Day Five
Old Trafford, Manchester

AUSTRALIA 235 AND 8–395 (DECLARED) DEFEATED ENGLAND 162 AND 200 (JP CRAWLEY 83, GD MCGRATH 4–46, JN GILLESPIE 3–31, SK WARNE 3–63) BY 268 RUNS.

THE MOOD WAS JOVIAL and confident as we limbered up in the rooms this morning. There was no rain in sight and only five wickets separated us from a comprehensive victory. When play began it wasn't Shane Warne, but the thoroughly professional Glenn McGrath who claimed four of the five wickets to fall. Warne again bowled superbly, but without the wheel of good fortune turning in his favour.

John Crawley could consider himself to be a bit stiff, when he dislodged a bail while fending off a short ball, but the rest of the batsmen were simply not good enough on the day. Robert Croft, in particular, looked a mess at the crease. He seemed ready to be pummelled by the short ball, as he knows his technique isn't going to cope with the onslaught. Some hard work awaits him in the nets during the off season.

The winning margin was a whopping 268 runs, one that will give the English squad plenty to think about in the future Tests. The celebrations afterwards were moderate by our normal standards, because we know there is a long way to go. The journey has just begun.

Again, I was summoned to the press conference by the media, along with Tubs. I was covered in beer, champagne and red wine, and sat shivering with cold while every question was directed at Mark. What a waste that press conference was for me. Then it was time for that sweetest of all times, the team song, which was again sung with such gusto and pride one was immediately covered in goosebumps.

It was farewell to Mum tonight. She flies back to Australia tomorrow, after spending four weeks touring the country. I was glad Mark and I rewarded her with some runs in this match, even though I know she would have been a nervous wreck watching us play.

ENGLAND V AUSTRALIA

Third Test- 3rd-7th July, 1997 at Old Trafford

Umpires: G. Sharp/S. Venkataraghavan   Standby: J. H. Hampshire

Match Referee: R. Madugalle   *TOSS WON BY: Australia who elected to bat.*

50p

Scorers: M. J. Proctor (England)/M. K. Walsh (Australia)
Man of the Match Adjudicator: P. J. W. Allott

ENGLAND

		FIRST INNINGS		SECOND INNINGS	
1	M. A. Butcher	st. Healy b. Bevan	51	ct. McGrath b. Gillespie	28
2	M. A. Atherton*	ct. Healy b. McGrath	5	l.b.w. b. Gillespie	21
3	A. J. Stewart+	ct. Taylor b. Warne	30	b. Warne	1
4	N. Hussain	ct. Healy b. Warne	13	l.b.w. b. Gillespie	1
5	G. P. Thorpe	ct. Taylor b. Warne	3	ct. Healy b. Warne	7
6	J. P. Crawley	ct. Healy b. Warne	4	Hit Wicket b. McGrath	83
7	M. A. Ealham	Not Out	24	ct. Healy b. McGrath	9
8	R. D. B. Croft	ct. S. Waugh b. McGrath	7	ct. Reiffel b. McGrath	7
9	D. Gough	l.b.w. b. Warne	1	b. McGrath	6
10	A. R. Caddick	ct. M. Waugh b. Warne	15	ct. Gillespie b. Warne	17
11	D. W. Headley	b. McGrath	0	Not Out	0
		Extras b-4 lb-3 w- nb-2	9	Extras b-14 lb-4 w-1 nb-1	20
		TOTAL	162	TOTAL	200

BOWLING ANALYSIS	O	M	R	W	WD	NB	O	M	R	W	WD	NB
McGrath	23.4	9	40	3			21	4	46	4		
Reiffel	9	3	14	0		2	2	0	8	0		1
Warne	30	14	48	6			30.4	8	63	3		1
Gillespie	14	3	39	0			12	4	31	3		
Bevan	8	3	14	1			8	2	34	0		

Fall of Wickets:

1-8 2-74 3-94 4-101 5-110 6-111
7-122 8-123 9-161

1-44 2-45 3-50 4-55 5-84 6-158
7-170 8-177 9-188

AUSTRALIA

		FIRST INNINGS		SECOND INNINGS	
1	M. A. Taylor*	ct. Thorpe b. Headley	2	ct. Butcher b. Headley	1
2	M. T. G. Elliott	ct. Stewart b. Headley	40	ct. Butcher b. Headley	11
3	G. S. Blewett	b. Gough	8	ct. Hussain b. Croft	19
4	M. E. Waugh	ct. Stewart b. Ealham	12	b. Ealham	55
5	S. R. Waugh	b. Gough	108	ct. Stewart b. Headley	116
6	M. G. Bevan	ct. Stewart b. Headley	7	ct. Atherton b. Headley	0
7	I. A. Healy+	ct. Stewart b. Caddick	9	ct. Butcher b. Croft	47
8	S. K. Warne	ct. Stewart b. Ealham	3	ct. Stewart b. Caddick	53
9	P. R. Reiffel	b. Gough	31	Not Out	45
10	J. N. Gillespie	ct. Stewart b. Headley	0	Not Out	28
11	G. D. McGrath	Not Out	0	Did Not Bat	
		Extras b-8 lb-4 w-0 nb-3	15	Extras b-1 lb-13 w- nb-6	20
		TOTAL	235	TOTAL (for 8 dec.)	395

* Captain
+ Wicket-keeper

BOWLING ANALYSIS	O	M	R	W	WD	NB	O	M	R	W	WD	NB
Gough	21	7	52	3		1	20	3	62	0		2
Headley	27.3	4	72	4		1	29	4	104	4		
Caddick	14	2	52	1			21	0	69	1		4
Ealham	11	2	34	2		1	13	3	41	1		4
Croft	4	0	13	0			39	12	105	2		

Fall of Wickets:

1-9 2-22 3-42 4-85 5-113 6-150
7-160 8-230 9-235

1-5 2-33 3-39 4-131 5-132 6-210
7-298 8-333 9-

Hours of Play: 11.00 a.m. to 6.00 p.m. or after 90 overs have been bowled whichever is the later. On the last day, a minimum of 75 overs have to be bowled. The captains may agree to stop play at 5.30 p.m. on the 5th day if there is no prospect of a result. Lunch: 1.00 p.m- 1.40 p.m. Tea: 3.40 p.m. - 4.00 p.m. (The fielding team can claim a new ball if they wish, after 80 overs.)

AUSTRALIA WON BY 268 RUNS

(Man of the Match - S. R. Waugh)

THE FINAL OFFICIAL SCORECARD FROM THE THIRD TEST.

DAY 60 JULY 8

Newcastle

AUSTRALIANS 7—290 (BP JULIAN 106)
DEFEATED MINOR COUNTIES 9—281
(I COCKBAIN 82, MJ SLATER 1—7,
JL LANGER 1—19) BY 9 RUNS.

WHOEVER PENCILLED THIS MATCH into our itinerary has obviously never been part of a winning side before. To have to front up to this politically correct fixture against the Minor Counties XI the day after a Test win and after two-and-a-half hours on the motorway is so ridiculous it defies logic. All we could do was take the attitude of 'Oh well, we're here now and we have a job to do'. Today was captain's day for me, as Tubs was having a breather (something which I probably should have had as well, considering the state of the painfully swollen joint between my right thumb and index finger). In fact, I have assumed the captaincy role for this leg of the tour while Tubs linked up with the captains of all the Test-playing nations for a meeting in London to discuss various issues and concerns of the players.

This type of match isn't popular with the players for a number of reasons. One, the opposition is nothing like what we face at international level. Two, while such a fixture is okay at the start of a tour, when we are still finding our feet, by the tour's half-way mark tough opposition is required so we can fine-tune our game. And, three, it is assumed that we will win in convincing fashion — if we don't the doomsday clouds come from all around, usually in the form of headline-seeking journalists.

Fortunately for us, we had no such problems. This was thanks largely to the prodigious hitting of BJ, who, after we batted first, looked as if he was playing with his brothers in the backyard on his way to 106 off just 89 balls.

Quite often in these uninspiring encounters the lads make their own fun, and today our entertainment came from the generous odds our 12th man, Jason Gillespie, offered the lads on a variety of matters such as our final scoreline, sixes struck and wickets taken.

Everyone had a go picking our innings total, with the winner taking all. Tony Smith, our always hard-working baggage man, used his 26 years in the job to great effect by

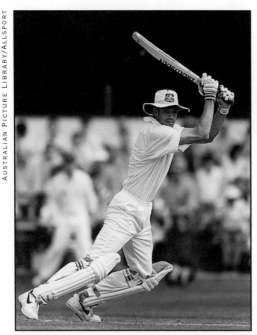

BJ HITS OUT DURING HIS SPECTACULAR CENTURY.

nominating 289 as our final score, just a single away from being spot on but easily close enough to collect the winning prizemoney.

More exciting was the odds Dizzy offered. On hitting a six:

3–1 Blewett, Bevan and Ponting

5–1 Langer, Julian and Elliott

On taking a wicket:

7–1 Slater

10–1 Langer

BJ's odds were quickly shown up to be as ridiculous as we first thought. He cleared the ropes not once, but eight times! Surprisingly, Herbie didn't have many backers in his corner, so it was with great personal delight that he sweetly lifted a pull shot into the adjoining terraced houses and promptly swivelled around to signal triumphantly to the disbelieving troops. However, Dizzy unexpectedly collected after Bevan, Blewett, Langer and Ponting were unable to deliver maximums, so it appeared as if the goateed one was on track for a very profitable day's work. Fate, though, was about to deal him a nasty, unexpected double blow.

With the game safely in our keeping and much to the crowd's delight, I let loose the 'rodeo clowns', Lang and Slats, to bowl the last two overs of the match. Slats was first to strike, with a slower ball that, according to the bowler, dipped wickedly. All eyes immediately turned to the balcony, where Gillespie, head in hands, contemplated the loss of 20 trips to the Golden Arches.

The arrival of Lang at the bowling crease sent the full house into chants of 'Langer! … Langer! …' His response was immediate. His action was strong and eager, his follow through unstoppable. The result: a catch taken on the deep mid-off boundary by Paul Reiffel that sent the crowd into wild celebrations and the players into uncontrollable fits of laughter. By now Dizzy was out of his chair, standing in a somewhat distressed state with arms wide apart, pleading for mercy. It was with some sadness that Lang couldn't repeat his success with the remaining five balls, but even so these final two overs did cap off what had developed into a very enjoyable afternoon.

Normally a winning captain will get a few pats on the back and some nice words, but all I received was abuse when I entered the change rooms. In front of me was one cash-strapped 12th man, who angrily wanted to know why I had put the game into disrepute by bowling the five-foot-plus-not-much, tearaways. My reply was straight to the point,

'I had faith in the boys and they didn't let me down!'

End of story.

On a personal note, I may have created a record as skipper today by claiming no wickets, not facing a ball and taking no catches. Obviously the captaincy brings out the best in my game!

With most of the families joining us on this section of the tour, it made a pleasant change to get out of the hotel atmosphere and enjoy a barbecue in the fresh air. It was something we should do more often, as it bonds not only the players but the families, too — if you can keep everyone happy you are well on the road to success. To cap off the night, the Blewetts were surprised with an engagement cake, but hopefully what then happened isn't an omen because it was soaked by a thunderstorm that arrived unexpectedly.

SLATS (LEFT) AND LANG (CENTRE) ARE HAPPY TO POSE WITH THEIR DEJECTED BOOKIE, AFTER THEIR SPLENDID BOWLING EFFORTS AGAINST MINOR COUNTIES.

DAY 61 | JULY 9

Edinburgh

PHILIP BROWN

GREG BLEWETT AT DALMAHOY GC.

THE WAUGH FAMILY LOOKED a bit shabby as we loaded our ever-growing luggage into our Toyota sponsored van. Once again, we had endured an interrupted sleep due to the absence of an air conditioner combined with the ridiculous central heating that made conditions so hot and humid it was hard to breathe.

Rosie didn't enjoy the sweltering temperatures. It's becoming increasingly noticeable that she is not coping well with the constantly changing routine, with different hotels, long car trips and noisy rooms. She isn't able to shake the slight bout of flu she's been carrying around, and I'm beginning to think that she's better off at home with Lynette, even though I love having them touring with me.

The two-and-a-half-hour trip was made worthwhile by the sight of the Dalmahoy Hotel, which is set among a pristine looking golf course on the outskirts of Edinburgh. While most of the lads ventured out onto the course, I took Rosie to the nearby leisure centre for a swim. This is an activity she seems to have a real liking for. Perhaps she'll be a future Olympic champion, although I fancy she'll be a tennis or squash player because her birthday coincides with two Australian greats, Heather McKay and Evonne Cawley.

DAY 62 JULY 10

Edinburgh

MY FIRST TASK TODAY as captain was to front up at a press conference which was staged to try to help promote our upcoming fixture and cricket in general in Scotland. In general, it was quite an enjoyable hour-long interrogation, but one question did stand out. It came from somewhere near the back of the room, from a middle-aged man who appeared to know what he was talking about. That was until he quizzed me on Shane Warne. He inquired, 'What is wrong with Shane Warne, he doesn't seem to turn them any more. Has he lost it?'

Considering Warney had claimed nine wickets in the third Test only last week and bowled numerous unplayable deliveries that spun at times viciously, I couldn't quite believe what I had heard. My response was brief and enjoyed by all except the bloke who asked the question.

'Don't you own a TV?' I asked. 'Didn't you watch the last Test?'

Amid the growing laughter, he admitted that he had been on holidays in France and missed the action. I'm sure he now regrets his lack of preparation for today.

If I get a free day on tour, I love nothing more than to visit the local zoo. I find it relaxing, therapeutic and as far away as possible from anything related to cricket. And having Rosie with me means such a venture is now doubly enjoyable, for every animal she sees and every smell she senses are new to her. To see the gorgeous, ever-curious look on her face is something that rivals anything I can achieve on the sporting field.

With the sun not setting here until around 10pm, you can squeeze a lot into one day. The extra daylight tonight provided the opportunity for me to visit the hotel complex's driving range, in preparation for our journey tomorrow to golf's equivalent of Lord's — St Andrews. However, judging from the resting spot of my 50 practice balls, I'm a good thing to make it three hundreds in a week, with the duck hook and pushed drive two shots certain to feature prominently after I get on the first tee in the morning.

DAY 63 JULY 11

Edinburgh

AT ABOUT THE SAME time the team bus was heading for golf's Mecca, both Warney and Gilly were about to board a jumbo that was heading back to Australia. The diagnosis on Gilly's left knee was a severely stretched medial ligament, which requires rest and then much strengthening work in order for him to enjoy a complete recovery. It was such a shame to see him leave, as he was a very popular team member and a guy destined for higher honours (which I'm sure will still come so long as he treats this setback as a test of character and not something that will permanently damage his career). Victorian keeper Darren Berry has been called up as his replacement. Warney, by contrast, was going home because of some good news. The tour hierarchy had allowed him to spend a couple of days back in Oz, so he can see his new-born baby in the flesh.

This is an initiative that is new in cricket circles, but I'm glad he's going home because he'll have a chance to bond with his daughter and see her in the flesh, rather than having to make do with the couple of photos that have been sent over. I just hope the Australian press give him a couple of days peace with his family.

Arriving at St Andrews is heaven for golf freaks. Every second shop sells everything to do with the game and there is a whole chain of links courses in the close vicinity. Among our squad, Punter and Blewey were particularly excited about the prospect of today's round — especially Ricky, who already has two sub–70 rounds to his name this tour, one of them on the Belfry's championship course.

First stop was a guided tour of the renowned St Andrews clubhouse. The only catch was the need for a jacket and tie, which quite a few of the lads had forgotten to bring along. However, the boys somehow managed to scrounge together the necessary items to enable them to make the tour. BJ was quite a sight, dressed in a vertically-striped tie nestled atop a horizontally-striped shirt and finished off with a diagonally-striped jacket. Next to that outfit, the highlight of the clubhouse tour was seeing the oldest ever painting depicting the game of golf, which hung unobtrusively in the members' sitting room with a value of over £2 million attached to it.

The only downer for the day was that we weren't playing the historic 'Old Course' but the 'New Course' (which was first played on in 1895). Having played the Old Course in 1989, this wasn't the huge disappointment for me that it was for some others.

The surprise packet of the day was Justin Langer, whose group took out the team prize ahead of the more fancied combinations. Blewey had a shocker by his standards, shooting in the high 80s. Late into the evening, he was still shaking his head in disbelief as he struggled to come to terms with 'taking the gas on the big occasion', as he put it. Punter was steady, carding a 77, which sounds impressive until you discover just how good this guy strikes the ball.

Smithy, meanwhile, was confirming my theory that if someone hasn't any co-ordination at ball sports they take up fitness work to cover their deficiencies. His score was of epic proportions, 137 strokes in all. Knowing Smithy, he would have enjoyed every one of them, if only because of all the walking he did to retrieve his wayward balls.

To cap off a great day, most of the team snuck out into the Old Course just before dusk to play the famous 17th hole — the Road Hole. The sceptics said it wasn't possible, but these rebels succeeded in doing so before any of the course marshals spotted their efforts. Like Lord's, there is strict protocol and rules here that must be obeyed by all, especially the law that requires you to be on the first tee 10 minutes before your scheduled starting time. Tragic stories have been told of overseas visitors arriving for their game only marginally late, and being given their marching orders. This would be an extremely severe blow, as you have to book 18 months ahead just to swing a club on the course.

AUSTRALIAN PICTURE LIBRARY/ALLSPORT

THE 1997 AUSTRALIANS AT ST ANDREWS.

DAY 64 | JULY 12

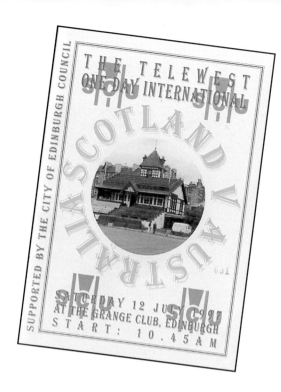

Edinburgh

AUSTRALIANS 9–278 (MJ SLATER 95,
JL LANGER 46, KLP SHERIDAN 5–65)
V SCOTLAND 6–95 (MS KASPROWICZ
3–28) NO RESULT.

IN THE MAIL THIS morning I received a letter which I will always treasure. It was dated July 9 and read as follows …

> *Dear Steve,*
>   *Welcome to the A.T.C.C., the Ashes Two Centuries Club. You can be President and I'll be the C.E.O., as we are the only two left!*
>   *Future Australian members can be assured of a warm welcome and, let's face it, we could do with some more.*
>   *Congratulations on all your performances and best wishes to the two Marks and the team for a successful tour. Regards.*
> *Sincerely*
> *Arthur Morris*

An unexpected full house came to the impressive Grange Cricket Club for the eagerly awaited clash between the Australians and the latest team to qualify for cricket's 1999 World Cup. The success of the Scots at the recent World Cup qualifying tournament in Malaysia has increased the profile of the sport here ten-fold, to the extent the story of their success kicked soccer off the newspaper back pages, if only for one day.

Going out to toss was, inevitably, a major event, with cameras from Sky Television and various local stations, plus journalists from the print media, joining George Salmond, the local captain, and myself as the coin went up. The toss even had to be re-enacted for one cameraman, who happened to miss this momentous event the first time around.

The unwritten rule in these types of games is that we bat first, to set a big total and give the crowd value for money. This is exactly what occurred, even though Salmond called correctly on a placid looking strip that seemed ideally suited to batting. Slats then came out guns blazing and gave the opposing bowlers a lesson in how not to bowl to a player capable of executing the most ferocious pull shots known to man. After 15 overs, it looked as if a team total of 400 might be attainable, but this notion fell by the wayside when Slats fell five runs short of a century. Lang and Punter were the only other Australian batsmen to do themselves justice, as the middle to late-order handed the left arm orthodox spinner, Keith Sheridan, a gift 'five-for' and a guaranteed place in Scotland's cricket folklore.

My stint at the crease was a waste of time, as I was barely able to hold the bat, due to the stiffness and pain in my right thumb joints. The medicos tell me this is a problem that needs up to six or seven weeks rest to fully correct — a gap in the schedule that is impossible to find in a whole year, let alone on this tour.

Playing for a Test spot should always lead to excellence, and it was once again Kasper who put his hand up. He produced a decisive spell of quality outswing bowling that left the Bravehearts in dire straits after their first 10 overs at the crease. Dizzy was also impressive, but BJ's wretched run of luck continued. An infected ingrown toenail threw his approach off balance and led to a wayward spell that has probably condemned him to last place on the bowling queue.

Late in the day, just before the match was abandoned because of a torrential downpour, the cricket became a sideshow to the main event — a tandem streaking act. The male intruder was apprehended almost immediately, but his female counterpart somehow escaped the wrath of the security guards to frolic merrily across the outfield, much to the delight of the capacity crowd and some unnamed observers on the playing field.

The whole day was a great success for what has been until recently a 'remote' cricket outpost. If the game is to prosper into the next century it is the cricketers of these embryonic nations who must be fostered, to ensure the continued expansion of the game. We appreciated the opportunity to have a chat with the opposition after the game — not just because they're good fellas, but especially because they are eager to acquire as much cricket knowledge as they can so they can try to reach a competitive level during the 1999 World Cup.

After the post-match festivities, Slats, Heals, Kasper and I set off down the motorway for Birmingham — a minimum four hours — so we would be there for the start of the British Grand Prix at Silverstone tomorrow. One of Heals' sponsors, Foster's, are a major contributor to the Formula One events and when four guest spots became available to the team, the names of the petrol heads in the squad went into a hat. I was one of the lucky ones.

I've always wanted to see exactly how quick these cars go and what skills the drivers need to be successful. There's something about a major sporting event that always stirs my imagination. Maybe it's the thrill of the unknown outcome, or perhaps the aura and mystique that surround the spectacle. For me, I think it's the chance to observe the very best in action that separates these occasions from anything else.

DAY 65 JULY 13

Silverstone

FOLLOWING SLATS' INSTRUCTIONS, WE set off at 7.30am in search of a remote airfield on the outskirts of Silverstone. From there we were to be airlifted, via helicopter, to the race track. This, we had been told, was a very good move, as the circuit is inevitably surrounded by many kilometres of gridlocked traffic on the morning of the Grand Prix. However, we missed our designated lift-off time, which meant we didn't arrive until an hour later than we had hoped and therefore didn't get to enjoy a proposed tour down pit straight.

The race itself was highly entertaining, extremely loud and a very worthwhile experience. The only downer for me was that watching the race was somewhat repetitious in nature, because you can see only one section of the track. For Slats, this wasn't a concern. He was in revhead heaven. We certainly got the impression, though, that a lot of people come to this sport for the social life in the marquees and the 'celebrity spotting' opportunities rather than the sport itself. The Aussie boys were as guilty as anyone in this regard, as we enthusiastically pointed out, among others, Pierce Brosnan and Melinda Messenger (the 'Page 3' girl).

The power of the sport almost cost us dearly as we headed for London afterwards. Kasper's execution of a roundabout exit all but came to grief, due to what might be described as his 'overexuberance' at the wheel. Thankfully we all arrived at the Heathrow Excelsior Hotel in one piece, and set about preparing for tomorrow's one-day game at John Paul Getty's private estate.

ABOVE: AN ON-DRIVE DURING THE FIRST OF THE TWO HUNDREDS I SCORED IN THE THIRD TEST, AT MANCHESTER.

RIGHT: THIS WAS ONE OF MY MOST SATISFYING TEST CENTURIES, HIT AT A TIME WHEN THE TEAM DESPERATELY NEEDED SOMEONE TO MANAGE A BIG SCORE.

AUSTRALIAN PICTURE LIBRARY/ALLSPORT

AUSTRALIAN PICTURE LIBRARY/ALLSPORT

ABOVE: SHANE WARNE BOWLING TO GRAHAM THORPE ON THE SECOND DAY AT OLD TRAFFORD, WHEN HE SPUN THROUGH THE ENGLISH TOP-ORDER IN DEVASTATING FASHION.

LEFT: MARK WAUGH ON THE ATTACK DURING HIS SECOND-INNINGS HALF CENTURY IN THE THIRD TEST.

OPPOSITE PAGE

TWO ANGLES OF IAN HEALY'S REMARKABLE STUMPING OF MARK BUTCHER IN THE THIRD TEST.
TOP: HEALS HAS SCOOPED UP A QUICK, OVERPITCHED LEG-SIDE DELIVERY FROM MICHAEL BEVAN AND WHIPPED OFF THE BAILS.

BOTTOM: THE AUSTRALIANS WAIT FOR CONFIRMATION THAT OUR GREAT KEEPER HAS COMPLETED HIS 100TH DISMISSAL IN ASHES CRICKET.

THE THIRD AND FOURTH TESTS

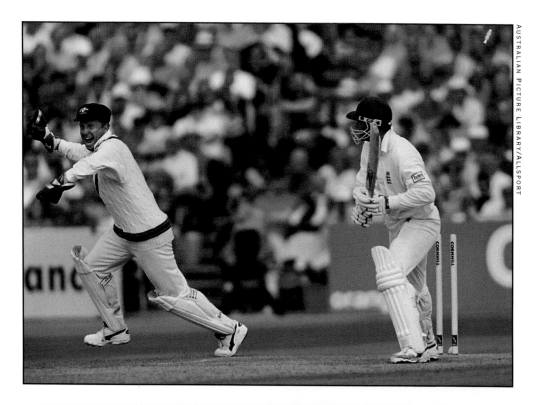

THE THIRD AND FOURTH TESTS

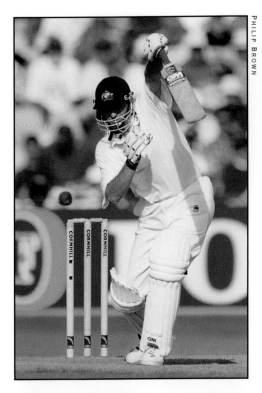

PHILIP BROWN

LEFT: FEELING THE EFFECTS OF MY DAMAGED RIGHT THUMB DURING OUR SECOND INNINGS OF THE THIRD TEST.

BELOW: WITH MARK TAYLOR IN THE OLD TRAFFORD DRESSING-ROOMS AFTER WE'D LEVELLED THE SERIES.

OPPOSITE PAGE

TOP LEFT: MATTHEW ELLIOTT ON HIS WAY TO 199 DURING OUR ONLY INNINGS OF THE FOURTH TEST, AT HEADINGLEY, HIS SECOND HUNDRED OF THE ENGLISH SUMMER.

TOP RIGHT: RICKY PONTING HOOKS DURING HIS FAMOUS PARTNERSHIP WITH ELLIOTT IN THE FOURTH TEST, WHEN THEY TOOK AUSTRALIA FROM A PRECARIOUS 4–50 TO A COMMANDING 5–318. PONTING'S 127, HIS FIRST TEST CENTURY, CAME IN HIS MAIDEN ASHES ENCOUNTER.

BOTTOM: RICKY STUART (LEFT PHOTO, IN CAP) AND COACH MAL MENINGA (RIGHT PHOTO, NOT IN CAP) WERE AMONG THE CANBERRA RAIDERS WHO CAME TO THE HEADINGLEY DRESSING-ROOM TO CONGRATULATE US ON OUR BIG WIN.

STEVE WAUGH

THE THIRD AND FOURTH TESTS

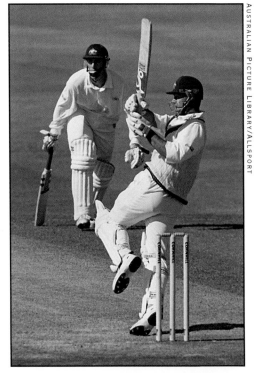

THE THIRD AND FOURTH TESTS

GLENN MCGRATH, WHO IS AT LEAST VERY, VERY CLOSE TO BEING A GENUINELY
GREAT AUSTRALIAN FAST BOWLER, ENJOYS HIS SUCCESS AT LEEDS.

THE THIRD AND FOURTH TESTS

JASON 'DIZZY' GILLESPIE, WHO 'CAME OF AGE' AT HEADINGLEY WHEN HE TOOK 7–37 IN ENGLAND'S FIRST INNINGS AND NARROWLY BEAT MATTHEW ELLIOTT FOR THE MAN-OF-THE-MATCH AWARD.

THE THIRD AND FOURTH TESTS

IAN HEALY IN THE HEADINGLEY DRESSING-ROOM, LEADING THE TROOPS IN ANOTHER STIRRING RENDITION OF 'UNDER THE SOUTHERN CROSS'.

THE TEAM SONGS CONTINUE DURING THE EARLY STAGES OF A PARTY THAT WENT LONG INTO THE NIGHT.

THE THIRD AND FOURTH TESTS

DAY 66 JULY 14

Ibstone

AUSTRALIANS 5–267 (DECLARED; MTG ELLIOTT 95, MG BEVAN 54) DREW
WITH JP GETTY'S INVITATION XI 4–237 (RA SMITH 57, MD CROWE 115,
MG BEVAN 4–85).

BEING A TOUR SELECTOR can have some advantages, particularly in these 'goodwill' fixtures where the off-field hospitality more than rivals the on-field action. Consequently, my duties today were strictly family orientated. Lynette and Rosalie had driven down from Scotland by themselves to be part of the festivities.

John Paul Getty's love of cricket has a rather unusual, perhaps even unique, origin. During a stint at a clinic for alcohol rehabilitation, Mr Getty (who is, of course, one of the world's wealthiest men) was introduced to the Rolling Stones' Mick Jagger — a man whose love of the game is legendary. Jagger suggested the billionaire recluse give cricket a try, and the rest is history. Soon, JPG was the owner of *Wisden*, the English equivalent of the *Bible*, and he had also donated a couple of million pounds to the MCC to help finance the renovations at Lord's.

In fact, Mr Getty fell for the game so badly that he built his own ground at his private retreat, which is situated about an hour's drive from London. The winding narrow road which leads to his magnificent property offers no clue as to the majesty of this ground. Then, suddenly, it's there in front of you — a beautifully manicured outfield, scoreboard complete with thatched roof, a traditional quaint clubhouse with 'bat-and-ball' railings, and ample space for spectators to laze about on the lush hillsides which surround the playing surface. Throughout the day, a Queen's regiment band played tunes in the background, while an ice-cream vendor handed out free cones to anyone who felt the urge. This highly enjoyable day also included a guided tour of Mr Getty's personal library, which has an estimated value of more than £15 million and features historic items such as the first-ever atlas of the world and scrolls that were written by monks in the 11th century. Among the celebrity guests in attendance were Mick Jagger and Marianne Faithfull, but for me the highlight was meeting Mr Getty himself.

Out in the middle, Matt Elliott continued his love affair with English bowling attacks and further enhanced his rapidly growing status in the process, but without question the innings of the day came from New Zealand's best-ever batsman, Martin Crowe, who caressed his way to a superb 115. Martin is retired now, yet he made his ton using one of my bats, which he had never picked up until five minutes before he walked to the crease.

As late as we dared, the Waughs hit the bitumen to journey to Manchester. I have four days off, which we will be spending with our old friends from the Nelson CC. I must say I'm looking forward to spending some worthwhile private time with my family, who have faithfully followed the team around the country, always supporting me but never being able to enjoy a steady routine because of the constant changing of hotel rooms and endless hours on the road. Rosie is missing her own bed and doesn't like not having enough room to move — I'm pretty sure she and Lynette will leave for home earlier than we originally intended. Asking them to continue this process is not fair on them when they can't get a decent night's sleep.

In the meantime, I'm going to have four days off from writing my diary. In my absence, Justin Langer will keep you up to date.

STEVE WAUGH

I TOOK A NUMBER OF PHOTOS OF ROSIE DURING HER TIME IN ENGLAND. THIS IS MY FAVOURITE. IN THE FOREGROUND IS A BOX OF DUMMIES SHE'S NOT QUITE SURE WHAT TO MAKE OF. MEANWHILE, IN THE BACKGROUND, THE CRICKET CONTINUES ON JP GETTY'S PRIVATE ESTATE.

DAY 67 JULY 15

Cardiff

LAST NIGHT, WE LEFT the Wormsley CC for a three-hour journey to Cardiff, where we are to play Glamorgan tomorrow. As you can imagine, most of the guys were pretty tired after the day's play and spent the trip watching *A Few Good Men*, playing cards or sleeping.

Although Heals didn't play yesterday, he had spent the day playing with his kids, socialising with the crowd and going for a five-kilometre run with Smithy, Kasper and Swampy. So he was as worn out as the rest of us by the time we boarded the coach.

At 11.30pm, we reached the Copthorne Hotel in Cardiff and everyone eagerly went straight into the reception desk, checked in and were comfortably asleep in their hotel beds ... dreaming about runs, wickets and run outs. Everyone that is, except Heals, who had fallen asleep at the back of the coach and, unbeknown to his team-mates, had been left asleep in his seat!

As is standard practice Huey, the driver, parked the coach, locked it up and went to his room for a well-earned sleep. However, as luck would have it, he had left something behind in the coach and went to retrieve it about an hour after we had checked in. While searching for his toothbrush in the luggage compartment, Huey made enough noise to wake Heals, who was still locked inside. Who knows, Heals may still be there now if Huey hadn't gone back to the coach well after midnight last night.

Warney arrived back in the UK this morning, smitten with his little girl, Brooke Victoria. It is great to have him back on the tour — not only for his bowling, but also for his presence around the team. Most people would be suffering from jet-lag by now, but this didn't stop Warney getting out onto the golf course this afternoon. I am not sure what he loves most — his two girls, Simone and Brooke, his cricket, his cards or his golf.

I wouldn't like to ask him!

Until tomorrow, Justin Langer.

RICKY PONTING, DESPITE THE HEIGHT ADVANTAGE JUSTIN LANGER HAS GIVEN HIM, SMASHES THE VOLLEYBALL INTO THE NET. THE THIRD MAN IN THE PHOTO IS DARREN BERRY.

DAY 68 JULY 16

Cardiff

AUSTRALIANS 4—369 (DECLARED; MA TAYLOR 71, GS BLEWETT 54,
RT PONTING 126*, JL LANGER 50*) V GLAMORGAN 0—30.

THE SINGING AND 'ABDOMINAL' sensation, Peter Andre, is staying here at the Copthorne Hotel. Talk about groupies! There are beautiful, young women everywhere, trying to catch a glimpse of their heart-throb hero. We cricketers have decided that we must be in the wrong business, judging by the following of young female admirers who melt at the mere thought of catching a glimpse of their Aussie star. Even though Peter talks with an English accent, he still claims to be a 'proud Australian'. The biggest surprise for me was that he is one of the few men in the world that I am taller than ... that is, besides Steve Smith, of course!

Today turned out to be a good, solid, batting practice exercise for the team. All the guys spent time in the middle and enjoyed batting on a very flat wicket at the Sophia Gardens cricket ground, home of the Glamorgan County Cricket Club.

Ricky Ponting batted superbly. His feet have been moving well for the last couple of weeks and it's no surprise that he finally cashed in with a big undefeated century. He is a determined young man, who works very hard to ensure that he makes the most of his wealth of natural ability. Others with unlimited, natural ability often fall into the trap of relying solely on the gifts they were given by their parents. I don't think Punter will ever go to his grave, or come to the end of his career, wondering if he could have done more with his ability or talent. He is a hungry young cricketer who I am sure will play a lot of very good cricket in the next decade.

Until tomorrow, Justin Langer.

DAY 69 JULY 17

Cardiff

AUSTRALIANS 4—369 (DECLARED) AND 5—100 (PR REIFFEL 35*)
V GLAMORGAN 254 (SP JAMES 91, PR REIFFEL 5—60).

FIFTEEN WICKETS AND 300 runs in a day's cricket isn't bad going for a match which seemed last night to be destined for a mundane finish. If you had predicted after yesterday's play that The Sophia Gardens wicket would start playing tricks today, I would have considered you to be an Aussie Rules commentator, rather than a cricket expert.

The wicket started to get a little uneven after lunch, and Pistol showed why he is such an important part of the Australian bowling attack by cleaning up the Glamorgan tail and helping himself to five wickets. Bevo bowled as well as he has all tour and had the Glamorgan batsmen playing all around his wrong'uns and top spinners. When he's bowling well, Bevo is a very difficult package, who presents the batsmen with challenges they very rarely have to face on a day-to-day basis. India's Anil Kumble is considered to be one of the world's best bowlers, and Bevo is in the same mould. They can be more than a handful.

Cricket can be such a frustrating game! As if in slow motion, I watched the ball roll off my thigh pad and dribble towards my leg stump so slowly that I could almost see the seam of the 10-over old ball ticking over towards its target. In a desperate attempt to stop the ball from dismantling my left bail, I tried a series of 'Maradona-like' moves, but because of my ordinary soccer skills I failed to stop the metal from reaching the magnet. Call it unlucky, but at the end of the day the scorebook says, 'Langer bowled 10.'

Life goes on! A win for the good guys tomorrow will ease my frustration.

Until tomorrow, Justin Langer.

DAY 70 JULY 18

London

AUSTRALIANS 4–369 (DECLARED) AND 7–217 (DECLARED; PR REIFFEL 56)
DREW WITH GLAMORGAN 254 AND 3–211 (SP JAMES 79, MP MAYNARD 45*).

I AM WRITING THIS on the morning of the game with Middlesex. Last night, the team was announced for the three-dayer at Lord's and I wasn't in the XI. When the combination was read out, I was sitting on the coach next to Slats. He's been left out, too, so we are both feeling pretty down in the dumps at present.

I guess the hardest thing about this 'dream tour' of England is that for every game six players have to sit on the sidelines. Unfortunately for those six guys, it means that time has to be spent off the ground simply thinking about the game rather than playing it. Believe me, this is hard to come to terms with, especially when you love playing the game as much as I do.

First thing this morning, it was the time of the tour when our green, gold-and-red-striped blazers were worn with our cleanest whites and polished shoes and shown off in public for the official Ashes team photograph. As usual, there is no such thing as a 'simple' team shot. Among other things, the same recurring problems of player placement, staring into the glare, a photographer who wishes he was a clown, too much sunlight, too much cloud … It happens every time! We posed in front of Tower Bridge, with Japanese tourists taking as many snaps of the team as was the official photographer. I wonder if they know what they were taking photos of? Eventually, after 15 to 20 minutes of waiting for the perfect light, the photographer, who reminded us of Dudley Moore in *Arthur*, decided it was time to 'click' away and the job was done.

Receiving the photograph at the end of the tour will be a moment to be cherished by all the players. In years to come, we can show our grandchildren and anyone else who is interested exactly who played in the successful 1997 Ashes Tour. It was a shame, though, that Adam Gilchrist and Andy Bichel weren't with us this morning.

They have as much right to be in this photo as the rest of us.

Regards, Justin Langer.

London

MIDDLESEX 305 (MR RAMPRAKASH 76, MW GATTING 85, GD MCGRATH 4–61) V AUSTRALIANS.

I HOPE LANG HASN'T shown me up too much over the past four days. For me, it is back to the Westbury Hotel … and goodbye once again to Lynette, Rosie and the in-laws (who we picked up yesterday at Manchester airport after they had enjoyed a 10-day adventure around Ireland). As I have explained earlier, the Australian squad's policy is that wives and girlfriends can stay with us during Tests, but during our matches against the counties the team must bunk together and the girls have to find their own accommodation. This generally works okay, but in London a hotel bed can be hard to find at short notice and they are always outrageously expensive (upwards of £150 per night).

After our team photo was taken, we headed to Lord's to face Middlesex. If there's one game against a county that every member of an Australian Ashes team wants to play it's this one. Firstly, the game is played at the Home of Cricket. Secondly, the lunches are the best in the country. And, thirdly, Middlesex always put out a competitive XI, which ensures we receive good match practice before a Test match.

As always, Lord's was in immaculate condition. In fact, the wicket looked to be a much better one than the Test-match strip. Middlesex's captain is Mark Ramprakash, English cricket's biggest underachiever at Test level but County cricket's best batsman, and he won the toss and wisely decided to give his batsmen first use of the wicket.

By close of play it was Middlesex's two most experienced and classy batsmen who had cashed in on the ideal conditions. The ever-expanding Mike Gatting, now, of course, a Test selector, contributed an inspiring 85, which was made more impressive by the way he handled Warney (as well as anyone has done all summer), while 'Ramps' once again put his name in front of the English selectors by compiling a textbook 76.

Perhaps Warney held back a bit today. I'm sure 'Gatt' would have been looking for a chink in his armour or a few pointers that might help his lads in the upcoming Test.

At the other end, Pigeon again showed us that he now has that rare ability to take wickets even when he's not at his best. This, for us, is a huge advantage because 'positive-body-language-intimidating' types don't come around all that often.

Tonight, for the first time, the whole of my travelling family went out for dinner as one. Rosie, of course, isn't accustomed to eating out, especially Italian, and she barely made it through her vegies before deciding she'd had enough. As a consequence, we all took turns showing her the sights around Marble Arch, while the others completed their meals. Rosie really is growing up quickly over here. She interacts extraordinarily well with people and kids she's never met, appearing to bond with them immediately. I'm so glad she's over here — I would have missed out on so much of her growing up if she had stayed at home.

I can imagine what it would have been like if we had been reunited at Sydney Airport in late August after I'd been away for four months. It would have been like two strangers, introducing themselves to each other.

SHANE WARNE (RIGHT) TRIES TO FIND OUT WHAT THE ENGLISH TACTICS WILL BE FOR THE NEXT TEST, DURING A QUIET CONVERSATION WITH ENGLAND SELECTOR AND MIDDLESEX VETERAN MIKE GATTING.

DAY 72 | JULY 20

London

MIDDLESEX 305 V AUSTRALIANS 6–351 (MTG ELLIOTT 83,
ME WAUGH 100*, SR WAUGH 57).

IT WAS A REFRESHING change to be able to play with the sun beating down on our backs.

I think the sunshine acted like an instant source of power for all the boys and we batted as an Australian side should — aggressively, positively and creatively. The day was capped off superbly by a Mark Waugh single off the penultimate ball of the day, which left him unbeaten on the triple figures. This was a confidence-restoring innings. Others to enjoy themselves were Herb, who scored 83, and yours truly, with 57. In fact, all bar Tubs and Punter gorged ourselves on the local attack, while no-one missed out on the banoffe pie and ice cream at the lunch break.

For Angus Fraser, of Middlesex and English renown, this was his last throw of the dice in the hope of a Test recall, but it wasn't to be. This highly-respected professional ended up wicketless and close to a sidecar (100 runs) at the end of the day. However, he had a much better time of it afterwards, when a wine-tasting benefit function was held in his honour at the ground.

AUSTRALIAN PICTURE LIBRARY/ALLSPORT

WARNEY AGAIN, THIS TIME SIGNING AN AUTOGRAPH FOR ONE OF HIS MANY FANS IN ENGLAND.

London

MIDDLESEX 305 AND 6–201 (MW GATTING 47, KR BROWN 48*, SK WARNE 3–55) DREW WITH AUSTRALIANS 7–432 (DECLARED; ME WAUGH 142*).

JUNIOR CONTINUED HIS PILLAGE of the Middlesex attack into the second hour of the morning, before Tubs decided to let our quicks loose on the county's top order. Mark's unbeaten knock will hopefully be the turning point for him as far as Test scores go, as this has been a disappointing tour for him, run-wise, to date. He is a real confidence player who thrives on striking the ball well. If the runs aren't coming as naturally as he'd want, his confidence level falls significantly.

Our victory bid was thwarted by Mike Gatting, who looked set for back-to-back fifties until I was called on to make a rare bowling appearance and sent him packing with a useful off cutter which broke my tour duck with the ball.

The Poms have included the uncapped Gloucestershire bowler Mike Smith in their squad for the next Test. In my opinion, this is a move that won't improve their chances, even if he's the 'form' bowler in the county championship. While Smith does have the ability to swing the ball, he looks to me to be a metre short of the pace needed to trouble top-class players. Time will tell if I'm right, and there have been many players picked in the past who have elevated their games to levels not many thought they would. Mark Taylor is a prime example. Back in the '80s, Tubs was seen by many as being a steady cricketer with not quite enough shots or talent to make the step up from Shield to Test cricket. But once he got the chance, he confounded those who doubted his credentials.

In Phil and Ethel, Lynette and I had ready-made babysitters, so tonight the two of us headed off to see the 'Phantom Of The Opera'. It was my fourth and Lynette's third visit, but it was still a buzz to see the curtain lift up and the performance begin, especially as the star of the show is the Australian, Peter Cousens, and another of the performers is a lad from Panania, in Sydney's Western Suburbs, where we were brought up. It was a superb show, and to cap off the evening, we enjoyed a backstage chat with the cast, who, judging by their inquisitive questioning, are all cricket mad.

DAY 74 JULY 22

Leeds (via Buckingham Palace)

DROPPING A PLAYER FROM the Test XI is always a gut-wrenching experience, not only for the unfortunate player but also for the selectors involved. I'm sure Bevo must have known it was coming and, in a funny kind of a way, he'll be relieved to know he now has a chance to sit on the sidelines, re-group and gather his thoughts so that he can come back a stronger player and person. Once we'd made up our minds that Ricky Ponting would come into the starting side, Swamp, Tubs and I sat with Bevo, and talked to him about his game and his ambitions. He knows what he has to do to come back and, for the sake of Australian cricket, let's hope he does so — he has a rare talent that has yet to be tapped at Test level.

This morning, before we headed north to Leeds, we set off for a rare treat — a visit to Buckingham Palace. There were definitely a few nerves among the boys as we entered the gates at the Palace, driving slowly past the hordes of tourists who were waiting to watch the changing of the guard. The boys certainly looked the part, dressed in our official tour blazers. And we were keen to make a good impression, especially as it was well over 20 years since an Australian side had been invited to have morning tea with the Queen.

We were escorted to one of the official meeting rooms, the 'Bow Room', at which time tea, orange juice and biscuits were made available. Some 15 minutes later we were told to assemble in a semi-circle, for a meeting with the Queen. I've never seen Mark Taylor so anxious and on edge, so I tried to comfort him by saying, 'Geez Tub, I hope you don't forget anyone's name.' He just smiled and said, 'Thanks a lot, Tugga.' as he tried to dry his sweaty palms on his trouser leg.

When the big moment finally arrived, it was like watching a movie — except we were in it. Her Majesty walked into the room, followed by Prince Andrew. Both were looking formal, yet relaxed. Tubby did the introductions, at which time the royal hand was extended and met with a 'Ma'am' or a 'Your Majesty'. Heals, standing directly next to me, on my left, was like a schoolboy up in front of the headmistress for the first time. He presented the Queen with a painting by his six-year-old daughter, Emma, drawn especially for the Queen's Birthday. She seemed genuinely pleased to accept the gift.

Pleasantries exchanged, it was time to throw off our formal hats and have an informal chat with the Queen and Prince Andrew. Speaking to her was like chatting with one's grandmother; at least she reminded me of my father's mother, not only by her looks but also by her chatty disposition. Much of our conversation is a blur for me, as I was slightly overwhelmed by actually having this special opportunity.

The most unusual question of the day — and perhaps the tour — came from Kasper, who asked the Queen, 'Did you watch the Military Tattoo versus the Gladiators on television last night?' 'Yes I did,' she replied. Kasper pressed further with this follow-up question, 'Was it your idea to go on the Gladiators?', which drew a response, 'We didn't do too well did we?' Trying to cover for her team, the Queen showed the lads a couple of moves that led to their downfall, at one stage putting her right foot forward and showing the technique used.

This was a meeting to remember. We all came away very impressed by both members of the Royal Family and their comforting natures, which made us feel more at ease than we had originally expected.

Cricket-wise, I feel as if I'm approaching something like peak form. Everything is hitting near the middle of the blade and I can't see any reason why I shouldn't finish the tour off strongly. My only concern is the swelling and continual sharp pain that is emanating from in and around my right thumb joint. Hooter has tried to combat this by devising a pad that can fit inside my glove and take some of the impact. I only hope that by the end of the Test I've got one sore and swollen thumb, because that will mean I've scored a few runs.

Fans are certainly nice to have on your side, and most are loyal and true through good and bad times. I'm sure I have the most dedicated supporter of any cricketer in the world. Her name is Suchitra and without fail she faxes me before each match, while regular goodwill messages are usually accompanied with cards and occasionally presents. She was at Headingley today, having saved enough money to make the trip from Madras to watch Mark and I play our 50th Test together. In recognition of this milestone, Suchitra presented us with an inscribed silver tray, which is something that I will always appreciate. And then, to confirm just what a true fan she is, she handed over a bottle of Southern Comfort, some chocolates and a 'good luck' gold coin.

It is gestures such as these that make me realise that I have an obligation to my supporters to give it my all, all the time. I know how much it means to them to have an association with their favourite players.

Back at the hotel, my family had checked in and tried to make themselves comfortable. To get out of the stuffy atmosphere, I gave Rosie another opportunity to swim around in the hotel pool, which, of course, she loves. I'm sure she gets frustrated by the lack of space in the hotel rooms.

DAY 75 JULY 23

Leeds

IT WAS A SLEEPLESS night all round for the Waugh family, owing to Rosie's reaction to the impatient eyeteeth which are forcing their way through her gums. She must have woken five or six times, and each time Lynette got up so that I could get enough sleep to prepare for the upcoming Test match. This is just another example of the sacrifices she's made and makes for the sake of my career and for which I am truly grateful.

Yesterday at practice, following a schedule agreed upon by both coaches, Geoff Marsh and David Lloyd, we stepped into the nets before the Poms. Today, they had the first option, which gave us the chance to watch the conclusion of their hit-out. It appeared that the English session was noticeably quieter and flatter than ones we'd watched in the past on this tour, while we are looking sharp and focused. We can all feel the momentum shifting in our favour.

The only problem with our session was the lack of nets at our disposal. Normally, you would have three or four to enable you to get through the batting order in a reasonable space of time, but with only two in use here, it takes an eternity to get through 17 players. Thankfully, the local cricket academy helped us out by providing a group of net bowlers who all charged in with a commitment that augers well for their future.

My obligations to Channel 7 are usually completed by the day before a Test, but because of our late arrival here yesterday, following our detour to Buckingham Palace, I had to interview Warney and Junior this morning. This would normally contravene team policy, but an exception was made because of the circumstances. Interviewing my brother is seen as something of a comedy for others, as we don't often speak directly to each other on tour (although we generally eat out and socialise in the same groups). For me, though, it's much harder to keep a straight face when asking Warney a question or two and I've cost Channel 7 a fortune in wasted film because of the 'bloopers' I've created.

Tonight's team meeting was, I believe, the best of the tour so far. It was brief, uncomplicated, informative and motivational. We are now entering the crucial phase of the tour, when all the hard work we've done should hold us in good stead. We've designated the remaining four-and-a-half weeks as a 'mini-tour', to which we must devote our full attention — there is no time to contemplate returning home or for our desire and commitment to finish off the job to slacken. Swampy has given us the challenge of performing better than our opposite number in this match, which means I am 'taking on' the talented but inconsistent Graham Thorpe. This type of motivational element is something that Swampy encourages and believes in, and one that has, in my opinion, been of benefit to all on tour to varying degrees.

The meeting was enhanced by some inspirational footage of our two most recent Test successes at Headingley (1989 and 1993), intertwined with footage of The Don and other Aussie greats. I must say I feel relaxed, knowing that my previous two Tests here have both produced unbeaten 150s. Here's hoping I can make it three in a row!

With the hotel fully booked out, partly because the Canberra Raiders super league team is in town for the 'World Club Challenge', it was impossible to upgrade to a family suite, which is what we wanted so that Rosie would have a separate room and I could get the necessary sleep to be ready for a Test match. Thankfully, Crommo came to the rescue when he offered his managerial suite to us, a gesture that shows how keen he is to help in any way to secure the Ashes for Australia.

ENGLAND'S CHAIRMAN OF SELECTORS DAVID GRAVENEY (SECOND FROM RIGHT) STUDIES THE NEW TEST PITCH. THE LATE CHANGE OF STRIPS CAUSED GREAT CONTROVERSY RIGHT UP UNTIL THE START OF THE MATCH.

DAY 76 JULY 24

Fourth Test — Day One
Headingley, Leeds

ENGLAND 3–106 (MA ATHERTON 34*) V AUSTRALIA.

IT'S NOT UNUSUAL TO see wickets tailored to suit the home side's needs. In fact we'd been stitched up last October in New Delhi by a wicket that looked five days old before the Test started. That pitch was dry, cracked and close to falling apart, but, most significantly, ready-made for India's three-pronged spin attack.

You couldn't really compare the late change of wicket here to that situation, because at Headingley the Test wicket has been swapped for another to try to stop one of our bowlers from gaining an advantage. We have heard that the English chairman of selectors, David Graveney (formerly a left-arm orthodox spinner at county cricket level), checked out the intended wicket and was very concerned about how dry it was and its lack of grass cover. Obviously, such a wicket would suit Shane Warne down to a tee. Graveney decided that a change of wicket was necessary, to give his selected team a better chance of success. A new wicket was chosen, and prepared to the best quality possible in the three days the groundsman had to work on it. This is fair enough if the groundsman believes he has misjudged the timing of his pitch preparation, in regards to watering or rolling the surface, but for a chairman of selectors to throw his hat into the ring was unacceptable.

Our management have formally objected to Graveney's involvement in the switch, via a letter from team manager Alan Crompton. The whole episode has led to denials from everyone who has had a finger pointed at them, but one brief conversation leads me to believe our information is correct. Walking over to have a look at the new, decidedly green, well-covered pitch, I crossed paths with Graveney, who said to me, 'You should have seen the other one they'd prepared. I could have turned it square on that!'

After the pre-match conjecture over the late change of wicket, the pitch turned out to be one with more than average grass covering, but still less grassy than the over-sporting one we had encountered in the Test at Old Trafford.

Mark Taylor continued his golden streak with the toss, but this time wasn't as bold with his choice, choosing to send the opposition in on what looked to be a bowler-friendly wicket. But on a day that was continually interrupted by the vagaries of Yorkshire's weather, England clawed their way to 106 for the loss of three wickets in front of a crowd that were desperate to get vocal but had very little to get excited about.

This was a frustrating day all round. Our attack bowled too short, as can often happen when the wicket is expected to suit the quickies. They were aware we expected them to get the breakthrough and consequently pushed too hard for success. This was certainly the case for Glenn McGrath, who would have hoped to have had three or four scalps on his belt, but instead had to settle for just one and an 'economy' rate of over three runs per over — a rare statistic for this miserly master. Paul Reiffel, though, was again a model of consistency, making the batsmen earn every run as he probed away looking for a chink in their techniques.

For England, Atherton showed his undeniable value to his team in difficult situations and conditions by riding out the initial storm before settling in for the long haul. He was looking a little apprehensive, but was still good enough to put the loose ball away.

Mark Butcher looked the most comfortable we'd seen him, before he clipped one off his toes only to see Greg Blewett take a freakish catch (or fortunate catch, depending on which side of the fence you're sitting) at short leg. Not long after, Greg gobbled up a spooned catch off the handle of Alec Stewart's blade, to even out the difficulty of the two snares, but soon after he discovered the perils of his position. Nasser Hussain forced a certain boundary straight into our short leg's visor, to remind him of the suicidal tendencies that one needs to be successful in such a despised position. David Boon turned fielding in this spot into an art form; I'm not sure if Blewey wants to make it a long-term position.

The Gods must have been smiling upon us when Hussain perished after the clock had forged past 7pm — a time normally associated with dinner being served on the table, not with having to fend off a McGrath 'throatseeker'.

I rated today as an even contest, with neither side doing enough to take an advantage into the second day's play. By the time we got back to the hotel room, it was 'nighty night' to Rosie and off down the road in search of some Chinese takeaway for Lynette and me.

One other thing I had to do, as I do each night of a Test, was report to radio station Triple M, back in Sydney, to fill them in on the major events of the day. Today, such events weren't easy to find.

Fourth Test — Day Two
Headingley, Leeds

ENGLAND 172 (MA ATHERTON 41, JN GILLESPIE 7–37) V AUSTRALIA 4–258 (MTG ELLIOTT 134*, RT PONTING 86*).

IT WAS VOLLEYBALL FOR the warm-ups this morning, which would have undoubtedly raised a few eyebrows in this traditional cricketing post in the north of England. But it didn't do the trick for us straightaway, as nightwatchman Dean Headley dug in to give his tenacious captain valuable support.

But then Jason Gillespie began what will be remembered as one of the greatest spells of express bowling ever seen in these parts. First to go was the 'nightwatchy', snapped up by the 'lightning' reflexes of the man in the gully. What followed was almost procession-like in the way the English batting order came and went, all blown away by what Ian Healy later described as 'the quickest spell of bowling I've ever kept to'.

Gillespie had it all. Those huge strides and that loping run came together at the crease for a back-straining coiled delivery and release. This is all accompanied by a monumental follow-through that sees his head almost come into contact with the turf while his bowling hand extends to behind his left ear. It's a graceful yet brutal action that can produce genuine pace and a lethal late outswinger. Headingley looked as if a typhoon had made its presence felt, with casualties everywhere — Headley 22, Thorpe 15, Crawley 2, Croft 6, Gough 0, Smith 0. Mark Ealham survived the onslaught, but came away with a bloodied brow after trying to pull a good-length ball from Paul Reiffel, only to top edge it into his helmet grill. The shot Mike Smith played to register a duck on his Test debut was one he won't want to invite friends around to sit and watch on the video. It can best be described as a timid-looking attempt to swat the ball away.

Only Mark Butcher and John Crawley could consider themselves a little hard done by. This was particularly so in the case of Crawley, who was caught at short leg after a firm leg-side shot cannoned off Greg Blewett's boot up into the air for Greg to complete a freakish dismissal that turned the tables well and truly in our favour. England were 6–163 before Crawley's demise. Nine runs later they were all out.

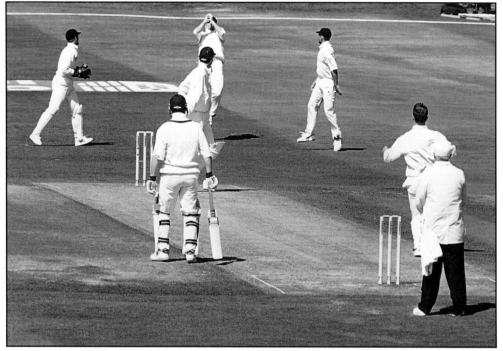

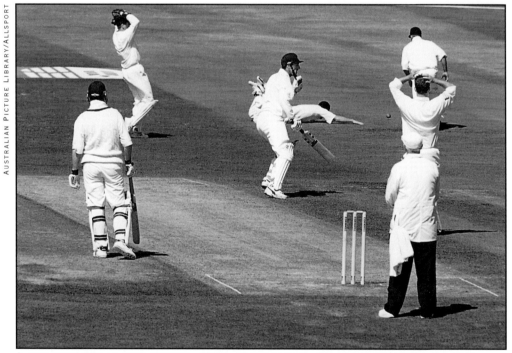

A KEY MOMENT IN THE SERIES. WITH AUSTRALIA 3–50 IN REPLY TO ENGLAND'S 172, GRAHAM THORPE AT FIRST SLIP DROPS MATTHEW ELLIOTT OFF MIKE SMITH. WITH THE FIRST BALL OF THE FOLLOWING OVER, I WAS CAUGHT AT SHORT LEG. BY STUMPS, AUSTRALIA WERE 4–258.

A golden opportunity was ours to take advantage of, after rolling England for around 150 short of what they would have expected after the first day. However, it appeared we were heading down the same treacherous path when we lost four wickets for 50. But our young guns, Matthew Elliott and Ricky Ponting, then took control.

Our top-order collapse had begun when local hero Darren Gough sent the crowd into a frenzy by getting a shortish ball to brush the glove of a retreating Mark Taylor before our captain had scored. Blewett went soon after, driving late at an outswinger, while the Waugh boys spooned catches that resulted from a lack of pace in the wicket and a lack of soft hands by the batsmen. To be caught at bat-pad off a 'nothing special' type of ball is a waste, and if I could have kicked my own backside I would have given it a real going over. A centimetre or two either way of fieldsman Crawley and I was safe, but in all honesty I deserved the fate that befell me. Wasting good form is a crime and I was guilty of it here.

Our precarious position of 4–50 would have been worse had Thorpe not grassed a sitter off Elliott's blade from Mike Smith's bowling the ball before I departed. Perhaps Thorpe was snoozing at slip, because it certainly didn't seem likely there was going to be a chance coming his way. Smith looked nervous and unsure, but I felt he was handled poorly considering he is a new-ball swing bowler. He should have been given an opportunity to show off his skills and excellent recent form without having to wait too long for his chance. By the time he did get that opportunity, the ball had lost its shine, the breeze was against his natural swing and he was running up the hill and into the wind. For his sake, tomorrow had better see a marked improvement or else he'd better begin to savour every moment of what will be his only Test appearance.

At the close, we had taken control of the game. Ponting and Elliott's superb partnership is already worth 208 runs, with the prospect of many more tomorrow. Both players looked class acts today, displaying excellent techniques, fine judgment and a natural talent to seize opportunities at the appropriate times. Both are fine exponents of the hook and pull shots, a fact obviously unknown to our opponents, who must have sensed a weakness in there or had been given dud mail by their spies. Strangely, Mark Ealham was again underbowled, and must be wondering what he's done wrong. Whenever he's been used he's performed very well and has never let his side down.

One of the more amusing incidents on tour happened today, while we were slicing through the English batting. On the fall of each wicket, our supersubs run out onto the ground with drinks and words of encouragement. Lang is always an eager contributor, sprinting on and off the field looking after the on-field players' needs while at the same time setting an example to opposition sides about our commitment. Today, though, he may have overdone it. He raced down the players' enclosure steps and began to sprint onto the ground, but caught his foot on the boundary rope. Down he went, after struggling for a step or two to retain his balance, composure and pride. It was certainly a show stopper — the crowd loved it and so did we, and while it was a trifle unsettling for Lang it at least solved that most difficult question to answer in player-profile questionnaires …

'What is your most embarrassing moment in cricket?'

Fourth Test — Day Three
Headingley, Leeds

ENGLAND 172 V AUSTRALIA 5–373 (MTG ELLIOTT 164*, RT PONTING 127).

DISAPPOINTINGLY, TODAY WAS TO be a day of frustration, with more action happening in the next-door gymnasium of the local Leeds Rhinos super league team and on the card tables than out in the middle. There was, however, enough time to see Ricky Ponting bring up a masterly 'beyond his years' century before he was dismissed for a memorable 127. This was the only wicket to fall during the whole day.

In many ways, Ricky's century reminded me of my first Test century, scored some eight years ago on the same ground. It was a hundred full of attacking shots, scored off a relatively low number of balls and one that helped set the side up for victory. At the other end, Matthew Elliott continued his marathon — crushing every attempt the Poms could muster to dismiss him, while at the same time growing stronger as each ball passed.

I wouldn't like to be in Graham Thorpe's shoes right now. Every run Elliott scores must be like a dagger through his heart, with the tally being 135 runs since that fateful chance was put down. At the end of the day's play, we had moved on to 5–373. We are the only ones with any hope of a win, which may end up being the psychological advantage that will guide us to victory.

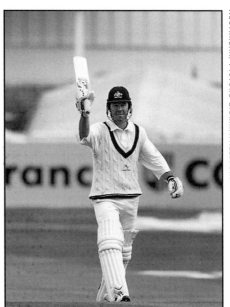

RICKY PONTING REACHES HIS CENTURY.

Fourth Test — Day Four
Headingley, Leeds

ENGLAND 172 AND 4—212 (N HUSSAIN 101*, JP CRAWLEY 48*)
V AUSTRALIA 9—501 (DECLARED; MTG ELLIOTT 199, PR REIFFEL 54*,
GD MCGRATH 20*, D GOUGH 5—149).

ROSIE HAD HER FIRST full night's sleep of her tour last night, much to the relief of Lynette, who doesn't get into a deep sleep for fear of Rosie crying and disrupting my slumber during a Test match. But as soon as the match is over, to even out the ledger a little, it's my turn to look after Rosie in the mornings.

The papers this morning gave England little chance of survival. They predicted the worst, showing no faith whatsoever in the home team's ability to fight back. On the field, Elliott continued where he'd left off, in complete control as he picked up the tempo whenever he wanted. His level head and hunger for more runs drove him onwards towards the revered double hundred club. Following his effort at Lord's, once again he managed to score more himself than England did in their first innings. But just when the team was ready to acknowledge a magnificent 200, a searing Gough yorker ripped his stumps apart.

Paul Reiffel again underlined his value to the side with a cameo of real class, timing his way to an undefeated 54 off 72 balls. And he was capably supported by the batting bunny, Glenn McGrath, who outscored Messrs Taylor, Blewett, M. Waugh, S. Waugh, Warne and Gillespie with an impressive knock of 20 not out. McGrath and Reiffel added an unbeaten 40 for the last wicket before a declaration was made during the lunch break.

For the third successive Ashes tour, Australia had compiled more than 500 at Headingley, dispelling the myth that the square is a batsman's nightmare and a seamer's paradise. Even more remarkable is the fact that each of the top seven in the Australian batting order have scored their maiden Test hundred against England. In fact, if you add Michael Slater into the equation, every member of the Australian squad who has hit a Test hundred has hit their first against the Poms. This is a bit of a damning statistic for the county and Test bowlers doing the rounds in this country. For McGrath, his innings was notable in that it was only the third time in his Test career that he'd reached double figures, which, realistically, is like most batsmen scoring a century.

A sizeable first-innings lead allowed us the luxury of setting attacking fields and making aggressive bowling changes that we might not have tried if the match was more evenly poised. Sensing the moment, McGrath sprinted in down the hill with added zest and duly removed both Butcher and the tormented England captain before the crowd had settled back into their seats after the lunch break.

The wicket of Butcher was a beautiful piece of bowling. We have been regularly aggrieved to see the ball pass the outside edge of the Surrey left-hander's blade. But we've noticed that Butcher continually plays the same line, which means that if the ball moves off the wicket, or goes

AUSTRALIAN PICTURE LIBRARY/ALLSPORT

BUT FOR THE EFFORTS OF NASSER HUSSAIN (ABOVE) AND JOHN CRAWLEY, THE FOURTH TEST MAY WELL HAVE BEEN ALL OVER BEFORE STUMPS.

across him from a right-handed bowler's normal angle from over the wicket, he will too often play and miss. Bowling around the wicket negates that angle, while making the batsman wary of leaving balls just around the off stump. In other words, Butcher now had less room for an error in judgment, and it was this new angle that led to his downfall. He again played the same tried and trusted defensive prod, only to see the ball catch the edge instead of flying harmlessly through to the keeper.

Alec Stewart was the victim of a low shooter that snuck under his guard, but if he is brutally honest he'll admit he should have been on the front foot and not stuck to the crease, in batting's 'no-man's land'. The vital wicket of Thorpe was taken by another swift Gillespie 'exocet', before Hussain and Crawley began an excellent backs-to-the-wall counterattack. From a precarious 4–89, the home team reached a respectable 4–212 by the close of play, but hopefully the not out batsmen have only delayed our victory celebrations. For England to escape with an honourable draw they will have to not lose a wicket for a session, the same feat they achieved late this afternoon with considerable skill and courage.

Fourth Test — Day Five
Headingley, Leeds

ENGLAND 172 AND 268 (N HUSSAIN 105, JP CRAWLEY 72,
PR REIFFEL 5—49) LOST TO AUSTRALIA 9—501 (DECLARED).

ALL WAS IN READINESS for later celebrations as I sat in a chatty and animated dressing-room minutes before we were due out onto the field this morning. A bottle of Southern Comfort was on the nearby afternoon tea table, my John

STEVE WAUGH

THE DEPENDABLE JUSTIN LANGER IS ON
HAND TO MAKE SURE OUR POST-TEST
CELEBRATIONS DON'T GET OUT OF HAND.

Williamson and Cold Chisel CDs were ready for the call and I'd even remembered to have a couple of towels handy, to protect my gear when the champers and beer began to flow. I think deep down we all expected only one outcome from the day, but at the same time we knew we had to make it happen, not sit back and expect someone else to do it for us.

Hussain's departure to a loose shot early on signalled the beginning of the end. Mark Ealham then fell to a superb reflex catch by Mark Waugh that said to all of us — let's go for the jugular, it's our day. The brittle lower half of England's batting order was being found wanting in the commitment department again, and once their only ray of hope, John Crawley, was out there was no stopping us.

MARK TAYLOR IN THE HEADINGLEY DRESSING-ROOM AFTER OUR BIG WIN, BELTING OUT COLD CHISEL'S 'BOW RIVER' FOR THE BENEFIT OF HIS TEAM-MATES.

Except for the luncheon adjournment. This came with England nine-down and was a huge blessing in disguise, as it enabled us to fully prepare for the mandatory dressing-room debacle that was to follow. Robert Croft obviously had plans to get on that motorway for the long drive back to Wales as soon as possible, for he played a 'shot' to the first ball after the break that was more likely to catch a fish than repel a cricket ball. We now led the series 2–1.

Making our celebrations just that little bit extra special was the presence of the Canberra Raiders super league team, who had come to the ground to support us dressed in shorts, singlets and outrageously coloured wigs. It was a fabulous couple of hours sharing the victory with football greats such as Mal Meninga, Laurie Daley and Ricky Stuart and a time we will cherish and long remember. Not satisfied with the festivities at the ground, we kicked on to the bar area of our hotel, where family, friends and Raiders gathered for a long night.

It was here in the relative safety of the bar area that I not only contemplated but executed one of the most foolhardy acts ever witnessed. Feeling that added strength and invincibility that one gets from alcohol, I challenged Big Mal to take myself, Junior and a couple more of my braver team-mates on. His objective was to try to run through us and score an imaginary try between the two guest sofas situated some two metres behind us. A Foster's can was in Mal's hand, as the 'footy', but all I saw were two hairy 'oak trees' pumping in unison at good pace heading straight for me. (Mal Meninga, as everyone knows, is a very big man.) With pride and reputation at stake, I went in head first, full of tenacity but mainly hope, only to be sent catapulting through the air after a bone-shattering confrontation.

We dusted ourselves off, shook hands, and headed for the bar for a beer and chat. It wasn't until a couple of hours later that turning sideways began to present problems and I realised that I might be spending tomorrow morning searching around town for a neck brace. Later on, I was minding my own business as I was heading for the men's room, when the nightmare resurfaced. Big Mal was in my face again, this time catching me off guard in a crunching tackle, pick-up and pile-driver. Of course, I did the manly thing and attempted a reply, with hitman Healy in support, but I was further humiliated.

All in all, it was a night to savour. I feel privileged to have been injured by one of the best of all time.

SLATS TAKES TO THE HEADINGLEY STAGE, HAVING BEEN WISE ENOUGH TO DISGUISE HIMSELF AS A CANBERRA RAIDER BEFORE HE BEGAN TO SING.

Taunton

ABOUT A WEEK BACK, the notion of conducting a signing session at this point of the tour, rather than in the frantic final days of the trip, seemed like a good idea. It wasn't. I can assure you it's an arduous task, signing signature after signature with a hangover as your companion.

Then it was onto the bus. Up until now, we have been driving around Britain in what is usually Manchester United's team coach. But with the Premier League season about to begin, we've had to give it back, for a somewhat downmarket model. I'm not sure today was the right time for a change of scenery, a fact we made sure our owner-driver was fully aware of. Five hours in a bus is uncomfortable at the best of times, and given our parlous physical state, a faulty air-conditioner and lack of fluid-replacing refreshments on board, the journey to Taunton developed into the nightmare leg of the tour.

The trip was only made bearable by the good reading to be found in today's sport sections. And when we arrived, Swamp proved he is human after all, by taking pity on the squad and ordering an afternoon off, much to everyone's joy and obvious relief. Further good news arrived in the form of a palatial room, complete with double bed, in the Castle Hotel, a famous old castle which dates back to the early 16th century and has been converted into modern accommodation. Meanwhile, Lynette and family bunked themselves in at the less salubrious 'Travel Inn', which is located a couple of kilometres down the road.

This will be the last leg of their journey. Originally, Lynette and Rosie were planning on seeing out the tour, but because of the stresses of travelling that can't be overcome, we've agreed that they should go home early — even though it will be hard to be so far apart again. Thankfully, Rosie's first birthday is in two days time, so at least we can finish their travels together on a high note.

DAY 82 | JULY 30

Taunton

ONE PLAYER WHO HAS been impressive lately at training is Slats, who's like a caged-up tiger, just waiting so he can take his chance. It's been an extremely frustrating period for him, because he's lacked chances due to rain and selections. Making it doubly difficult for him is the fact that he's scored seven Test hundreds and averages over 47 in Test cricket — he knows he can do the business. Obviously, he was dropped for a reason and I'm sure as soon as he comes to terms with this fact he'll be on his way back better than ever. It seems to me that he's in so much of a hurry at the moment that he's not 'crossing his Ts and dotting his Is', which he has to do to become the automatic selection he once was. It would be great to see both Slats and Lang do well, along with Kasper and BJ, who, right from the very first day, have all been very patient and understanding of the team's needs and our selections.

Days off on tour are precious and one was upon us today. Most of the single lads on tour opted for a round of golf, while the couples either hit the pavement in search of a bargain or indulged in a spot of sightseeing. For the travelling Griswalds (aka Waughs), we headed off to the historic city of Bath, which is no more than an hour from our current location. Inevitably we missed a couple of vital turnoffs and added a significant amount of travel time to the excursion, but at least the countryside was pleasantly relaxing and the weather invitingly warm. An enjoyable day was had by all, especially by Lynette who uncannily tracked down a shop that stocked miniature collectibles and doll's house items that just happened to be the ones she'd been looking for without luck in recent times. Activities such as today are invaluable on a cricket tour, because they not only get you out of the hotel and into the fresh air, they also get you away from the team.

This is important — we virtually live out of each other's pockets all year round and constantly socialise together. In some ways, it's an environment where the 'real world' almost doesn't exist.

DAY 83 JULY 31

Taunton

TO HEAD OFF THE threat of complacency in the camp, the team split up into two groups at training this morning. With Tubs enjoying some R&R, I looked after the batting group, while the bowlers were in coach Marsh's capable hands. During the batting group's chat, we emphasised the need to finish the tour off strongly. In recent times, the team's ordinary performances in the last Test of a series that has already been decided have been a direct result of the batsmen under-achieving. The fact that we batsmen have acknowledged our responsibility is in itself a breakthrough, because it would be easy to blame outside factors or even the bowlers. Taking further the approach we first adopted in the lead-up to the fourth Test, starting from tomorrow we have decided to knuckle down and treat the last four first-class games of the tour, including the last two Tests, as a separate entity to all that has occurred to date.

Unfortunately the practice wickets today, like so many we have put up with on tour, were not up to standard. These were very well grassed and offered the keen-to-impress local net bowlers a lot of movement both vertically and horizontally, which is fine if you are seeing the ball well but destructive if you are struggling with your form.

Being captain for this fixture against my former county (I played two seasons with Somerset, in 1987 and 1988) gives the game an extra edge for me. From a team point of view, it would be great to keep the momentum going and achieve a third victory over a county team on this tour.

With the captaincy comes the added responsibility of dealing with the media and today was no exception, with local and international crews all jostling for an interview after practice. The problem for me today was the lack of time I had available for the cameras and the journos, because I had a young lady's first birthday party to organise. Interviews over, I dashed into the nearest Marks and Spencer department store, and thus began a mad scramble in the food section, shopping basket under one arm while the other scooped items off the shelves at impressive speed. Already in my hotel suite were drinks, balloons, streamers, courtesy of the hotel's concierge who had gone searching on my behalf. And, of course, there was a birthday cake …

Amazingly, it all went like clockwork. All I needed now was the birthday girl and the guests. Soon after, Rosie's eyes lit up like beacons when she crawled past the door to be mesmerised by the sea of balloons. She somehow sensed that all that was in front of her was because of her. Seeing her smile was all the thanks I needed and made me realise how lucky I was to have her with me on her first birthday.

Not long after it was a full house, with players, wives, girlfriends and presents all crammed into the room. Rosie tore into the wrapping paper to find a collection of dolls, clothes and collectibles. It was great to have most of the team together enjoying a family day, although it can have the effect of making you homesick — you tend to think you've been transported back home for the day. Slats then put the icing on the cake when he wooed everyone with his guitar skills and silky voice while singing 'Happy Birthday to Rosie'. This somewhat pacified Rosie after her earlier scare, when she had come face to face with her gorilla cake.

For Lynette and I, this was a perfect last day together as a family. It was desperately difficult to bid a final farewell as they left for their own hotel. The last six weeks have been a whole new experience for both of us, with Rosie putting a whole new complexion on touring life. Fortunately, Phil and Ethel have been a tremendous help as always, but still it's been tough for everyone to adjust to family life on the road with a touring team.

SHANE WARNE IN THE NETS AT TAUNTON, TRYING TO RETAIN THE BATTING FORM THAT SAW HIM SCORE HIS FIRST HALF CENTURY IN ASHES CRICKET AT LEEDS.

DAY 84 AUGUST 1

Taunton

SOMERSET 284 (KA PARSONS 71, RJ TURNER 58, SK WARNE 5–57)
V AUSTRALIANS 4–182 (SR WAUGH 51*).

TODAY'S CROWD WAS THE biggest seen at Taunton since Bradman's 1938 Australians played here, proving again that there's nothing better for the English game than an Ashes tour. Not only do the television rights, ticket sales and sponsorship bring in 'telephone numbers' for the ECB, the counties clean up, too, through the large attendances, then those players enjoying benefits back their trucks up and try to get everything they possibly can autographed.

One man's day was ruined by the late withdrawal of Ricky Ponting, who has a bout of the flu that worsened quite significantly overnight. Pigeon's day off was now a day of toil and sweat, especially after the coin landed cruelly for the away team's skipper. Glenn's day was made worse when, after just seven overs the match-starved new-ball combination of Julian and Kasprowicz had earned the groundsman's wrath — he knew he was in for some serious panel beating of the advertising boards at the conclusion of play — while I was considering retirement from the captaincy. The score after 35 minutes of 0–72 was nothing short of disastrous, and no matter how hard I tried to convince myself that the wicket was a belter, the outfield slick, and the ground small in size, it didn't hide the fact that we were in desperate need of a breakthrough.

Responding as he always does, McGrath gained a wicket early in his spell and, in tandem with Warney, changed the tempo and complexion of the game. But even with this reversal in fortunes, the West County lads still went to lunch with the amazing return of 4–143.

For a captain, these games are a difficult balancing act at times. Every game on tour is played with the intention of winning, but the main priority is the Test matches. With this in mind, you have to monitor your bowlers very carefully, being particularly watchful of the amount of overs they're bowling. On occasions, a bowler will want a heavy workload to allow him to settle into a steady rhythm or to gain some match

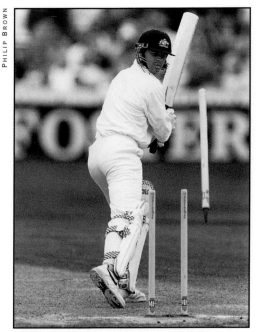

GREG BLEWETT LOSES HIS MIDDLE
STUMP TO ANDY CADDICK.

practice and confidence. However, at other times, that same man may want a short spell, just to stay sharp or to perhaps prevent an injury that his gut feeling suggests may be in the offing.

Today was a day where Pigeon needed a relatively brief stint at the crease, as he knows he's in good form and his body yearned for a reduced workload. Keeping our main strike bowler away from the bowling crease provides opportunities for others, but it also allowed the Somerset batsmen to continue on their merry way, scoring at around four-and-a-half runs per over.

There was, however, some joy for us as Warney continued to inflict pain on the Pommy batsmen, creating new nightmares for fresh-faced opponents and re-opening old wounds for those he's bowled to before.

Cricket is such a mind game. Players can sense apprehension and fear in opponents, if they read body language with any authority. One player who is obviously carrying some excess emotional baggage is Mark Lathwell, a guy who made his Test debut against us back in 1993. Then he was seen as the next wonder boy. Unfortunately, his constitution wasn't quite up to scratch at the highest level and the system gobbled him up. He walked to the crease today looking as if he knew he wasn't going to last, and in Shane Warne we had the perfect executioner.

Warney ended up getting what the bowlers these days call a 'Michelle' (as in 'Pfeiffer', for 'five-for'), but disconcertingly for us we conceded 52 extras, made up primarily of no-balls, the scourge of captains and coaches. Still, Somerset's total of 284 represented a fine comeback by us and a series of wasted opportunities for the locals.

The carnage continued in the final session of play, as all our lads managed solid-looking starts without going on with the job. I was the exception, striking the ball with perhaps the most authority I've shown on tour. This was truly an amazing day's cricket, which saw 14 wickets fall, 466 runs scored, 28 no-balls bowled and 70 boundaries struck. And all in front of a capacity crowd. This sort of positive cricket will guarantee the future success of the game and must be encouraged by everyone involved with the sport.

PHILIP BROWN

CAPTAIN MARK TAYLOR (RIGHT) WITH FITNESS GURU STEVE 'TATTOO' SMITH.

AUSTRALIAN PICTURE LIBRARY/ALLSPORT

STEVE WAUGH

LEFT: GREG BLEWETT AT BRANDS HATCH.
RIGHT: COACH GEOFF MARSH IN NOTTINGHAM, ENJOYING ANOTHER ASHES TRIUMPH.

THE 1997 AUSTRALIANS

THE 1997 AUSTRALIANS

TOP: SHANE WARNE AT OXFORD, WAITING TO DISCOVER IF IT'S A GIRL OR A BOY.

BOTTOM: SHANE AGAIN, SOON AFTER, WITH MANAGER ALAN CROMPTON. WARNEY'S CIGAR IS FAIR DINKUM, CROMMO'S WAS SUPPOSED TO EXPLODE SOON AFTER IT WAS LIT.

RIGHT: PAUL REIFFEL, AT HIS FIRST TRAINING SESSION, TRYING TO ADAPT TO ENGLISH TIME.

BELOW: JUSTIN LANGER (LEFT), RICKY PONTING (CENTRE) AND DARREN BERRY, DURING THE VICTORY CELEBRATIONS IN LEEDS.

PHILIP BROWN

STEVE WAUGH

THE 1997 AUSTRALIANS

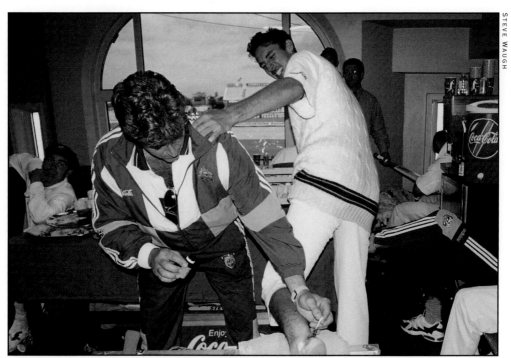

DIZZY GILLESPIE ENDURES PHYSIO ERROL ALCOTT'S CURE FOR BLISTERS.

MICHAEL BEVAN'S FAMOUS SINGING VOICE TAKES CENTRE STAGE. SHANE LEE (LEFT) IS ON GUITAR.

THE 1997 AUSTRALIANS

LEFT: THE UNLUCKY ANDY BICHEL, ON THE BALCONY AT TRENT BRIDGE FOR THE GAME AGAINST NOTTS, PONDERING HIS IMMINENT FAREWELL FROM THE SQUAD. **RIGHT:** MATTHEW ELLIOTT, SHOWING JUST HOW STRONG HE REALLY IS.

MICHAEL SLATER (RIGHT), ON THE TEAM BUS WITH INXS'S TIM FARRISS.

THE 1997 AUSTRALIANS

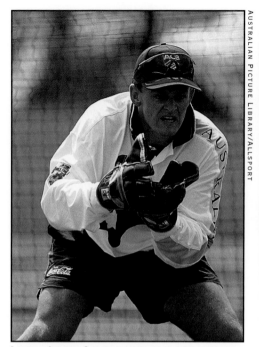

LEFT: ADAM GILCHRIST, ALMOST CERTAINLY A FUTURE TEST STAR.
RIGHT: BRENDON JULIAN IN THE LORD'S DRESSING-ROOM DURING
THE SECOND TEST.

GLENN MCGRATH IN FRONT OF THE HONOUR BOARD AT LORD'S, WHICH FEATURES
THE NAMES OF THE OVERSEAS BOWLERS WHO HAVE TAKEN FIVE WICKETS IN A TEST
INNINGS AT THE GROUND. WE'D ALREADY ADDED PIGEON'S NAME TO WHAT IS A VERY
EXCLUSIVE LIST.

LEFT: SHANE LEE DISPLAYS HIS AFL SKILLS. **RIGHT:** SHAUN YOUNG (LEFT), WHO, LIKE LEE, WAS CALLED UP TO THE SQUAD AFTER PAUL REIFFEL RETURNED HOME AND BRENDON JULIAN WAS INJURED, RECEIVES HIS FIRST TEST CAP AT THE OVAL.

MICHAEL KASPROWICZ ON THE MOBILE PHONE AT TRENT BRIDGE. AT THE OTHER END IS ANDY BICHEL, LISTENING AS WE BELT OUT ANOTHER VICTORY SONG.

THE 1997 AUSTRALIANS

WITH MY GREAT FRIEND AND GREAT TEAM-MATE IAN HEALY.

WITH BROTHER MARK AND THE FAMOUS BEDSER TWINS, ALEC AND ERIC, AT JOHN PAUL GETTY'S PRIVATE GROUND AT IBSTONE.

THE 1997 AUSTRALIANS

DAY 85 | AUGUST 2

Taunton

SOMERSET 284 AND 3—147 (RJ TURNER 65*, SC ECCLESTONE 47)
V AUSTRALIANS 323 (SR WAUGH 62, BP JULIAN 71, AR CADDICK 5—54).

SOMETIMES COUNTY FIXTURES LACK intensity and atmosphere. But not today. There was an air of excitement and expectancy about prior to the first ball being delivered, with many players having points to prove, most notably the man bowling this first over, Andy Caddick, and my partner in the middle, Michael Bevan.

Caddick had, of course, been quite amazingly left out of the English starting XI for the Test at Headingley. Judging by his impressive spell yesterday evening (3 for 30), he is determined to win his place back straightaway. Bevo, in contrast, is at a stage where he needs to rebuild some personal pride and confidence, rather than worry about forcing his way back into the side straightaway. He needs to be comfortable in himself and his game before he has another crack at Test level, but once this is achieved I'm sure his natural gifts will shine through.

For me, today represented a chance to build on a solid start. However, only Caddick would have been pleased with his efforts, finishing with five scalps. Bevo and I were dismissed early on, courtesy of two pretty useful deliveries from the 'human FA Cup'. This is why the Somerset man is a dangerous competitor, for he can produce the odd unplayable wicket-taking delivery.

Brendon Julian saved us from being embarrassed on a batting paradise, weighing in with a murderous 71 which further underlined his prodigious talent. But as the immortal Jack Gibson once said, 'What has talent ever won you?' Now is the time for BJ to seize the moment, convert his natural skills into match-winning performances at the top level, and give Australia a much needed world-class allrounder. Only he can make it happen!

A lead of 39 was only just acceptable, but the speed with which we scored our runs ensured we would have plenty of time to win the game in the fourth innings.

Somerset's approach to their second innings was much more sedate than their helter-skelter attitude on Day One. However, this relative serenity was soon to change beyond anyone's expectations or wishes, and much to the distress of many people at the ground.

Warm weather, warm beer, 'soccer-type' supporters and Shane Warne at the bowling crease proved to be a volatile cocktail. With Warney's high profile and continued success, he is always going to be a target for much adulation and, sadly, some ridicule. In just about every game on tour we have seen sections of the crowd continually yelling out and chipping away at Shane, to try to put him off his game.

Mostly this comes in the form of chants such as, 'Warney ... Warney ... You fat bastard, you fat bastard ... You ate all our pies!' Or another favourite, 'He's fat, he's round, he bounces on the ground ... Shane Warne ... Shane Warne.'

This type of thing is basically water off a duck's back for Shane. For all of us. However, today the 'fans' went way over the boundary, from fun and gentle sarcasm to constant, ugly abuse. These small minorities in the crowd, which would have been limited to three groups, each with around 15 or so people, began to get way out of control midway through Shane's second over. The usual harmless fun turned nasty and far too personal, with idiotic chants being the main focus of everyone's attention — purely because you couldn't avoid them due to their loudness and crudeness.

Choruses of 'Warne takes it up the !@#$!', 'Warne is a !@##$%!' and 'Aussies, we own your country, we own your !@#$%!' became so frequent that all the players were becoming angered and distracted by the drunken louts. Our concern was shared by the umpires, and it was Nigel Plews (a former policeman, who umpired two Ashes Tests in 1989 and one in 1993) who said to me, 'This is ridiculous, they've gone way too far.'

Taunton is a small ground, which may have 'amplified' the noises from our perspective, but, whatever, what was occurring beyond the boundary was now beginning to create friction out in the middle. It finally all came to a head at the commencement of another Warne over, when the chants began again even louder than on previous occasions. As captain, I believed it to be in the best interests of the decent spectators to be able to enjoy the cricket. Of course, I also wanted to stop Warney copping further degrading and derogatory remarks for no reason. The umpires agreed and the game duly came to a standstill.

The Somerset CC Chief Executive was summoned from the grandstands, and a conference ensued which resulted in Security being sent to the troublesome areas. We learnt later that two culprits received their marching orders.

These extreme measures quelled the brain-dead yobbos, and led to a relatively quiet last hour which was appreciated by the genuine cricket fans still at the ground.

Cricket crowds today want more for their money. This demand on the cricketers is fine, providing the stresses it creates are recognised and people realise we need some time to ourselves, particularly during breaks in play such as lunch and tea. But many cricket followers today expect players to sign autographs anytime, anywhere. 'Sorry, not now' is not an alternative. Only today, Warney was abused by a Somerset member in the committee rooms for not signing a kid's autograph during the lunch hour.

At the end of this controversial day's play, the game looked set for an exciting conclusion, particularly if the aggressive attitude of both teams continues. Inevitably, my day wasn't over even though the whites were off, as the press boys were hovering ominously outside the change room doors. There was no need for a nuclear scientist to work out their line of questioning. Some of the scribes pointed out that what had occurred was no different from what happens all over the world. But even if this was so, I argued, why should it be tolerated? Why would you bring your kids and wife to the game if you knew you would be subjected to loutish behaviour and constant swearing?

I'm not sure if they agreed with my line of thought, but I remained happy with my actions and felt I had done the right thing. That's all you can ask of yourself.

THE WHORTLEBERRY PIE, A LOCAL DELICACY THAT'S BEEN SERVED TO AUSTRALIAN CAPTAINS SINCE THE DAYS OF THE DON. ALAN CROMPTON SEEMS PRETTY PLEASED THAT HE'S NOT THE ONE ABOUT TO DO THE TASTING!

DAY 86 | AUGUST 3

Taunton

SOMERSET 284 AND 3—147 V AUSTRALIANS 323. NO PLAY.

THIS MORNING WAS DEFINITELY similar to what most Australians believe an English summer is like. It was grey, bleak and drizzly. You could tell by the weather that the prospects of any play were minimal, or by observing the upbeat mood around the breakfast table as the boys gathered around. Days off are precious, but to be truthful we could have done with a bit a workout today.

Taunton's 'The Castle' hotel has a unique tradition involving the Australian cricket team which dates back to the days of Bradman. It all started when The Don was set to play against Somerset in the '30s, but fell ill the night before the match. The locals came up with the idea of baking the great man a local delicacy to lift his spirits. The dish in

The reaction to my decision to stop play at Taunton has been overwhelmingly positive. There are a great number of cricket followers who, like me, are sick to death of the abuse of players that some 'fans' seem to think is acceptable. I won't put names to the generous comments that follow, but here is a sample of feedback I've received ...

'I had the misfortune to sit in the same stand as the mindless louts who appeared to take such great delight in hurling what I considered to be very abusive and offensive remarks at you and other members of your team. I left at about 5.30pm with my nine-year-old son, as I did not want to subject his ears to any more of the disgusting language which was coming from behind us ...

'I hope you will not all tar us all with the same brush. I suspect that 99 per cent of the crowd at Taunton on Saturday wanted nothing more than to watch good cricket ...'

'I am writing to inform you that the more agreeable part of the crowd at Taunton considered the recent match played there to be the most entertaining for a very long mind was a specialty of the area, baked with ingredients found growing wild in the nearby Quantock Hills. These tiny berries are known as 'whortleberries' and after being prepared with some skill by a local baker developed into the famous (or if you've tasted it, infamous) Whortleberry Pie.

In the days leading up to our game here, The Castle sent out a plea to locals, seeking help in picking the necessary whortleberries for the 1997 edition. 'As a last resort we could use commercial blueberries,' the hotel's owner was quoted as saying, 'but the flavour isn't the same and since we insist on using fresh, local produce in everything we serve, we're not prepared to compromise, even for the Australians.'

Fortunately a local farmer's daughter, Esme Redwood, came to the rescue ...

'It's not a very good season, but I managed to find about two pounds of fresh ones,' she explained. 'In a good year, I reckon I can pick about five pounds at a time. They're very fiddly because you have to pick them individually. My mother was a great one for whortleberries. She picked 300 pounds in one season when she was 82!'

As skipper, it was my turn to do the honours in 1997 — my role being to taste the delicacy and at the same time appear to enjoy it for the benefit of the snappers' cameras.

Many of the guys spent the rest of the day scouring the shops in the search of a bargain. Blewey is always keen to liven up his wardrobe, usually by way of a pair of curtains disguised as jeans or some 'lounge-suit cloth' that resembles a shirt. Each to his own, I guess, but Blewey would be far better off investing in a mirror so he can see some of his 'fashion statements' before he ventures out with them on. My afternoon was spent at a favourite haunt of mine, the cinema, where *Jurassic Park: The Lost World* was terrifying hordes of youngsters. They apparently expected something a bit tamer than the scenes of dinosaurs eating humans at the same speed Merv Hughes used to demolish hors d'oeuvres at official functions.

time. It also regrets the unfortunate reactions from the unfortunate section of the crowd.'

'As a cricket enthusiast who, with my son, made a 120-mile round trip to Taunton last Saturday to watch and enjoy the second day's play, I wish to offer my sincere apologies for the totally unnecessary events that took place ... There is no place for them in cricket whatsoever and the authorities may need to be much more robust in dealing with Counties who allow such yobbish behaviour to occur.'

'I hope you don't think these morons represent the English cricket supporter. How brave they all are when full of drink and surrounded by their mates ...

It is because of people like this that I stopped going to the cricket ...'

One letter Shane received commented, 'In a way it's a bit of a backhanded compliment that they barrack you so much. If you weren't so bloody good they wouldn't be bothered. Eric Cantona had exactly the same problem and he was a genius as well, so you're in pretty good company.'

DAY 87 | AUGUST 4

Taunton

SOMERSET 284 AND 3–147 V AUSTRALIANS 323. NO PLAY, MATCH DRAWN.

ALTHOUGH THE WEATHER WAS no better than yesterday, it was decided that both teams would venture down to the ground and wait until lunch before calling the match off, to presumably make sure that the corporate boxes were filled for the day. This was a sad end to what had been a spirited affair. Somerset must be congratulated for their approach, which was unlike that of quite a few other counties, who gave the impression that our game was no more than an opportunity to rest key players.

By this stage of the tour everyone has one thing in common — a hatred for packing bags — especially as there always appears to be more to be packed each time this chore is performed. This morning, it was bags down in the foyer by nine o'clock, so that our ever-reliable baggage-man, Tony Smith, could have them at our next hotel ready and waiting for our arrival later in the day.

Back on the bus and down the motorway, we all went in search of our next venue, which is situated on the outskirts of Nottingham.

Our management has made a change from the hotel we stayed at earlier in the tour, and now we found ourselves in a much more relaxed atmosphere. This hotel even has a 'health retreat' attached to it, but the biggest bonus for the lads comes in the form of a McDonald's which is located, literally, at cover point as you looked out from the reception area.

While most of the couples ventured out tonight for a spot of Chinese, we single lads enjoyed a relaxing drink together. And we caught up with John Cornell ('Strop' from the old Paul Hogan shows and one of the key off-field figures in the formation of World Series Cricket in the 1970s). John is a friend of the team who has helped out with player contracts in the past, and he's a guy well worth listening to if you want to learn about business and dealing with people.

DAY 88 | AUGUST 5

Nottingham

THE GRIND OF MODERN day cricket is relentless and it was in the nets we found ourselves again this morning. To their credit, our management have tried to vary training sessions as much as they can, but as Allan Border once said, 'To win cricket games you have to bat well, bowl well and catch well. There are no magic formulas.'

A normal session for us begins with a jogged lap and a few short sharp exercises, intertwined with some sit-ups and push-ups supervised by Steve Smith. Errol Alcott will then guide us through our stretching routine, which takes 20 to 25 minutes, before handing us back over to Smithy for a more intense workout — usually some sort of 'circuit work' with different activities at each 'station' (stopping point in the circuit). After this, we might take part in a game of volleyball or some other group activity, to get the energy levels up. Then it's either into the nets for the real thing or a solid fielding session, involving a couple of drills for the entire squad followed by some more specific work, such as catches for the guys who field in the catching cordon on game day.

Our efforts at practice today indicated to me that we are ready to finish off England in the fifth Test. The quality of our work was as

JUSTIN LANGER, NO. 17 OF THE WEST COAST EAGLES.

AUSTRALIAN PICTURE LIBRARY/ALLSPORT

good as we've produced all tour. The only downer was an injury to BJ, who got 'cleaned up' by an enthusiastic net bowler and needed ice on his left wrist. I hope the blow hasn't caused any serious damage, as his left arm is, of course, his bowling arm.

For my Test preview for Channel 7, the network's cricket anchorman, Jim Wilson, lined up an afternoon of clay target shooting and quad runner bike races. The winner of the target events, Ricky Ponting, wasn't a surprise, considering the way he's been seeing the cricket ball. The quad runners were an opportunity for some retribution for Slats, who still seethes when reminded of his reckless driving disqualification at the go-karts earlier on in the tour. Using scurrilous tactics and with no concern for his or anyone else's safety, he left a field of six eating his dust.

Tonight's team meeting revolved around what tactics we should employ against the Hollioake boys, who have been included in the English side. They've obviously been selected for their temperament and attitude. We agreed that they will be expecting a bit of chat from us, to welcome them into the fold, which more than likely will inspire them to perform at their best. So, using a bit of reverse psychology, we have decided to give them 'the silent treatment'. This can put many a batsman off, because they then know their opponents are totally focused and planning their downfall, rather than wasting their energy on talk and gestures. Hype and talk are poor substitutes for class and technique — if the Hollioakes are good enough they'll swim, if not they'll sink.

My gut feeling is that they'll be in for a bit of a struggle in the upcoming Test, especially if they think that the pressures of Test cricket are no different from those in One-day cricket. They are worlds apart.

ADAM (LEFT) AND BEN HOLLIOAKE, ENGLAND'S ANSWER TO THE WAUGHS.

DAY 89 | AUGUST 6

Nottingham

TUBS TURNED IN ONE of his best net sessions of the tour this morning, hitting the ball with some authority and looking positive — which is exactly how he should be playing to ensure he comes out of his dry run of the last two Tests.

Earlier on, before we hit the nets, the 'Sherrin' (AFL ball) came out of the kitbag and you should have seen the boys go. I'm telling you this little red item could be the breakthrough of the decade for the medical profession — the answer to a wide variety of ailments. In one short session, a remedy was found for Herbie's dodgy knee, Warney miraculously lost all stiffness in his body and Blewey was obviously cured of the knee pain that has dogged him for some time. The remainder of the lads leapt out of the ground to take spectacular marks, in between feigning hand passes and throwing dummies as if they were in line for the Brownlow Medal.

A quiet evening was had after Lang and I arrived too late to catch a flick at the cinemas. Instead, we settled for a feed and a chat. Lang is a deep thinker on the game and life in general, and always makes for good conversation over the dinner table — I, for one, believe he will eventually get the breakthrough at Test level he so desperately wants and deserves.

I called home tonight, and Lynette informed me that a visit to the doctor has confirmed that Rosie has been suffering from a dose of the flu for at least the past couple of weeks. This makes her unsettled sleep patterns easier to understand — it may have been wrong to blame them purely on the unfamiliar surroundings. Their trip home was a lengthy affair, after typhoons left them holed up in Hong Kong for two days, but thankfully Rosie travelled much better on the return leg than she did coming over.

Fifth Test — Day One
Trent Bridge, Nottingham

AUSTRALIA 3–302 (MTG ELLIOTT 69, MA TAYLOR 76, GS BLEWETT 50, ME WAUGH 60*, SR WAUGH 38*) V ENGLAND

IT WAS A PENSIVE mood that permeated through the team bus as we made the 20-minute journey from the hotel to Trent Bridge, where we were once again greeted by an enthusiastic full house. For England, the loss of Darren Gough through injury is a major blow, but many were hoping that this setback would be offset by the dawn of a new era, courtesy of the Hollioake boys. Adam was always going to make his debut here, but we weren't sure about Ben until they both made their way onto the ground shortly before the toss, to be presented with their first Test caps by Mike Atherton.

Mark Taylor again guessed correctly, with tails again, to make it five tosses in a row. This good fortune caused much chagrin, not only for his adversary, but for the whole of the ground — a huge sigh went up as soon as it was obvious the Gods had smiled upon us.

Mark and Matthew Elliott then took full advantage, putting together their most impressive stand of the tour. Except for a couple of close lbw decisions that favoured them, they were in complete control, and the lunchtime score of 0–84 was exactly what we wanted. It is generally accepted that a scoreline of around 2–70 represents an evenly-shared opening session, so by that standard we were well on top.

Matty Elliott had eclipsed 1000 runs for the tour when he reached 31, an achievement which further confirmed his rapidly-growing status at Test level. The stand was surprisingly curtailed at 117, when the leaner of our two 'engine-room men' fell, and 43 runs later he was joined in the pavilion by our captain, not long after Mark had scored his 6000th run in Test cricket. He was only the sixth Australian to reach this mark (after Border, Boon, Greg Chappell, Bradman and Harvey), a very fine achievement from a very fine player.

Greg Blewett and Mark Waugh carried on the good work, although not convincingly early on. However, as they grew in confidence the crowd was treated to some glorious strokeplay. Ben Hollioake began nervously in his first spell at a Test bowling crease, going for 25 from his first three overs and quickly realising that here was a much tougher assignment than the under–19s 'Test' against Zimbabwe he'd been playing in only days earlier. To Atherton's credit, the England skipper took the teenager under his wing, bowling him in short spells, and they reaped a reward when Blewett offered a lazy jab to a ball pitched outside his off stump and left Stewart to do the rest.

The final session was safely negotiated by Australia's answer to the Hollioakes, leaving us handsomely placed at 3–302. We shouldn't lose from here.

Today was probably the best I've felt all series. The feet were moving nicely, I was comfortable and at ease without being complacent, and my timing and

AUSTRALIAN PICTURE LIBRARY/ALLSPORT

GREG BLEWETT ON THE WAY TO HIS SECOND HALF CENTURY OF THE SERIES.

placement were first class. I only wished we could have continued for a couple more hours, to keep up the momentum we had developed.

Tomorrow's first session will either see England fight hard to get back into the game by way of some pro-active cricket, or we will dominate proceedings totally if they allow us to set the tone. The overriding feature of today's play was the negative body language that the England team exhibited from the very first ball. It was as if the loss of the toss had wrecked their chances of winning.

One other notable event, from my point of view, was Adam Hollioake not wearing his newly-won England cap in the opening session. Some might say 'big deal', but wearing that cap is more than a gesture.

I believe it's a mark of respect to the country you're playing for and to those that have worn the cap before you. After all, it's an elite few who get the opportunity to represent their country — I believe you have an obligation to show your appreciation by donning the team's cap with that crest upon it, at least on the first morning, as a mark of solidarity and your commitment to the cause.

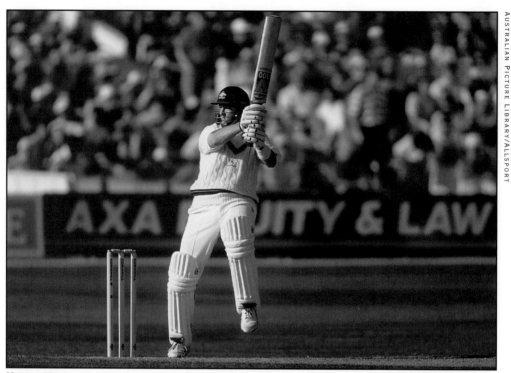

MARK (TOP) AND MYSELF BATTING LATE ON THE FIRST DAY, AS THE AUSTRALIAN
INNINGS TOTAL CLIMBED TOWARDS 300.

DAY 91 AUGUST 8

Fifth Test — Day Two
Trent Bridge, Nottingham

AUSTRALIA 427 (ME WAUGH 68, SR WAUGH 75, DW HEADLEY 4–87)
V ENGLAND 4–188 (AJ STEWART 87).

ONE THING THAT HAS continually amazed me throughout this Test series is how much time the England players spend in the nets. Every day, we arrive at the ground 90 minutes before play to find the opposition in the nets endlessly bowling, facing throwdowns and taking sharp catches. On top of this, they have long fielding sessions and 'team bonding' games, which add up to a real solid workout … even before they go into battle for the real thing. I couldn't believe they were at it again this morning, as the weather forecast predicted the sort of steamy, hot conditions where you need some extra fuel in the tank.

To the Englishmen's credit, they came out swinging in the first session and polished us off, 45 minutes after lunch, for the addition of only 125 runs. It was a superb comeback, easily the best by an England team on English soil in the past three Ashes series.

Scoring 75 was pleasing, but because I felt in such good nick it wasn't nearly enough, especially when I wasn't encountering too many problems when I was dismissed. I was taken down by Malcolm, who produced a pretty useful outswinger at good pace, but my downfall was primarily a result of me almost pulling away before the ball was bowled. I thought Devon had slipped, or lost his run-up just at the point of delivery, and switched off for a split second.

As we made our way out onto the field in single-file, I had to take a second look to make certain I wasn't imagining what I had just seen. On the edge of the ropes, inside the boundary, Andy Caddick and Dean Headley were being interviewed by a local television commentator. At the same time, the English openers were about to take the field. Quite clearly, they had not been in the dressing-room to wish their openers good luck, which to me is a very unprofessional thing to do. I interpreted their attitude as being 'I've done my job, now I can forget about the game until I'm required again.' They should have been backing up the guys involved in the immediate action.

As England were chasing 427 and needed to win this Test to keep the Ashes alive, we recognised that, from the home team's point of view, it was imperative that they got off to a steady yet positive start. Consequently, the blitzkrieg that Alec Stewart showered down upon us caught us by surprise. In the end, he fell 13 runs short of what would have been his first Ashes hundred and a much-deserved one. He'd faced just 107 balls and smashed 14 fours, and was taken brilliantly by Heals at the second attempt, which gave the world's premier custodian his 300th Test catch and his 100th Test catch against England.

Warney then dragged us back into the game with a great spell on an unproductive wicket for his art, taking 3–14 in the space of 39 balls. This return would have made up somewhat for the 100 he lost to Ian Botham earlier on in the day, after Shane failed to trouble the scorers. (At the start of the tour, 'Beefy' and Shane had agreed on the following bet — every time Warney scored more than 20, Beefy would pay him £5 for every run over 20. Every time Warney scored less than 20 Beefy would receive £5 for every run less than 20. Early on, Shane was way in front. Now, things are getting much closer.)

England's final scoreline of 4–188, after they had been 0–106, was a reflection of our gutsy fightback. But it would have been even better had the third umpire not panicked and given Graham Thorpe not out before the left-hander had scored. The TV ump was about the only person who believed the green light was the right option. But, as they say, 'the umpire's ruling is final, and always correct!'

Current Aston Villa and Australian goalkeeper Mark Bosnich popped into the change rooms after play, for a beer and to have a dig at Junior. Bosnich had backed my brother yesterday at 5–1 to score a hundred, but had been let down when the first wicket of the day fell in the morning's third over.

FOR ONE OF THE FEW TIMES IN THE SERIES, MIKE ATHERTON DOESN'T FALL TO GLENN MCGRATH. THIS TIME HE WAS CAUGHT BEHIND OFF SHANE WARNE.

DAY 92 | AUGUST 9

Fifth Test — Day Three
Trent Bridge, Nottingham

AUSTRALIA 427 AND 4–167 (MA TAYLOR 45, GS BLEWETT 60)
V ENGLAND 313 (GP THORPE 53, AJ HOLLIOAKE 45, GD MCGRATH 4–71,
SK WARNE 4–86).

THE EARLY BREAKTHROUGH WE so desired was not forthcoming, although it would have been except for the guy in the gully who dropped a sitter off Thorpe from McGrath's bowling.

An impressive debut knock by Adam Hollioake suggested his selection was an inspired move rather than simply speculative. However, he was out with his score on 45 and the England total on 243, as did his partner (for 53) on the same total. This double blow left the capacity crowd stunned, and us well on top.

Young gun Ben Hollioake, with his laid-back approach and almost trance-like appearance, reminded me a little of David Gower at the crease. He certainly didn't look ruffled while scoring 28, in fact he looked as if he needed a good slap in the face to get him going. He also displayed a lot of talent and a dislike for leaving any deliveries at all. I'll go out on a limb and say he'll end up a better batsman than bowler.

Robert Croft walking to the wicket reminded me of a bull walking into the ring ... surrounded by 11 matadors.

Glenn McGrath was given first throw of the spear. Croft, realising his strength isn't against the short, fast ball, went for glory against Warne. He raced to 18 through a variety of innovative and lofted shots, but it was only a matter of time before he went down and again it was a shortish ball that brought him to his knees. He was caught by Greg Blewett, close in on the leg-side.

The English tail showed a bit of fight for the first time this series, a struggle that culminated in a thoroughly entertaining innings of 12 from Devon Malcolm which brought the house down. His three boundaries were horrific-looking strokes, but full of effort and enterprise. It's hard to hit an off drive with your eyes closed and your front foot nearly a metre outside the leg stump, but this man pulled it off, in the process showing what a class bowler and quick thinker he is.

AUSTRALIAN PICTURE LIBRARY/ALLSPORT

SHANE WARNE GETS GRAHAM THORPE, AND ENGLAND HAVE LOST THEIR SECOND WICKET OF THE MORNING.

McGrath finally bamboozled the 'wood-chopping' one with a slower ball similar to a delivery I used to produce with success in One-day cricket. He and Warne again shared the spoils, grabbing a further four well-deserved poles each.

Building quickly upon our 114–run first innings lead was what we needed. This objective was fulfilled in spectacular fashion, primarily by Elliott (37) until he fell to the catch of the series by a diving John Crawley at deep backward-square. From 1–51, although we lost wickets at regular intervals, we kept up a healthy scoring rate to finish the day at 4–167. Ricky Ponting and I are at the crease.

All up, it was a pleasing day's work. From a spectator's point of view, I, like many others, felt that this match has developed into far and away the best Test match of the summer. It is no coincidence that it is being played on the best wicket by a 'country mile' we've seen during the series.

A couple of interesting by-plays between members of each team occurred today. At one point, Robert Croft was admiring his straight six off Warney on the ground's huge replay screen, unaware that Shane was ready to bowl his next delivery. Finally, in exasperation, Warney called down the pitch, 'Hey Crofty, don't worry, you will be able to see the replay again in a couple of minutes … in the dressing-room.'

Shane was right!

Earlier on, the younger Hollioake had become intrigued by his own stroke play while watching that same giant monitor. As we stood silently around, someone suddenly asked, 'Is there any chance of you facing up? This isn't second XI cricket, mate.'

DAY 93 AUGUST 10

Fifth Test — Day Four
Trent Bridge, Nottingham

AUSTRALIA 427 AND 336 (RT PONTING 45, IA HEALY 63)
DEFEATED ENGLAND 313 AND 186 (GP THORPE 82*, GD MCGRATH 3–36,
JN GILLESPIE 3–65, SK WARNE 3–43) BY 264 RUNS.

ON THE DAY THAT English cricket was to be 'reborn', courtesy of the ECB blueprint entitled 'Raising the Standard', by Lord MacLaurin, we had in mind a further lowering of its status.

Lord MacLaurin's proposals were to be revealed to the public during the day, but, to me, the timing of such a document's release was very inappropriate. 'Raising the Standard' virtually admits that England isn't good enough to compete at the top level and that the state of the game across the country is in chaos. Surely such a demeaning report could have been tabled and discussed at a more suitable time, either before the series had begun or after its conclusion? But not in the middle of an Ashes series.

Being not out overnight almost always means a fairly light workout in the nets before play, with not too much physical activity, because I'm hoping to save my energy for a long stay out in the middle. Normally, I'll simply have a short net session followed by some throwdowns from Swampy, to feel the middle of the bat on the ball. Finally, I might receive some short, sharp catches to get my reflexes and hand-to-eye co-ordination going.

However, today my plans for a long innings were sadly mistaken. In the day's opening over I gloved a sharply lifting delivery from Andy Caddick to second slip, after hitting the previous ball through the covers for four. In a situation such as this, you find yourself back in the change rooms before you realise what has happened, almost as if it's not true. If only I could have turned back time and started all over gain.

England were certainly excited about my wicket, but in getting that vital breakthrough they lost their focus. In Ian Healy, we had the perfect man to capitalise on such a lapse, and he produced an innings of 63 off just 78 balls. The first hour of the day produced 75 runs from 12 overs, which put England out of the game when not so long before they had been right back in it.

Healy is a hugely frustrating player to bowl to. In one innings he looks as if he could get out every ball, in the next he'll produce quality strokes normally associated with the best batsmen in the game. The one constant with Healy is his scoring rate, which is consistently the best in our side. This is a valuable attribute for a No. 7, as it provides added impetus to an innings and more often than not changes the course of the game.

Unfortunately, for the second time in the series, it appeared that one of our players had been caught on the first bounce. Ricky Ponting was playing a vital supporting role when he pushed at an Adam Hollioake outswinger, got an edge and was scooped up by Alec Stewart behind the stumps. To be fair to Alec, he is a very honest and admirable adversary and I have no doubt he thought he caught the ball. However, a super-slow-motion replay, which honed in on the catch, suggested the ball might not have carried all the way.

My point is this: A player shouldn't be blamed when such an incident occurs. After all, he genuinely believes he has caught the ball. But rather than putting the onus on the catcher, why don't we use the third umpire to judge decisions that aren't clear to the human eye. And a second thing — the way these affairs are dismissed as being part of the game (I bet the local papers don't even give the Ponting dismissal the time of day) is a little frustrating to us. I'm sure that if Ian Healy or Steve Waugh had been involved (remember the headlines my catch of Brian Lara caused in the Caribbean in 1995) there would have been an uproar.

England's momentous task began reasonably, although the early loss of Stewart virtually snuffed out any thoughts they may have had of an unlikely victory, especially

AUSTRALIAN PICTURE LIBRARY/ALLSPORT

BEN HOLLIOAKE FALLS TO WARNE, AS ENGLAND DISINTEGRATE LATE IN THE DAY.

IAN HEALY, MAN OF THE MATCH AFTER TAKING SEVEN CATCHES AND SCORING A
FANTASTIC, VITAL 63 THAT PUT THE GAME OUT OF ENGLAND'S REACH.

as his fall came so soon after Glenn McGrath had dismissed Mike Atherton once more.
A positive start had been their only chance at getting a grip on the chase that lay ahead.
Then Jason Gillespie began a spell that captains dream of when they have plenty of
runs to play with — Gillespie claimed wickets at regular intervals even though he was
conceding a lot of runs between his successes. It didn't matter about the runs but the
wickets were priceless. Jason's spell was made all the more remarkable by the fact that
he was obviously suffering from back pain which had required plenty of painkillers,
just to get him to the bowling crease.

After the third wicket (Hussain, bowled for 21) fell, I turned to Matty Elliott, my
companion in the gully region, and stated, 'We'll win this tonight.' There was just over
an hour of play remaining at this stage. These words turned out to be prophetic, as
England's inexperienced and brittle batting line-up crumbled at the hands of a
rampaging attack, supported by advancing fieldsmen, all sensing an historic win.

The conditions of this Ashes series stated that we could ask for an extra half-hour, if
we believed we could end the Test in that time. We duly called for such an extension
and Devon Malcolm obliged with a slashing cover drive that found its way into Mark
Waugh's hands at second slip. Had Malcolm survived that ball, there were only seven
balls left in the day. Graham Thorpe had played a great rearguard innings, remaining
82 not out at the death, but he probably should have tried to shield the strike in the last
couple of overs, to try to force us back tomorrow to win the game. You never know
when it might rain all day.

Our joy and ecstasy were there for all to see, as we carried on like a soccer team who had just scored the winning goal in a Cup Final. It had been a superb team performance from a great side who had dominated nearly every session of the series since the disastrous first Test. This victory meant we were the first team in Ashes history to win five series in a row. Heals, Tubs and myself are the only three Aussies to have played in all these series.

Brother Mark inadvertently gave me a nice memento of the occasion when he threw the ball in the air after taking the series-winning catch, and then forgot about it. The ball was left on the ground as the advancing crowd charged onto Trent Bridge like the Scottish warriors in *Braveheart*. Fortunately for me, an Aussie named John Sandy swooped on the ball and then presented it to me when he saw I was after it — a fine gesture indeed!

Needless to say the celebrations were very animated, with Heals, because it was a series win, giving us three verses of *Under the Southern Cross*, our winning team song, instead of the usual two. Phone calls to Bic and Gilly were made, as these lads are still very much a part of the squad and our success, while Slats, Lang and myself made a vow to wear our green baggys for the next four days straight. Alcohol can make you do strange things! It was 4.30am before a day that we'll all long remember and be proud of for many years to come came to a close.

Boy, it was great to be part of the Aussie cricket team!

MICHAEL KASPROWICZ, JASON GILLESPIE AND ME, ALL IN THE BAGGY GREEN, SOAKING UP OUR ASHES TRIUMPH IN THE TRENT BRIDGE DRESSING-ROOM.

DAY 94 | AUGUST 11

Nottingham

ONE THING YOU DON'T want, when you've only had a couple of hours' sleep, and your head feels like it doesn't belong to you, is a succession of early-morning phone calls from the press.

I decided to attack the situation and head down to the pool for a spot of swimming. The only trouble with this plan was that the warm, muscle-relaxing spa loomed just to the left of the pool and it didn't take long for me to convince myself what the best option was.

At a special team meeting tonight, we learnt that Pistol will be heading home to be with his wife, who is experiencing some complications during the latter stages of her pregnancy.

More bad news came when we were told that Jason Gillespie has been diagnosed as suffering from stress fractures in his back and will need a lengthy rehabilitation to ensure the problem doesn't flare up again.

This makes Dizzy's effort in the second innings of the fifth Test even more meritorious. It proves, too, that he possesses great inner strength and courage by being able to play through the pain as he did.

STEVE WAUGH

DIZZY GILLESPIE, WITH HIS UNIQUE 'AUSTRALIA'S MOST WANTED' LOOK.

TODAY'S PAPERS WERE SCATHING IN THEIR CONDEMNATION OF THE ENGLISH SIDE
TO THE POINT OF RIDICULING THEM TO AN EMBARRASSING LEVEL. I GUESS THIS TYPE
OF JOURNALISM SELLS PAPERS BUT IN MY OPINION IT SHOULDN'T BE TOLERATED.

DAY 95 | AUGUST 12

Londonderry

IT WAS FAREWELL TO Pistol, and goodbye to Dizzy and Hooter, too. The latter pair are heading down to London to get a further diagnosis from specialists on our paceman's injured back. It is vitally important Dizzy gets his rehabilitation right, for his own sake and for the future well-being of Australian cricket. This guy is another McGrath in the making and he's still only 22 years old!

It seems like we're never off that damn bus, and yet another hour was clocked up before we reached Manchester Airport. Once there, we underwent a very thorough

BROTHER MARK IN LONDONDERRY WITH A COUPLE OF NEW-FOUND FRIENDS.

JUSTIN LANGER, CLEARLY ENTRENCHED AS AUSTRALIAN CRICKET'S NO. 1 ANGLER.

and strict inspection, before beginning our trip to Belfast. Quite a few of the boys have been apprehensive about travelling to this perceived hot spot, but for most of us it has become quite normal to visit cities and countries that most tourists are advised are best bypassed.

Our trek wasn't over when we arrived in Belfast, for we still had an hour's drive to our hotel in Londonderry to endure. Thankfully, this was broken up by a pit stop at a favourite waterhole of our liaison officer. Warney was particularly grateful for the diversion, as he spotted his favourite snacks, 'Bacon Bites' hanging in their plastic bags from the wall. He was so pleased, in fact, that he relieved the proprietor of a whole strip of these snacks — 15 bags in all!

We finally reached our hotel after half a day's travelling. Half the lads were eager to get on the golf course, while the rest of us went in search of some salmon in the meandering streams just down the road. One could say the fishing expedition was a dismal failure — the only sign of success came the way of Kasper, but he let his chance of glory escape when the fish headed for the safety of the rocks and reeds before losing the hook and dashing off to freedom.

My efforts were somewhat hindered by the six stinging nettle bushes that nestled up against my arm as I threw my most impressive cast for the day. For the next 15 minutes I rummaged through the bushes, in search of a leaf that I was told would nullify the pain if it was rubbed on my skin shortly after contact. Unfortunately, I never found one, the sting didn't ease up at all, but at least I had an excuse for my lack of success on the salmon front.

DAY 96 | AUGUST 13

Londonderry

THE ADULATION WE ARE receiving from the Irish is quite unexpected. We are especially pleased to learn that they are on our side, hoping and praying that the Poms are going to cop a hiding.

We had the huge honour today of playing golf at Royal Portrush. This is a course that Gary Player, the legendary South African golfer, said only last week, while winning a Seniors event, was the best links course he'd ever played. If Gary was here today, he would have been horrified by some of the atrocious tee shots that were played on the first tee. Crommo started off with two glorious cover drives, one of which scooted across the members' car park, while Tattoo looked like a dog playing with a soccer ball as he hacked his way in zigzag fashion down the first fairway.

Royal Portrush lived up to its billing, with well-thought-out holes, carpet-like greens and manicured fairways adjoined by rough that requires you to break a wrist if you want to get the ball out. Punter was again the star, carding a 75. He finished just in front of Smithy, who played only nine holes less.

The evening was spent soaking up the hospitality of these extremely hospitable people. I can tell you the Guinness hit all the right spots.

AUSTRALIAN PICTURE LIBRARY/ALLSPORT

RICKY PONTING, TRYING TO BREAK PAR AT THE MAGNIFICENT ROYAL PORTRUSH.

DAY 97 | AUGUST 14

Londonderry

AUSTRALIANS 7–303 (JL LANGER 57, RT PONTING 117*) DEFEATED
IRELAND 164 (WK McCALLAN 64*, RT PONTING 3–14) BY 139 RUNS.

THEY SAID IT COULDN'T be done. Well, they didn't count on the love affair Lang has with his cherished baggy green cap. To everyone's astonishment, some four days after the Southern Comfort had done the talking in our victorious dressing-room celebrations at Trent Bridge, Lang is still proudly sporting his cap, a fact which wins him a bet neither Slats nor I could fulfil. But at least we didn't have an odour any skunk would have been proud of, or a permanent red ring around our melons from the elastic band inside the rim of the cap. This was another morale-boosting effort from Lang, who always does those little things that help bond a side together.

Today was a day in 'sheet city'. Having been excluded from the starting XI, I made the most of it — the only effort exerted came after the doorbell rang for room service or when I flicked over the pages in John Grisham's latest novel, *The Runaway Jury*.

Bad news did, however, make its way back to the hotel when an urgent message filtered through that either Pigeon or Warney was required to dash down to the ground to replace BJ, who couldn't bowl a ball during warm-ups because of that knock he received in the nets back at Trent Bridge. It was confirmed later that he has suffered a hairline fracture, thus ending his chance of a recall for the sixth Test, at The Oval, which was virtually guaranteed after the loss of Gillespie and Reiffel.

It's certainly been a tough tour for *Cleo's* former 'Bachelor of the Year' runner-up. First, it was a neck injury that damaged BJ's chances early in the tour, and now this. For the sake of his sanity, he must make something positive out of this setback. Like Bic, Gilly and Dizzy, he must make sure that the injury makes him hungrier when he next steps onto the field; perhaps it will increase his focus on the first game of next season.

Down at the ground Punter continued his rich vein of form with an exquisite exhibition of classy stroke-making, while the highly-impressive Darren Berry claimed five catches and one stumping in another polished display.

DAY 98 | AUGUST 15

Canterbury

TO CAP OFF A battery-recharging couple of days, I ventured out with Warney and 'Chuck' Berry onto the hotel's golf course this morning for a game of 'skins'. The trio nearly became a duo at the fourth, after Shane lost control of our golf cart while careering down a steep fairway. He ended his descent with a wild 360-degrees spin, before safely pulling up slapbang next to his ball.

The golf developed into a titanic tussle. Walking up the 18th, Warney had five skins, Chuck, 'the burglar', had six, and I had six. You would have thought there were millions at stake the way we played the hole, such was the 'gas taking' all round, but all arguments were resolved when I rolled in a sloping eight-footer for a five (on a straightforward par 3). While the standard of golf wasn't anything to write home about, the company, atmosphere and surroundings certainly were, and it made for a morning well spent.

Shortly after it was back on the merry-go-round — bus, plane, bus and finally our arrival at what is reputably the No. 1 rated hotel in Canterbury. It may well have been highly regarded during the winter months, but now that a mini drought has hit England the absence of air-conditioners left us trying to survive in stifling, almost unbearable conditions. The absence of fresh air gives the whole place the atmosphere of a gymnasium sauna.

It's hard enough trying to squeeze in a 'players' association' (or, to give it its proper name, the Australian Cricketers Association) meeting during the Australian season. It's harder still finding time for one on this Ashes tour, but miraculously all things fell into place and we found ourselves seated around a large table in the conference room of the hotel. Those who had made the journey to Kent for the meeting were ACA Chairman, the former Test off-spinner and my good friend, Tim May, the ex-CEO of the Australian Cricket Board, Graham Halbish, and a special guest, James Erskine, formerly of IMG (the International Management Group). The ACA has taken a full two years to become a reality. Maysie, Heals and I had begun the ball rolling and Warney played a supporting role, by providing many important introductions to business people. Tubs, because of his seniority, became involved at a later stage. Maysie has done an outstanding job, sacrificing endless hours in the quest to make this the first players' association to actually provide a role that is much needed by all cricketers.

The purpose of tonight's meeting was to bring the players in the squad up-to-date on the advancements we've made and what our objectives are for the future. The reason Erskine was here — which was, incidentally, a complete surprise to all of us on tour — was so he could put forward a proposal to the ACA for him to represent us in all negotiations. The meeting went extremely well, with all players committed to following through on the solid base that has been created. Even after three hours, we still had plenty to chat about, so it was resolved that we'd assemble again tomorrow night to round off proceedings and vote on whether we want Erskine to represent us in future dealings with the ACB.

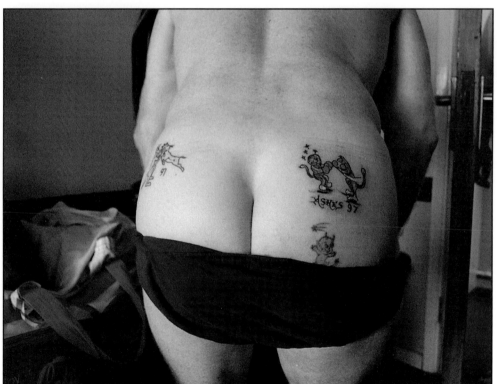

STEVE WAUGH

TATTOO LIVED UP TO HIS NICKNAME BY ADDING ANOTHER PIECE OF ART TO HIS BACKSIDE, THE DEED FITTINGLY BEING DONE IN THE LAND OF HIS PREDECESSORS ON THE FIRST DAY OF OUR STAY THERE. AFTER OUR TREMENDOUS WINNING SERIES IN SOUTH AFRICA, HE HAD ADDED A SPRINGBOK BEING BOOTED THROUGH THE AIR ONTO HIS LEFT BUTTOCK. NOW A BULLDOG HAS SUFFERED THE SAME FATE ON HIS RIGHT. WHAT AN INDICATION OF HIS LOYALTY AND LOVE FOR THE TEAM!

DAY 99 | AUGUST 16

Canterbury

KENT 201 (MV FLEMING 67, MS KASPROWICZ 4–72, S LEE 4–27)
V AUSTRALIANS 5–207 (SR WAUGH 94*).

THE ST LAWRENCE GROUND at Canterbury is quite unique, in that a huge oak tree is situated on the ground inside the boundary. It's a sight that is remarkable if you haven't seen it before. I think it's great because it gives the ground a real sense of character.

Once again, a ground for a tour match was sold out. To my fellow players' dismay I lost the toss and we found ourselves in the field, on a warmish English summer's day, bowling on a wicket as good as any we've seen for the whole tour. On paper at least, this was probably the most inexperienced attack we've put on the field all tour, but the desire and commitment of these guys was firstrate. Kasper troubled all the batsmen, while one of our two 'new' tourists, Shane Lee, claimed four wickets. The other 'debutant', Shaun Young, looked to be trying too hard, which is understandable considering what probably awaits him — a spot in the XI for the final Test. But he still managed to keep a tight check on the run rate.

Bowling one of the better county sides out on such a good track for only 201 was a great performance, highlighted by our

TASMANIA'S SHAUN YOUNG, AT HIS FIRST TRAINING SESSION WITH THE TEAM.

AUSTRALIAN PICTURE LIBRARY/ALLSPORT

best catching display of the tour. The slips cordon looked like a school of sharks eager for a feed. On such a wicket, I thought I'd be able to settle into the comfort of the change rooms. Instead, I barely had time to sort my gear out before I was facing Alan Igglesden, a former Test opening bowler, who had claimed three wickets for five runs in a destructive 11-ball spell.

As I faced my first over, I felt half asleep for some reason — perhaps because I only slept for about half an hour last night due to the unbearable heat. But once this initial settling-in period was safely negotiated, I began to feel in really good touch and with Bevo added 101 in quick time before the close of play.

Tonight's second half of the Players' Association meeting was an historic affair. It confirmed that everyone is thinking along the same lines and committed to following on from the hard work that has already achieved so much. A secret ballot was held, which unanimously decided to appoint James Erskine as our chief negotiator.

The only stumbling block was having to then negotiate with the negotiator about his percentages and control over the whole scheme of things. Once again, John Cornell came to our rescue. He acted on the players' behalf to gain the best deal for us, which leaves us with the power to hire and fire whoever we want.

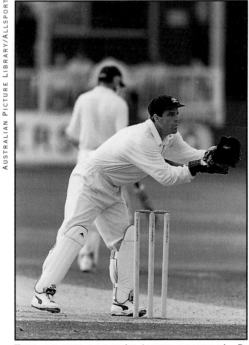

TWO OF THE SQUAD'S 'LATE COMERS', DARREN BERRY (LEFT) AND SHANE LEE, AT THE ST LAWRENCE GROUND IN CANTERBURY.

DAY 100 | AUGUST 17

Canterbury

KENT 201 AND 5–234 (TR WARD 68, AP WELLS 65) V AUSTRALIANS 315 (SR WAUGH 154, MG BEVAN 55).

IT TOOK ME FOUR balls to reach my century this morning, which was ideal after I'd had all night to think about the six runs needed to reach the landmark, and how I was going to get them. Overall, though, we were disappointing with the bat again, managing only 315 — a pretty unsatisfactory result when you consider we had Shaun Young at No. 8 and Shane Lee at No. 9, both of whom average over 40 in first-class cricket. This undisciplined display is exactly what we didn't want in the lead-up to the sixth Test and exactly what we said we wouldn't do when we sat down at Somerset to talk about how we wanted to finish the tour. Hopefully, our second innings will be a more professional effort. I was very satisfied with my 154 but slightly aggrieved to be the last man out, even though the ball I got from their Zimbabwean leggie, Paul Strang, gripped and turned out of the rough. One can only imagine what Warney would have done on this wicket. At one point, I went forward to play what was almost a half volley and ended up wearing it flush on the peak of my helmet, after it spat out of a foothole.

In Kent's second innings our fielding and bowling was top notch once more. We had no luck whatsoever early on, but gained the rewards shortly before the close of play, when two wickets fell in the last 10 overs.

Tonight gave the media guys a chance to air their 'bloopers tape' of the tour. Blunders from Healy, S. Waugh and Warne featured prominently, along with some candid and sometimes embarrassing camera shots of the lads on tour. The Channel 7 and Channel 9 boys have been great company all tour and are so well known to everyone they are almost part of the squad. The Aussie journos also said a word of thanks — in general, we've had a pretty good working relationship with them during the tour. That said, I think it's important to keep some distance between players and the media. We both have a job to do and opinions are bound to vary on different issues, many of which can be personal.

DAY 101 | AUGUST 18

Canterbury

KENT 201 AND 343 (MA EALHAM 85, S LEE 4–86) LOST TO AUSTRALIANS 315 AND 4–231 (MJ SLATER 47, RT PONTING 56*, MG BEVAN 47*) BY SIX WICKETS.

A LIGHT WARM-UP WAS all that was required before play, especially as the sun continued to shine as if trying to make up for the time lost when it deserted us all. Once the initial, crucial breakthrough was achieved in the morning session, the rest of the order succumbed under the pressure we began to exert. Shane Lee again bowled as well as he's ever done, claiming a further four wickets (which would have been his first-ever five-wicket haul in a first-class match, but for a high ball that was grassed by Slats). 'China' Young settled into a much better rhythm in this innings than he had in the first, and in doing so probably gave himself the nod for a Test jumper. Overall, it was an encouraging performance in the field and one that gives me great confidence going into our last match.

During my first-innings century my thumb problem resurfaced in a big way, and I am now struggling to hold the bat with any authority. Considering the Test is only three days away, I took on the role of McGrath and slotted in at No. 11 for the second dig. We looked a little shaky at 3–95 before tea, but in the end got home comfortably on the backs of Punter and Bevo, who overcame a few nerve-racking moments to give us only our third victory over a county on tour.

The win took longer than we had hoped. That fact, combined with the obligatory signing session for all those avid autograph collectors at the gate and a quick chat we enjoyed with the former New Zealand opener (and now coach of Kent), John Wright, meant that we arrived in London sometime around 8.30pm. After a quick feed, we hit the sack.

After all the troubles I'd had earlier in the tour organising satisfactory accommodation for my family at the Westbury, this time, now that I'm a 'single man', they've given me a penthouse suite (valued at £750 a night). No doubt this is a clerical error, but there was no way I was going to inform them of that.

RIGHT: MARK TAYLOR AT TRENT BRIDGE, SCORING 76 ON THE OPENING DAY OF THE FIFTH TEST.

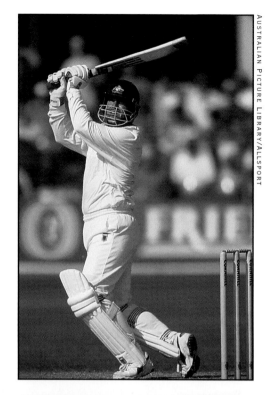

BELOW: ENGLAND'S ANDY CADDICK CAN ONLY DESPAIR AS BROTHER MARK AND I PILE ON THE RUNS LATE ON THE FIRST DAY AT NOTTINGHAM.

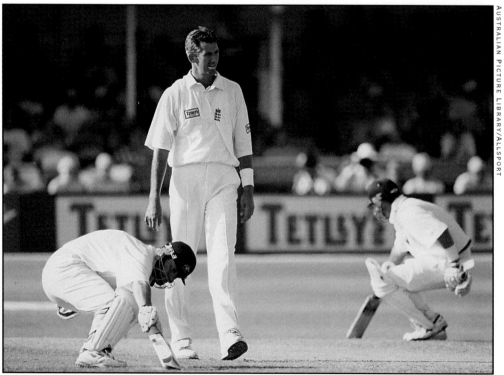

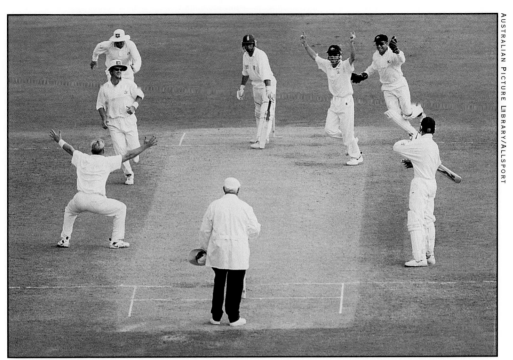

NASSER HUSSAIN'S TWO DISMISSALS AT TRENT BRIDGE. IN THE FIRST INNINGS (ABOVE) HE WAS BOWLED BY AN ABSOLUTE BEAUTY BY SHANE WARNE. IN THE SECOND (BELOW), HE AIMED A BIG DRIVE AT JASON GILLESPIE AND LOST HIS LEG STUMP.

THE FIFTH AND SIXTH TESTS

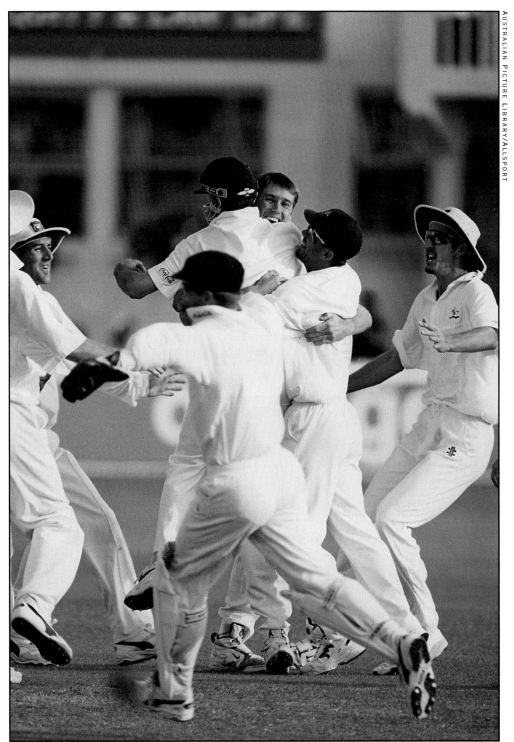

LET THE CELEBRATIONS BEGIN. DEVON MALCOLM HAS JUST EDGED GLENN MCGRATH TO MARK WAUGH AT SECOND SLIP AND AUSTRALIA HAVE RETAINED THE ASHES.

THE FIFTH AND SIXTH TESTS

WARNEY, WHO WAS LATER TO COP PLENTY OVER HIS VICTORY CELEBRATIONS, DOUSES HIS COMRADES IN CHAMPAGNE ON THE TRENT BRIDGE BALCONY.

WITH THE FORMALITIES ON THE BALCONY OVER, THE JUBILATION REACHED FEVER PITCH IN THE AUSTRALIAN DRESSING-ROOM.

THE FIFTH AND SIXTH TESTS

TWO STUNNING REFLEX CATCHES. **TOP:** IAN HEALY PERFORMS A BACKFLIP TO CATCH ALEC STEWART AT TRENT BRIDGE. **BOTTOM:** STEWART REACTS QUICKLY TO GRAB A HALF-CHANCE FROM GREG BLEWETT DURING OUR FIRST INNINGS OF THE SIXTH TEST, AT THE OVAL.

MICHAEL KASPROWICZ ACKNOWLEDGES A SHARP CATCH BY HIS CAPTAIN
(IN FOREGROUND), TO DISMISS THE DANGEROUS GRAHAM THORPE AT THE OVAL.
THIS WAS ONE OF KASPER'S SEVEN WICKETS IN THE INNINGS.

THE FIFTH AND SIXTH TESTS

SILLY MID-OFF MARK BUTCHER WEARS A COVER DRIVE DURING THE FINAL TEST.

THE FINAL WICKET OF THE SERIES. GLENN MCGRATH HAS JUST SPOONED MAN OF THE MATCH PHIL TUFNELL TO GRAHAM THORPE AT MID-OFF.

THE FIFTH AND SIXTH TESTS

MARK TAYLOR AT TRENT BRIDGE, AFTER LEADING HIS TEAM TO AN UNBEATABLE 3—1 SERIES LEAD.

WITH TUBS (CENTRE) AND HEALS AFTER RETAINING THE ASHES, OUR FIFTH STRAIGHT SERIES WIN. WE WERE THE THREE MEMBERS OF THE '97 SQUAD WHO HAD PLAYED IN ALL FIVE SERIES, DATING BACK TO OUR SUCCESS IN ENGLAND IN 1989, WHEN ALLAN BORDER LED US TO A FAMOUS 4—0 TRIUMPH.

THE FIFTH AND SIXTH TESTS

DAY 102 | AUGUST 19

London

ONLY TWO PRACTICE DAYS to go on tour … and that was exactly how we trained, with no energy and lack of purpose. We probably would have been better off having a day off and Mark Taylor said as much after training was completed. My session was a non-event — I've been told not to hit any balls in order to give my hand every chance to heal as best it can before the game. Matty Elliott had a shocker, being dismissed on three or more occasions, something he very rarely does in the nets as he is a very disciplined cricketer.

It will be interesting to see whether the theory 'practice makes perfect' rings true, or whether we can turn in a shoddy net session and still go out and produce the goods.

To be honest, the boys were probably looking forward to this afternoon's two options of R&R. Golf is always a popular choice among cricketers, as a way of relaxing and taking a few bucks off each other while bonding even further as a unit. Courtesy of Coke, we also had an opportunity to go racing at the Brands Hatch motor-racing circuit — an experience that I wasn't about to pass up.

It was basically in at the deep end for all of us. First up, we were tutored in the techniques of cornering and braking for a full 15 minutes (which was enough time for Chuck Berry to feel light-headed and go sweaty all over). Next thing we knew, we were in a BMW on the driver's side doing laps at good pace, with an instructor in the passenger seat clinging gamely to the dashboard.

I must say that with their guidance we all improved much quicker than any of us could have imagined. Next, it was the pros' turn to give us a demo and, boy, didn't they up the skill level by about 100-fold as they tore the track apart at speeds one couldn't have imagined possible.

It was now assumed that because we hadn't put any of the 'Beamers' into the safety barriers, or given the instructors whiplash, that we were apparently good enough to

MICHAEL SLATER, CHECKING WHAT THE BRANDS HATCH TRACK RECORD IS WHILE HE SECURES HIS HELMET.

handle driving a Formula Three car. These vehicles are a much smaller version of a Formula One car, and sit only inches from the track. Strategically-placed cones on the track were there to be used as guides for turning and braking, and they certainly made the job feel much easier, but even so I was shocked to look at my speedo and see 100mph and five-and-a-half thousand revs staring back at me. I reckon the reason they only give you three laps is that by lap two your confidence level has reached the point that no doubt, sooner or later, you will try something out of your depth.

Slats, of course, was in heaven amid the smell of octane and the screeching of tyres. 'Chuck', meanwhile, had settled into a steady rhythm once he realised he wasn't going to end up being ferried away by an ambulance. Blewey couldn't get enough, but the faces of McGrath, Kasprowicz, Julian and Elliott told a sorry tale. Being taller than average, they couldn't squeeze into the driving seat — although the whisper was that Herb could have if he really wanted to but the memories of his appalling road-sense on the go-karts was obviously preying heavily on his mind.

It was a day to remember, capped off by two 'white-knuckle' laps in the passenger seat of a 'souped-up' thing driven by Mark Webber, an Australian who is being touted as our next Formula One driver. We all agreed that this was a great way to get away from the grind of touring life and vowed to get back here as soon as we can.

Hopefully, tomorrow.

DESPITE MY DAMAGED HAND, I WAS DETERMINED TO FIND OUT JUST HOW FAST I COULD GO. THE ANSWER? A LITTLE TOO RAPIDLY, APPARENTLY (SEE MY REPORT CARD, BELOW).

NIGEL MANSELL
Racing School

43007

DATE 19/8/97   NAME Steve Waugh   CLASS IT

LAP No	LAPTIME	FLAG SIGNALS GIVEN	REMARKS				
1	✓		A bit too quick				WEATHER
2	✓	Y/F	at this stage				
3	✓						
4	✓	WY/F	Y/F = Yellow Flag,				BMW 318i SE
5	✓		W = Waved				
6			R = Red,				
7			Y/L = Yellow Light etc.				FORMULA FIRST
8			G = Green				14
9				POOR	FAIR	GOOD	
10			LINE			✓	INITIAL TRIAL ANALYSIS
			PACE	✓			85%.
			HANDLING			✓	

London

REASURINGLY, TODAY'S SESSION WAS much better than yesterday's and more like what we expect of each other. I was again limited in my preparations, only facing a dozen or so throw downs after trying to bat in the nets with no great success. I'm glad this Test will be the last match of the tour, because this hand problem is beginning to be a real inconvenience, mainly as I can't get any power through my shots.

WARNEY AT THE OVAL, PRACTISING TO BE SUPERMAN.

AUSTRALIAN PICTURE LIBRARY/ALLSPORT

Trying to have a quiet afternoon is near impossible at the conclusion of a tour, because everyone seems to want to see you for an interview or some sort of favour and last-minute details have to be attended to in order to make the trip home.

Our team meeting was pretty brief. We emphasised the need for everyone to dig deep for one last effort and for each player to set himself certain goals and objectives. For the Poms, big Devon Malcolm will be playing a 'do or die' Test, while pace bowler Peter Martin, spinner Phil Tufnell and middle-order batsman Mark Ramprakash will be making their first Test appearance of the summer. Surprisingly, John Crawley has been dropped, only one game after being considered good enough to be elevated from No. 6 to No. 3. Mark Butcher comes back to open the innings on his home turf, a move which shoves Alec Stewart back down the order.

THIS WAS THE LAST TIME TUBS WAS REQUIRED TO DO THIS BACKBREAKER ON TOUR.

It seems to me that the English selectors have got themselves into a huge tangle. This is probably best exemplified by the dropping or 'resting' of the teenage wonder boy, Ben Hollioake, after only one game. This said, it's always a dangerous thing to pay too much attention to the opposition line-up, instead of getting your own shop in order. Our biggest danger will be our batting, as I'm just sensing that it is a little carefree at the moment — in direct contrast to our bowling, which is looking in great shape.

Tonight represented my last opportunity to pull off a memorable team dinner and the boys certainly did their part, ordering 30 lobsters between them as we tucked into a mountain of tucker at one of London's better Japanese restaurants. I went to bed hoping my pre-match worries are just that. Only time will tell!

Sixth Test — Day One
The Oval, London

ENGLAND 180 (GD McGRATH 7–76) V AUSTRALIA 2–77.

NOT FOR THE FIRST time on tour, the dressing-room was inadequate to fit our squad in comfortably, resulting in the reserves, gear and all, being banished to the shower recesses.

The mood of the camp was a little hard to define. It hovered between focused and relaxed as we did our normal pre-match warm-up. For the first time in the series, Mark Taylor called incorrectly and Mike Atherton had no option but to bat on what looked like a wicket made for runs. It did, though, seem to be a pitch that would take quite a bit of turn — it was drier than normal for a first-day wicket. England must have been tempted to play two spinners, but such is Robert Croft's lack of form and worn-down state of mind that he was always a non-starter, even though he was in their original squad. Only last week, Croft had an altercation with another ex-England player, Mark Illot, during an Essex-Glamorgan NatWest Trophy semi-final, that led to both players pushing and shoving each other. The £1000 fine these blokes copped was a joke to me, considering Shane Warne and Merv Hughes copped considerably more for lesser offences in South Africa in 1994.

This incident probably came about after Nasser Hussain mentioned in a newspaper interview that 'England's domestic cricket was soft and players needed to toughen up a bit'. Pushing and shoving isn't the answer, however. It's what occurs between the ears that makes the difference.

Complacency and thoughts of going home are our two biggest dangers in this Test (I know this from the experience of previous tours). Predictably, it was McGrath who led the way for us early, swatting aside Atherton like an annoying bee off a soft drink can. This was the seventh time he had claimed the England captain's wicket during the series. Before this, Butcher had perished to an ill-advised stroke — he must have been wishing he hadn't got a recall.

GLENN MCGRATH HAS JUST DISMISSED THE ENGLISH CAPTAIN FOR THE SEVENTH TIME IN THE SERIES.

Michael Kasprowicz, meanwhile, was looking a little out of sorts. He bowled too many 'four' balls, which allowed the pressure to be released from a batsman's point of view. Into the frame stepped Shane Warne. His first ball, a vicious, spitting leg break, would have sent shivers through the home team's camp. It was exactly what they didn't want to see.

Due to a combination of Warne's almost 'unscoreable' bowling and McGrath's vice-like grip on proceedings at the other end, England found themselves going nowhere in a hurry. The lunchtime score of 2–97 didn't reflect our control over proceedings and we knew if we continued on the same path in the next session we'd reap the rewards.

Picking up a wicket with the first ball after lunch is a dream start — it offers a chance to dominate from then on. Stewart was the culprit for England, not for the first time he fell to a delivery straight after a break, which suggests he takes a while to switch on.

The next two wickets both fell to well-conceived bowling plans. Hussain was caught at mid-on off a well-pitched-up delivery aimed at his leg stump, having been drawn across his stumps by McGrath to a point where he was overbalancing and ripe for the picking. Thorpe then had his leg stump clipped by a ball delivered from around the wicket. He, too, had been lured across his crease — this was a classic dismissal from a big quick's point of view.

Ramprakash went meekly, after which Caddick and Martin had a few slogs at Warne before sanity prevailed. In the end, McGrath claimed 7–76 from 21 overs of distinguished quality, while Warne went a little under-rewarded with just two wickets and Kasprowicz claimed the prize scalp of Devon Malcolm, who played the worst 'shot' I have ever seen. As always, Big Dev's bat looks as if it's allergic to his body when he grips it and seems to have a mind of its own. This could be his only explanation for an attempted sweep that crushed into his back leg just below his knee. It was a comical dismissal.

It was now time to put the boot in and make England pay for their undisciplined batting. A lead of anything over 150 should see us not having to strap the pads on again, so a scoreline of 2–77 at the close was a pretty fair effort. Taylor was looking impressively aggressive at the crease before he, like Matthew Elliott, was dismissed by Tufnell. The English spinner is already gaining appreciable turn and bounce out of the bowlers' footmarks.

Tomorrow's play will be vital to us. The wicket is showing signs of being far too friendly to the spinners, and the odd ball from the quicks is bursting through the surface, too. This sort of wicket is extremely hard to score on, as it gives the batsmen no confidence or trust to play their shots with any authority. It's just a shame we haven't got Neil Harvey in the side, as he no doubt would have made light work of the situation.

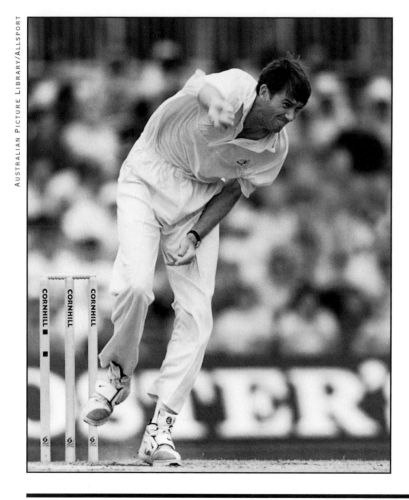

GLENN MCGRATH TOOK HIS WICKET TALLY FOR THE SERIES TO 36, WHICH, NEXT TO WHAT TERRY ALDERMAN ACHIEVED IN 1981 (42) AND 1989 (41) AND WHAT DENNIS LILLEE DID IN 1981 (39), IS AS MANY WICKETS AS ANY AUSTRALIAN HAS EVER TAKEN IN AN ASHES SERIES IN ENGLAND.

DAY 105 | AUGUST 22

Sixth Test — Day Two
The Oval, London

ENGLAND 180 AND 3–52 V AUSTRALIA 220 (GS BLEWETT 47, RT PONTING 40, PCR TUFNELL 7–66, AR CADDICK 3–76).

I MUST ADMIT I found today's warm-up of team volleyball a little strange. We haven't done that in any of the previous Test matches, but it certainly got the lads together and feeling relaxed about the day ahead. More unusual and disturbing were the number of people walking by our viewing enclosure, the amount of unnecessary talk, and the fact that some of our guys were playing 500 during the morning's session.

Now, I'm not saying you can't do what you want to do, but these are things that didn't happen during the first five Tests so I don't see why they should be transpiring during this game.

Sure enough, this slight loss of focus led to a day where England fought back admirably. Heading their charge was the 'artful dodger', Phil Tufnell, who claimed 7–66, his first 'five-for' in 20 Tests, in a display that left many wondering why he'd been sent packing down the motorway in each of the previous five Tests. Having seen England self-destruct yesterday, we should have learnt our lesson. Unfortunately, we mirrored their efforts and in doing so put them well and truly back in the hunt.

During the last four Tests he's umpired us, Peter Willey seems to have developed a liking for raising the finger in my direction. I don't think I've survived an appeal yet, although I have given him plenty of chances to get rid of me. Today's outcome, though, was one I thought might have gone the other way. Scoring 22 is a batsman's nightmare — it means you've done the initial hard work and should be now accustomed to the pace and bounce of the wicket. The job should be a lot easier. In these circumstances, I reckon that on about 90 per cent of occasions a batsman will get himself out, by premeditating a shot, thinking about the previous ball or thinking too far ahead. If you can block these thoughts out and devote all your energies to the next ball, your chances of success are greatly increased.

SHANE WARNE POLITELY ASKS UMPIRE
PETER WILLEY WHETHER THE BATSMAN AT
THE OTHER END MIGHT BE LBW.

I think I'm a little more frustrated than normal today at getting out, because it only needed someone to go on to get a big score and the game was as good as over. Greg Blewett's 47 and Ricky Ponting's 40 were well-constructed digs, but not the big one we were looking for, while everyone felt for Shaun Young, who snared the dreaded globe on debut.

A lead of 40 was, in all honesty, no lead at all considering the wicket was deteriorating much quicker than anyone had anticipated (with the exception of Peter Willey, who mentioned to me that this is 'the driest Oval wicket I have ever seen'. Peter has been a Test and first-class cricketer or umpire for the best part of 30 years!

As we're batting last on such a wearing pitch, we don't want to be chasing anything more than 150, so it was with some relief that Kasprowicz picked up two quick wickets. This put the pressure back on England, who are in a precarious position at close, in reality 3–12.

The biggest downer for us is the groin strain Shane suffered late in the day, just when the scene had been set for him to run amok. The most important ice bag of the season was immediately applied to our spin-bowling champion when he entered the change rooms. One hopes it's not too serious and he'll be able to bowl to something like the standard we're accustomed to. Tomorrow, the game is there for the taking.

After taking something like 500 to 600 photos during the tour, I entertained the idea of a slide night tonight, which was well attended but had to be aborted after five minutes because of a blown fuse in the slide projector. I was left to lick my wounds, while the boys headed for a feed at one of the many nearby restaurants.

DAY 106 | AUGUST 23

Sixth Test — Day Three
The Oval, London

ENGLAND 180 AND 163 (GP THORPE 62, MR RAMPRAKASH 48, MS KASPROWICZ 7–36) DEFEATED AUSTRALIA 220 AND 104 (AR CADDICK 5–42) BY 19 RUNS.

WE COULDN'T HAVE HOPED for a better start to the day. In the very first over, Hussain played an airy shot to a Warne delivery, only to see it spoon to backward point. From here, though, England fought back well. Thorpe completed the first half-century of the match — further proof of the difficult nature of the wicket and the loss of confidence of batsmen in both sides — and Ramprakash, looking to book a spot on the plane for England's upcoming tour of the West Indies, confirmed his status as the best looking and best-organised cricketer in the county system.

It's quite amazing to think that Ramprakash is averaging only around 17 per innings from 19 Tests, which further underlines that much-heard statement, 'It's a mental game.' One could see he was a little overawed in the first innings, but sometimes such a problem can be solved as simply as by getting one convincing shot through the field. That's exactly what happened this morning. The Middlesex captain punched Warne off the back foot for a couple of fours and visibly grew in stature.

With Warne courageously battling through his groin strain, but still clearly hampered to the point where he was bowling like a human, it was Kasprowicz who put his hand up and said, 'I'm the man you're looking for.' Once Thorpe and Ramprakash went, the rest of the England batting order fell rather meekly again, with Big Dev bagging one of the worst pairs in the history of the game. To his credit, though, he doesn't have any pretensions to be a batsman and always has a swing. This either results in quick runs or a quick dismissal, which at least doesn't hold the game up.

If ever there was a player deserving of success it is Michael Kasprowicz, who has worked hard all tour, even after being dropped when he did nothing wrong. Circumstances at that time worked against him. To see him take 'seven-for' was a tour highlight for me and, more importantly, is the breakthrough he needed to give him the confidence and belief that he really belongs at the highest level. From now on he will

IAN HEALY STUMPS MARK RAMPRAKASH. THIS WAS HIS 26TH DISMISSAL IN THE SERIES — EQUAL TO WHAT HE MANAGED IN 1993. HE WOULD FINISH THIS ASHES SERIES WITH 27.

MICHAEL KASPROWICZ SPREADEAGLES DEVON MALCOLM'S STUMPS TO COMPLETE THE FINEST BOWLING PERFORMANCE OF HIS CAREER.

go into Test matches with a different attitude and with the self-belief that will enable him to go from strength to strength.

Chasing 124 sounds simple but we knew it wouldn't be quite that easy, particularly if we lost a couple of quick wickets. The key was reaching 50 without the loss of more than one wicket, because if we could have reached that point we felt the Poms would probably start thinking they were out of the match. However, we got off to a poor start, losing Elliott, who ill-advisedly failed to offer a shot to a Malcolm delivery that moved in and trapped him lbw. For a while Taylor and Blewett looked in control, until a fired-up Caddick trapped our captain in front. Mark Waugh quickly succumbed to his arch adversary, Tufnell, for the second time in the match. This was probably not what Mark was thinking when he mentioned before the series started that he didn't really rate 'Tuffers' as a danger. I guess it never pays to make too many statements about this game.

Blewett and I got through to tea. In the dressing-room during the break I lost my cool, giving everyone a bit of a blast because I thought we were heading in the wrong direction, that is towards a loss. I thought by doing so I might ignite a bit more passion, or trigger a more committed approach to knocking off the runs, but looking back, the move definitely backfired on me because I became too fired up to finish the job.

Back at the crease after tea, I wasn't fully in control of my game, and fell victim to a shot of poor selection which gave Caddick my scalp for the sixth time in the series, and gave further impetus to England. It was a catalogue of disasters from here on in, as we chased our target in a scatterbrain fashion, obviously getting too far ahead of ourselves rather than playing the moment. The only remaining batsman to show the spirit and application that was needed to win the game was Shaun Young, who fought hard and played each ball on its merits, even though he remained only 4 not out.

This was a weird match, won in the end by England by 19 runs. It included 10 lbw decisions and a couple of dismissals via balls that 'burst' through the pitch surface. The wicket was basically a disgrace, and again didn't allow Test cricket to be played properly. On such a poor wicket, bowlers can look better than they are and gain inflated results, while batsmen need luck to survive. This creates a situation where the good players don't necessarily influence the game as they would on a good wicket. Bad wickets, because of a lesser need for class and skill, generally bring the quality of the contest down and definitely bring the teams closer together. Having said this, the better team won this Test.

Surely, this time, lessons will be learnt from our point of view. Our record in these so-called 'dead rubber Tests' is atrocious. I, for one, don't believe the theory that 'dead' Tests don't matter as much — just pulling on the baggy green should make it a very 'live' Test.

Losing here takes the edge off our great comeback. To win 4–1 sounds and looks a lot better than 3–2, but a series win is still a great achievement especially away from home. As usual after a series, the teams got together for a drink and a chat in the change rooms, and the jovial and friendly atmosphere was in keeping with a series devoid of any real nastiness and ill-feeling.

It was great to be part of a successful Ashes tour again. I hope I can make one more!

MARK TAYLOR AT THE OVAL WITH A REPLICA OF THE ASHES TROPHY. THE REAL THING REMAINS LOCKED IN ITS CASE AT LORD'S.

London

IT WAS WITH A feeling of acute disappointment and a nasty headache that I awoke the morning after our unbelievable capitulation in the final Test. Although there was no use dwelling on the events of that fateful third day, it is vitally important we learn from them, so that if we are faced with a similar situation in the future we can handle it in a better fashion.

SECTIONS OF THE ENGLISH ESTABLISHMENT DIDN'T REACT TOO KINDLY TO THE SUGGESTION THAT THE TROPHY SHOULD COME HOME WITH US.

ON THE TUESDAY BEFORE OUR DEPARTURE (AUGUST 26) WE WERE OBLIGED TO
TAKE PART IN UNDOUBTEDLY THE WORLD'S BIGGEST SIGNATHON. JUST ABOUT
ANYTHING THAT MOVED — BATS, PADS, T-SHIRTS, POSTERS, YOU NAME IT —
NEEDED AN AUTOGRAPH.

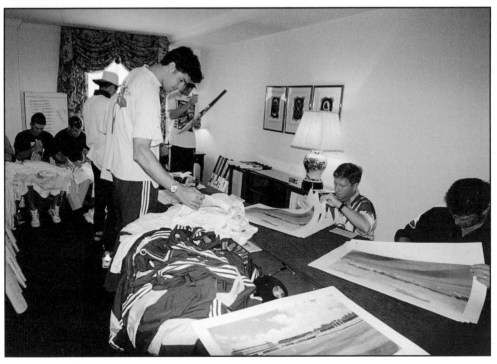

The final days of the tour were very much a winding-down period, for we had been on the road for 26 of the last 29 weeks following back-to-back tours of South Africa and the UK. There were lazy afternoons in beer gardens, a team sponsor's cruise down the Thames one night, a huge team signing session that everyone in London must have heard about, judging by the amount of items stretched out in the manager's room and halfway down the corridor. In between, I had media interviews to do — mostly as a summary of the tour and how things went for myself and the team.

As a team, I thought we came back superbly after the first Test loss and the 3–0 drubbing in the One-dayers. After these setbacks we never really 'lost' a day's cricket until the final day of the tour, which in my opinion showed a lot of character and will to win. My tour was one where, along with most batsmen, I didn't really feel as if I got into the series. This was due to some excellent bowling, but also many poorly-prepared wickets, which tested everyone's confidence to the maximum. I was however, very pleased to score hundreds in each innings of the crucial Manchester Test — that will always be a fond memory for me.

We managed to pull the creams out for one last day, a six-a-side corporate tournament in London on August 27, the day before we left England. And half a dozen of us even squeezed in an appearance at the Ian Botham Leukemia Appeal-sponsored corporate day at The Oval on the day of our departure. Then, finally, we headed for Heathrow, for the first leg of our long trek home.

Home!! A place we all couldn't wait to see.

1997 ASHES TOUR STATISTICS

TOUR SUMMARY

Date	Venue	Opponent	Result for Australia
May 11	Hong Kong	#World XI	Won by 4 wickets
May 15	Arundel	#Duke of Norfolk's XI	Won by 113 runs
May 17	Northampton	#Northamptonshire	Won on run rate
May 18	Worcester	#Worcestershire	Lost by 5 wickets
May 20	Chester-le-Street	#Durham	Abandoned
May 22	Leeds	#England	Lost by 6 wickets
May 24	The Oval	#England	Lost by 6 wickets
May 25	Lord's	#England	Lost by 6 wickets
May 27–29	Bristol	Gloucestershire	Drawn
May 31–June 2	Derby	Derbyshire	Lost by 1 wicket
June 5–8	Birmingham	ENGLAND	Lost by 9 wickets
June 11–13	Nottingham	Nottinghamshire	Drawn
June 14–16	Leicester	Leicestershire	Won by 84 runs
June 19–23	Lord's	ENGLAND	Drawn
June 25–27	Oxford	Universities	Abandoned
June 28–30	Southampton	Hampshire	Won by innings & 133 runs
July 3–7	Manchester	ENGLAND	Won by 268 runs
July 8	Jesmond	#Minor Counties	Won by 9 runs
July 12	Edinburgh	#Scotland	No result
July 14	Ibstone	#J.P. Getty Invitation XI	Drawn
July 16–18	Cardiff	Glamorgan	Drawn
July 19–21	Lord's	Middlesex	Drawn
July 24–28	Leeds	ENGLAND	Won by innings & 61 runs
August 1–4	Taunton	Somerset	Drawn
August 7–10	Nottingham	ENGLAND	Won by 264 runs
August 14	Eglinton	#Ireland	Won by 139 runs
Aug 16–18	Canterbury	Kent	Won by 6 wickets
August 21–23	The Oval	ENGLAND	Lost by 19 runs

(# Denotes not first-class)

Matches	Played	Won	Lost	Drawn	No Result
Tests	6	3	2	1	–
Other First-class	10	3	1	5	1
One-day Internationals	3	–	3	–	–
Other Non First-class	9	5	1	1	2

AUSTRALIANS V WORLD XI KOWLOON CRICKET CLUB, HONG KONG
11 MAY 1997 — TOSS: WORLD XI

World XI

*SV Manjrekar c Warne b Bichel	80
L Klusener b Julian	30
AP Gurusinha c Healy b Julian	6
Aamer Malik c Warne b Kasprowicz	36
R Gavaskar not out	51
BM McMillan b Bichel	11
SM Pollock c Healy b Julian	3
SJ Brew c Healy b Blewett	7
+JP Fordham c Julian b Bichel	2
Mohsin Kamal not out	1
Extras (lb 3, w 12, nb 3)	18
Total (8 wickets, 40 overs)	**245**

DNB: RK Chauhan.

FW: 1–72 (Klusener), 2–81 (Gurusinha), 3–167 (Aamer Malik), 4–174 (Manjrekar), 5–195 (McMillan), 6–208 (Pollock), 7–217 (Brew), 8–229 (Fordham).

Bowling: Kasprowicz 8–0–60–1 (1nb, 5w); Bichel 8–0–56–3 (3nb, 1w); Warne 8–1–33–0 (2w); Julian 8–0–44–3 (1nb, 4w); Blewett 8–0–49–1

Australians XI

*MA Taylor c Fordham b Mohsin Kamal	4
ME Waugh c Chauhan b Gavaskar	116
SR Waugh c Aamer Malik b Klusener	45
GS Blewett c sub b McMillan	3
JL Langer b Klusener	13
RT Ponting not out	35
+IA Healy c Klusener b Gavaskar	11
BP Julian not out	9
Extras (lb 1, w 7, nb 4)	12
Total (6 wickets, 28.4 overs)	**248**

DNB: MS Kasprowicz, SK Warne, AJ Bichel.

FW: 1–7 (Taylor), 2–85 (SR Waugh), 3–100 (Blewett), 4–130 (Langer), 5–200 (ME Waugh), 6–222 (Healy).

Bowling: Pollock 4–0–26–0 (1nb, 2w); Mohsin Kamal 4–0–50–1 (3nb, 3w); Klusener 7–0–52–2 (2w); McMillan 5–1–25–1; Chauhan 4–0–39–0; Gavaskar 3.4–0–43–2; Brew 1–0–12–0

Umpires: M Walsh and R Fotheringham

Australians won by 4 wickets.

Glossary

In these statistics, the following abbreviations are used:
*   captain
+   wicketkeeper
FW   fall of wicket
DNB   did not bat

AUSTRALIANS V DUKE OF NORFOLK'S XI, ARUNDEL

15 MAY 1997 — TOSS: AUSTRALIA

Australians

MF Waugh c Ward b Whittall	46
*MA Taylor b Emburey	45
SR Waugh st A Flower b GW Flower	27
RT Ponting b Emburey	13
JL Langer c Ward b Radford	22
MJ Slater not out	50
+IA Healy not out	15
Extras (b 8, lb 3, w 5, nb 1)	17
Total (For 5 wickets, 50 overs)	**235**

DNB: BP Julian, JN Gillespie, MS Kasprowicz, GD McGrath.

FW: 1–101 (ME Waugh), 2–107 (Taylor), 3–143 (SR Waugh), 4–143 (Ponting), 5–190 (Langer).

Bowling: Radford 10–0–52–1; Foster 7–0–26–0; Whittall 10–0–45–1; Capel 4–0–21–0; Emburey 10–2–25–2; GW Flower 9–1–55–1

Duke of Norfolk's XI

GW Flower c Langer b Julian	26
JW Hall b Kasprowicz	4
TS Curtis c Healy b Kasprowicz	2
+A Flower b Gillespie	2
TC Walton c & b Kasprowicz	3
DM Ward c Healy b Gillespie	2
AR Whittall lbw b Gillespie	2
*JE Emburey c Gillespie b ME Waugh	29
DJ Capel c Langer b Gillespie	5
NV Radford not out	30
NA Foster c Healy b Julian	1
Extras (lb 4, w 11, nb 1)	16
Total (all out, 34.5 overs)	**122**

FW: 1–19 (Hall), 2–31 (Curtis), 3–39 (A Flower), 4–43 (Walton), 5–45 (G Flower), 6–47 (Whittall), 7–51 (Ward), 8–59 (Capel), 9–119 (Emburey), 10–122 (Foster).

Bowling: McGrath 10–1–37–0; Kasprowicz 7–0–17–3; Julian 7.5–1–20–2; Gillespie 6–2–21–4; ME Waugh 4–0–23–1

Umpires: R Palmer & T Clarkson

Australians won by 113 runs

AUSTRALIANS V NORTHAMPTONSHIRE COUNTY GROUND, NORTHAMPTON
17 MAY 1997 — TOSS: AUSTRALIANS

Australians

*MA Taylor lbw b Curran	76
MJ Slater b Taylor	33
MTG Elliott c Snape b Taylor	4
ME Waugh c Curran b Snape	38
RP Ponting b Penberthy	2
JL Langer c Sales b Hughes	20
+AC Gilchrist c Bailey b Taylor	40
BP Julian run out (Snape)	1
SK Warne c Bailey b Penberthy	1
MS Kasprowicz c Taylor b Curran	1
JG Gillespie not out	1
Extras (lb 4, w 10, nb 1)	15
Total (all out, 47.4 overs)	**232**

FW: 1–43 (Slater), 2–47 (Elliott), 3–126 (Waugh), 4–130 (Ponting), 5–168 Langer), 6–204 (Taylor), 7–209 (Julian), 8–210 Warne), 9–227 (Kasprowicz), 10–232 (Gilchrist).

Bowling: Taylor 8.4–0–44–3 (1nb, 6w); Hughes 7–0–57–1 (2w); Curran 9–2–34–2 (1nb); Penberthy 10–0–39–2 (1w); Snape 10–0–37–1 (1w); Bailey 3–0–17–0

Northamptonshire

A Fordham c Gilchrist b Gillespie	2
MB Loye not out	65
*RJ Bailey c & b Julian	10
KM Curran c Gilchrist b Julian	12
AL Penberthy c Waugh b Warne	19
TC Walton st Gilchrist b Warne	2
DJG Sales not out	11
Extras (lb 4, w 9)	13
Total (5 wickets, 35 overs)	**134**

To Bat: JN Snape, +D Ripley, JG Hughes, JP Taylor.

FW: 1–14 (Fordham), 2–40 (Bailey), 3–55 (Curran), 4–108 (Penberthy), 5–113 Walton).

Bowling: Gillespie 6–0–16–1 (4w); Kasprowicz 7–2–15–0; Julian 6–0–27–2 (2w); Ponting 4–0–22–0 (2w); Waugh 6–0–29–0; Warne 6–0–21–2 (1w)

Umpires: MJ Kitchen and P Willey

Australians won by 17 runs (Rain Rule)

AUSTRALIANS V WORCESTERSHIRE COUNTY GROUND, WORCESTER
18 MAY 1997 — TOSS: WORCESTERSHIRE

Australians

*MA Taylor c Rhodes b Haynes	14
GS Blewett b Haynes	22
SR Waugh c Rhodes b Haynes	21
MG Bevan c Rhodes b Haynes	8
JL Langer lbw b Leatherdale	15
AC Gilchrist lbw b Lampitt	10
+IA Healy not out	9
BP Julian c Moody b Leatherdale	1
SK Warne c Rhodes b Leatherdale	3
MS Kasprowicz c Lampitt b Leatherdale	2
GD McGrath c Rhodes b Leatherdale	2
Extras (lb 4, w 6, nb 4)	14
Total (all out, 35.0 overs)	**121**

FW: 1–33 (Blewett), 2–53 (Taylor), 3–64 (Bevan), 4–78 (Waugh), 5–104 (Langer), 6–104 (Gilchrist), 7–105 (Julian), 8–109 (Warne), 9–113 (Kasprowicz), 10–121 (McGrath).

Bowling: Newport 6–0–18–0 (1w); Haynes 10–1–40–4 (3w); Sheriyar 7–0–29–0 (2w); Lampitt 7–0–20–1 (2nb); Leatherdale 5–1–10–5

Worcestershire

WPC Weston c Julian b Warne	12
*TM Moody c Warne b Kasprowicz	32
GA Hick c Warne b Blewett	35
GR Haynes c Warne b Kasprowicz	0
VS Solanki c Gilchrist b Warne	6
KR Spiring not out	9
DA Leatherdale not out	8
Extras (b 5, lb 1, w 11, nb 4)	21
Total (5 wickets, 38.5 overs)	**123**

DNB: +SJ Rhodes, SR Lampitt, PJ Newport, A Sheriyar.

FW: 1–58 (Weston), 2–65 (Moody), 3–65 (Haynes), 4–87 (Solanki), 5–114 (Hick).

Bowling: McGrath 10–1–32–0 (1w); Kasprowicz 10–3–13–2 (1nb, 2w); Julian 6–3–13–0 (1nb, 2w); Warne 10–1–36–2 (3w); Blewett 2.5–0–23–1 (2w)

Umpires: R Julian and DR Shepherd

Worcestershire won by 5 wickets

FIRST ONE-DAY INTERNATIONAL HEADINGLEY, LEEDS
22 MAY 1997 — TOSS: ENGLAND

Australia

*MA Taylor c Stewart b Gough	7
ME Waugh b Headley	11
SR Waugh lbw b Ealham	19
MG Bevan run out (Thorpe)	30
GS Blewett b Gough	28
MJ Slater c & b Ealham	17
+IA Healy c Atherton b Hollioake	17
SK Warne c Thorpe b Hollioake	4
MS Kasprowicz not out	17
JN Gillespie not out	3
Extras (lb 7, w 9, nb 1)	17
Total (8 wickets, 50 overs)	**170**

DNB: GD McGrath.

FW: 1–8 (Taylor), 2–39 (ME Waugh), 3–43 (SR Waugh), 4–106 (Bevan), 5–106 (Blewett), 6–140 (Healy), 7–140 (Slater), 8–157 (Warne).

Bowling: DeFreitas 9–1–35–0 (4w); Gough 10–2–33–2; Ealham 8–3–21–2 (1w); Headley 8–0–36–1 (1nb); Croft 10–1–16–0 (1w); Hollioake 5–0–22–2 (1w)

England

NV Knight lbw b McGrath	12
*MA Atherton c Healy b Kasprowicz	4
+AJ Stewart lbw b McGrath	7
GP Thorpe not out	75
GD Lloyd run out (Blewett)	0
AJ Hollioake not out	66
Extras (b 1, w 6, nb 4)	11
Total (4 wickets, 40.1 overs)	**175**

DNB: MA Ealham, PAJ DeFreitas, RDB Croft, D Gough, DW Headley.

FW: 1–18 (Atherton), 2–20 (Knight), 3–32 (Stewart), 4–40 (Lloyd).

Bowling: McGrath 10–2–34–2 (1w); Kasprowicz 7–0–27–1 (1nb, 2w); Gillespie 8.1–1–39–0 (4nb, 1w); Warne 10–0–46–0; ME Waugh 2–0–16–0 (1w); Blewett 3–0–12–0 (1w)

Umpires: R Julian and P Willey
Third Umpire: JC Balderstone
Match Referee: RS Madugalle (SL)
Man of the Match: AJ Hollioake

England won by 6 wickets

SECOND ONE-DAY INTERNATIONAL THE OVAL, LONDON
24 MAY 1997 — TOSS: ENGLAND

Australia

ME Waugh run out (Croft)	25
*MA Taylor run out (Hollioake)	11
SR Waugh b Croft	24
MG Bevan not out	108
MJ Slater run out (DeFreitas)	1
AC Gilchrist lbw b Hollioake	53
+IA Healy run out (Lloyd)	7
SK Warne not out	11
Extras (lb 8, w 1)	9
Total (6 wickets, 50 overs)	**249**

DNB: MS Kasprowicz, JN Gillespie, GD McGrath.

FW: 1–35 (Taylor), 2–37 (ME Waugh), 3–94 (SR Waugh), 4–98 (Slater), 5–211 (Gilchrist), 6–226 (Healy).

Bowling: DeFreitas 8–0–47–0; Gough 10–3–42–0; Ealham 9–2–40–0; Giles 9–0–48–0 (1w); Croft 10–2–39–1; Hollioake 4–0–25–1

England

*MA Atherton not out	113
NV Knight lbw b Kasprowicz	4
+AJ Stewart b Warne	10
GP Thorpe c SR Waugh b Bevan	7
GD Lloyd c Warne b McGrath	22
AJ Hollioake not out	53
Extras (lb 5, w 8, nb 1)	14
Total (4 wickets, 48.2 overs)	**253**

DNB: MA Ealham, PAJ DeFreitas, D Gough, RDB Croft, AF Giles.

FW: 1–6 (Knight), 2–77 (Stewart), 3–104 (Thorpe), 4–158 (Lloyd).

Bowling: McGrath 9–1–46–1 (2w); Kasprowicz 9.2–0–58–1 (1w); Gillespie 8–1–42–0 (1nb, 2w); Warne 10–0–39–1; Bevan 9–0–43–1 (1w); SR Waugh 3–0–20–0 (2w)

Umpires: JH Hampshire and DR Shepherd
Third Umpire: B Dudleston
Match Referee: RS Madugalle (Sri Lanka)
Man of the Match: MA Atherton

England won by 6 wickets

THIRD ONE-DAY INTERNATIONAL LORD'S, LONDON
25 MAY 1997 — TOSS: ENGLAND

Australia

MTG Elliott c AJ Hollioake b Gough	1
ME Waugh lbw b Gough	95
*SR Waugh c Thorpe b Gough	17
MG Bevan c sub (NV Knight) b Gough	8
JL Langer run out (Silverwood)	29
AC Gilchrist lbw b Ealham	33
+IA Healy c Lloyd b Croft	27
SK Warne c Stewart b Ealham	5
MS Kasprowicz not out	28
JN Gillespie c Thorpe b Gough	6
GD McGrath st Stewart b AJ Hollioake	1
Extras (b 2, lb 10, w 5, nb 2)	19
Total (all out, 49.2 overs)	**269**

FW: 1–2 (Elliott), 2–52 (SR Waugh), 3–63 (Bevan), 4–142 (Langer), 5–184 (ME Waugh), 6–218 (Gilchrist), 7–228 (Warne), 8–242 (Healy), 9–268 (Gillespie), 10–269 (McGrath).

Bowling: Gough 10–0–44–5 (3nb, 1w); Silverwood 6–0–44–0 (1w); Ealham 10–0–47–2; Croft 10–0–51–1 (1w); BC Hollioake 7–0–36–0 (2nb); AJ Hollioake 6.2–0–35–1

England

*MA Atherton lbw b Kasprowicz	1
+AJ Stewart c Langer b ME Waugh	79
BC Hollioake c SR Waugh b Gillespie	63
JP Crawley run out (Gilchrist)	52
GP Thorpe not out	45
AJ Hollioake not out	4
Extras (lb 9, w13, nb 4)	26
Total (4 wickets, 49 overs)	**270**

DNB: GD Lloyd, MA Ealham, RDB Croft, CEW Silverwood, D Gough.

FW: 1–22 (Atherton), 2–113 (BC Hollioake), 3–193 (Stewart), 4–253 (Crawley).

Bowling: McGrath 9–2–45–0 (1nb); Kasprowicz 8–1–40–1 (1nb, 3w); Warne 9–0–44–0 (3w); Gillespie 10–0–55–1 (2nb, 2w); Bevan 3–0–27–0; SR Waugh 4–0–22–0 (3w); ME Waugh 6–0–28–1

Umpires: MJ Kitchen and G Sharp
Third Umpire: A Jones
Match Referee: RS Madugalle (Sri Lanka)
Man of the match: D Gough
Men of the series: MG Bevan and AJ Hollioake

England won by 6 wickets

AUSTRALIANS V GLOUCESTERSHIRE, COUNTY GROUND, BRISTOL
27–29 MAY 1997 — TOSS: AUSTRALIA

Australians 1st innings

*MA Taylor c Russell b Smith	0
MTG Elliott c Russell b Lewis	6
JL Langer c Russell b Lewis	6
ME Waugh c Smith b Davis	66
SR Waugh b Smith	92
MG Bevan c Wright b Lewis	18
+IA Healy not out	30
SK Warne c Young b Lewis	5
MS Kasprowicz b Ball	16
JN Gillespie c Hancock b Ball	3
GD McGrath b Ball	0
Extras (lb 3, nb 4)	7
Total (all out, 73.4 overs)	**249**

FW: 1–0 (Taylor), 2–10 (Elliott), 3–21 (Langer),
4–117 (ME Waugh), 5–184 (Bevan),
6–205 (SR Waugh), 7–217 (Warne),
8–241 (Kasprowicz), 9–249 (Gillespie),
10–249 (McGrath).

Bowling: Smith 11–3–26–2; Lewis 19–2–89–4;
Alleyne 7–2–26–0; Hancock 8–1–29–0;
Davis 11–3–20–1; Ball 17.4–3–56–3

Gloucestershire 1st innings

NJ Trainor c Kasprowicz b McGrath	121
AJ Wright lbw b Gillespie	16
RP Davis lbw b Warne	30
RJ Cunliffe c Kasprowicz b Warne	61
THC Hancock lbw b Kasprowicz	15
S Young c Healy b Kasprowicz	1
MW Alleyne c & b Gillespie	20
*+RC Russell c Bevan b Warne	20
MCJ Ball c & b Kasprowicz	25
AM Smith c Gillespie b Warne	4
JJ Lewis not out	7
Extras (b 4, lb 6, nb 20)	30
Total (all out, 107.2 overs)	**350**

FW: 1–52 (Wright), 2–103 (Davis), 3–243
(Cunliffe), 4–250 (Trainor), 5–257 (Young), 6–286
(Alleyne), 7–288 (Hancock), 8–339 (Ball), 9–339
(Russell), 10–350 (Smith).

Bowling: McGrath 19–11–31–1; Kasprowicz
21–2–101–3; Warne 35.2–10–97–4; Gillespie
20–4–66–2; Bevan 12–1–45–0

Australians 2nd innings

MTG Elliott lbw b Smith	124
*MA Taylor lbw b Ball	30
JL Langer not out	152
SK Warne b Smith	0
JN Gillespie c Russell b Lewis	7
ME Waugh not out	32
Extras (b 6, lb 2, w 1)	9
Total (4 wickets, 109 overs)	**354**

DNB: SR Waugh, MG Bevan, +IA Healy,
MS Kasprowicz, GD McGrath.

FW: 1–62 (Taylor), 2–254 (Elliott), 3–262 (Warne),
4–269 (Gillespie).

Bowling: Smith 13–5–18–2; Davis 29–6–101–0;
Lewis 18–5–59–1; Ball 28–9–89–1;
Alleyne 8–2–25–0; Trainor 3–2–8–0;
Hancock 5–0–26–0; Russell 3–0–15–0;
Young 2–0–5–0

Umpires: GI Burgess and P Adams

Match drawn

AUSTRALIANS V DERBYSHIRE RACECOURSE GROUND, DERBY
31 MAY, 1, 2 JUNE 1997 — TOSS: AUSTRALIANS

Australians 1st Innings
*MA Taylor c Aldred b DeFreitas	5
MTG Elliott c Adams b Dean	67
JL Langer lbw b DeFreitas	1
GS Blewett b Harris	121
SR Waugh c DeFreitas b Blackwell	43
MG Bevan b DeFreitas	56
+IA Healy not out	40
BP Julian not out	12
Extras (b 5, lb 2, nb 10)	17
Total (6 wickets declared, 85 overs)	**362**

DNB: SK Warne, AJ Bichel, JN Gillespie.

FW: 1–10 (Taylor), 2–15 (Langer), 3–147 (Elliott), 4–246 (Waugh), 5–260 (Blewett), 6–335 (Bevan).

Bowling: DeFreitas 14–3–61–3 (5nb); Harris 18–2–70–1; Dean 16–1–76–1; Aldred 12–3–26–0; Clarke 6–0–45–0; Blackwell 15–1–57–1; Jones 4–0–20–0

Derbyshire 1st innings
AS Rollins lbw b Julian	15
MR May c Waugh b Julian	67
P Aldred b Gillespie	8
CJ Adams lbw b Warne	7
*DM Jones b Warne	31
ID Blackwell c Blewett b Julian	0
VP Clarke c & b Bevan	20
+KM Krikken c sub (MJ Slater) b Gillespie	6
PAJ DeFreitas b Bevan	6
AJ Harris not out	26
KJ Dean not out	21
Extras (b 7, lb 6, w 3, nb 34)	50
Total (9 wickets declared, 65 overs)	**257**

FW: 1–55 (Rollins), 2–77 (Aldred), 3–114 (Adams), 4–158 (May), 5–168 (Jones), 6–168 (Blackwell), 7–198 (Clarke), 8–204 (DeFreitas), 9–206 (Krikken).

Bowling: Bichel 5–1–28–0 (6nb); Julian 20–6–88–3 (9nb, 3w); Gillespie 17–3–62–2 (2nb); Warne 14–2–45–2; Bevan 9–4–21–2

Australians 2nd innings
MTG Elliott b Harris	4
*MA Taylor c Krikken b Aldred	63
JL Langer lbw b Dean	12
MG Bevan not out	104
BP Julian c Jones b Dean	62
SK Warne not out	2
Extras (b 2, lb 4, nb 12)	18
Total (4 wickets declared, 66 overs)	**265**

DNB: SR Waugh, GS Blewett, +IA Healy, AJ Bichel, JN Gillespie.

FW: 1–5 (Elliott), 2–35 (Langer), 3–159 (Taylor), 4–260 (Julian).

Bowling: DeFreitas 10–3–31–0 (5nb); Harris 16–3–49–1; Blackwell 9–1–50–0; Dean 10–0–45–2; Aldred 15–1–64–1 (1nb); Rollins 2–0–12–0; Clarke 4–1–8–0; Blackwell 9–1–50–0

Derbyshire 2nd innings
AS Rollins lbw b Warne	66
MR May c Waugh b Julian	27
CJ Adams c sub (GD McGrath) b Warne	91
*DM Jones c Healy b Julian	56
ID Blackwell c & b Warne	5
VP Clarke c Julian b Warne	28
+KM Krikken c Bevan b Warne	21
PAJ DeFreitas c sub (ME Waugh) b Warne	26
P Aldred not out	15
AJ Harris lbw b Warne	5
KJ Dean not out	9
Extras (lb 4, w 2, nb 16)	22
Total (9 wickets, 68.3 overs)	**371**

FW: 1–49 (May), 2–191 (Adams), 3–197 (Rollins), 4–213 (Blackwell), 5–251 (Clarke), 6–291 (Krikken), 7–339 (DeFreitas), 8–343 (Jones), 9–360 (Harris).

Bowling: Gillespie 5–0–35–0 (2nb); Julian 21.3–1–126–2 (4nb, 2w); Waugh 1–0–8–0; Warne 23–2–103–7 (1nb); Bevan 10–0–60–0 (1nb); Elliott 8–0–35–0

Umpires: VA Holder and RA White
Man of the Match: SK Warne

Derbyshire won by 1 wicket

FIRST TEST EDGBASTON, BIRMINGHAM

5–8 JUNE 1997 — TOSS: AUSTRALIA

Australia 1st innings

*MA Taylor c Butcher b Malcolm	7
MTG Elliott b Gough	6
GS Blewett c Hussain b Gough	7
ME Waugh b Gough	5
SR Waugh c Stewart b Caddick	12
MG Bevan c Ealham b Malcolm	8
+IA Healy c Stewart b Caddick	0
JN Gillespie lbw b Caddick	4
SK Warne c Malcolm b Caddick	47
MS Kasprowicz c Butcher b Caddick	17
GD McGrath not out	1
Extras (w 2, nb 2)	4
Total (all out, 31.5 overs)	**118**

FW: 1–11 (Elliott), 2–15 (Taylor), 3–26 (ME Waugh), 4–28 (Blewett), 5–48 (SR Waugh), 6–48 (Healy), 7–48 (Bevan), 8–54 (Gillespie), 9–110 (Kasprowicz), 10–118 (Warne).

Bowling: Gough 10–1–43–3 (1nb, 2w); Malcolm 10–2–25–2; Caddick 11.5–1–50–5 (1nb)

England 1st innings

MA Butcher c Healy b Kasprowicz	8
*MA Atherton c Healy b McGrath	2
+AJ Stewart c Elliott b Gillespie	18
N Hussain c Healy b Warne	207
GP Thorpe c Bevan b McGrath	138
JP Crawley c Healy b Kasprowicz	1
MA Ealham not out	53
RDB Croft c Healy b Kasprowicz	24
D Gough c Healy b Kasprowicz	0
AR Caddick lbw b Bevan	0
Extras (b 4, lb 7, w 1, nb 15)	27
Total (9 wickets declared, 138.4 overs)	**478**

DNB: DE Malcolm.

FW: 1–8 (Atherton), 2–16 (Butcher), 3–50 (Stewart), 4–338 (Thorpe), 5–345 (Crawley), 6–416 (Hussain), 7–460 (Croft), 8–463 (Gough), 9–478 (Caddick).

Bowling: McGrath 32–8–107–2 (6nb); Kasprowicz 39–8–113–4 (5nb, 1w); Gillespie 10–1–48–1 (1nb); Warne 35–8–110–1 (1nb); Bevan 10.4–0–44–1; SR Waugh 12–2–45–0 (2nb)

Australia 2nd innings

MTG Elliott b Croft	66
*MA Taylor c & b Croft	129
GS Blewett c Butcher b Croft	125
SR Waugh lbw b Gough	33
MG Bevan c Hussain b Gough	24
ME Waugh c Stewart b Gough	1
+IA Healy c Atherton b Ealham	30
SK Warne c & b Ealham	32
MS Kasprowicz c Butcher b Ealham	0
JN Gillespie run out (Crawley/Gough)	0
GD McGrath not out	0
Extras (b 18, lb 12, w 2, nb 5)	37
Total (all out, 144.4 overs)	**477**

FW: 1–133 (Elliott), 2–327 (Taylor), 3–354 (Blewett), 4–393 (Bevan), 5–399 (ME Waugh), 6–431 (SR Waugh), 7–465 (Healy), 8–465 (Kasprowicz), 9–477 (Gillespie), 10–477 (Warne).

Bowling: Gough 35–7–123–3 (3nb); Malcolm 21–6–52–0; Croft 43–10–125–3 (2w); Caddick 30–6–87–0 (2nb); Ealham 15.4–3–60–3

England 2nd innings

MA Butcher lbw b Kasprowicz	14
*MA Atherton not out	57
+AJ Stewart not out	40
Extras (b 4, lb 4)	8
Total (1 wicket, 21.3 overs)	**119**

FW: 1–29 (Butcher).

Bowling: McGrath 7–1–42–0; Kasprowicz 7–0–42–1; Warne 7.3–0–27–0

Umpires: SA Bucknor (West Indies) and P Willey
Third Umpire: JW Holder
Match Referee: RS Madugalle (Sri Lanka)
Man of the Match: N Hussain

England won by 9 wickets

AUSTRALIANS V NOTTINGHAMSHIRE TRENT BRIDGE, NOTTINGHAM
11–13 JUNE 1997 — TOSS: AUSTRALIANS

Nottinghamshire 1st innings

GE Welton c Gilchrist b Julian	16
MP Dowman c Julian b Reiffel	22
U Afzaal lbw b Kasprowicz	34
NJ Astle c Elliott b McGrath	99
+LNP Walker c Bevan b Reiffel	5
*P Johnson c Elliott b Reiffel	6
WM Noon c Gilchrist b Julian	0
KP Evans c ME Waugh b McGrath	21
PJ Franks c Gilchrist b McGrath	1
RA Pick b McGrath	7
AJ Oram not out	0
Extras (b 1, lb 4, w 1, nb 22)	28
Total (all out, 70.1 overs)	**239**

FW: 1–39 (Dowman), 2–44 (Welton), 3–121 (Afzaal), 4–148 (Walker), 5–156 (Johnson), 6–173 (Noon), 7–203 (Astle), 8–221 (Franks), 9–236 (Evans), 10–239 (Pick).

Bowling: McGrath 18.1–4–63–4 (2nb); Kasprowicz 17–4–54–1 (1nb); Reiffel 10–3–15–3; Julian 18–1–70–2 (1w, 8nb); Bevan 7–1–32–0

Australians 1st innings

MTG Elliott b Afzaal	127
MJ Slater lbw b Evans	14
RT Ponting lbw b Pick	19
ME Waugh c Astle b Dowman	29
*SR Waugh c Afzaal b Dowman	115
MG Bevan not out	75
+AC Gilchrist not out	9
Extras (b 3, lb 3, w 4)	10
Total (5 wickets, 95.2 overs)	**398**

DNB: BP Julian, PR Reiffel, MS Kasprowicz, GD McGrath.

FW: 1–29 (Slater), 2–55 (Ponting), 3–133 (ME Waugh), 4–250 (Elliott), 5–382 (SR Waugh).

Bowling: Franks 18–3–54–0 (3w); Pick 13–0–62–1 (1w); Evans 15–1–51–1; Oram 5–1–14–0; Astle 13–1–37–0; Dowman 16–0–78–2; Afzaal 15.2–1–96–1

Umpires: JD Bond and BJ Meyer

Match drawn

AUSTRALIANS V LEICESTERSHIRE GRACE ROAD, LEICESTER

14–16 JUNE 1997 — TOSS: LEICESTERSHIRE

Australians 1st innings

MJ Slater c Sutcliffe b Ormond	16
*MA Taylor b Ormond	1
RT Ponting b Ormond	64
MG Bevan c Sutcliffe b Wells	11
+IA Healy b Ormond	34
ME Waugh lbw b Ormond	6
JL Langer not out	9
BP Julian c Maddy b Ormond	5
SK Warne lbw b Pierson	20
PR Reiffel not out	6
Extras (b 23, lb 14, w 7, nb 4)	48
Total (8 wickets declared, 61 overs)	**220**

DNB: GD McGrath.

FW: 1–10 (Taylor), 2–29 (Slater), 3–83 (Bevan), 4–158 (Ponting), 5–167 (Healy), 6–176 (Waugh), 7–182 (Julian), 8–212 (Warne).

Bowling: Mullally 14–1–55–0 (1w, 2nb); Ormond 20–7–54–6 (2w); Wells 9–3–24–1 (1w); Pierson 10–3–34–1; Maddy 7–1–15–0; Mason 1–0–1–0

Leicestershire 1st innings

DL Maddy b Reiffel	1
IJ Sutcliffe c Healy b Reiffel	3
GI Macmillan c Bevan b Warne	34
*JJ Whitaker c Langer b Reiffel	1
A Habib not out	11
+PA Nixon not out	2
Extras (b 2, lb 2, nb 6)	10
Total (4 wickets declared, 30.3 overs)	**62**

DNB: VJ Wells, J Ormond, TJ Mason, ARK Pierson, AD Mullally.

FW: 1–1 (Maddy), 2–24 (Sutcliffe), 3–30 (Whitaker), 4–59 (Macmillan).

Bowling: McGrath 12–4–24–0 (3nb); Reiffel 10–6–12–3; Warne 5–1–20–1; Julian 3.3–2–2–0

Australians 2nd innings

*MA Taylor c Macmillan b Mason	57
MJ Slater b Ormond	17
ME Waugh not out	16
MG Bevan c & b Mason	13
Extras (lb 2)	2
Total (3 wickets declared, 23.4 overs)	**105**

DNB: RT Ponting, JL Langer, +IA Healy, BP Julian, PR Reiffel, SK Warne, GD McGrath.

FW: 1–39 (Slater), 2–83 (Taylor), 3–105 (Bevan).

Bowling: Ormond 8–0–36–1; Maddy 7–1–13–0; Mason 4.4–0–21–2; Pierson 4–0–33–0

Leicestershire 2nd innings

DL Maddy lbw b Reiffel	7
IJ Sutcliffe c Healy b McGrath	31
GI Macmillan c Slater b Julian	25
*JJ Whitaker lbw b Warne	21
A Habib c Ponting b Warne	13
+PA Nixon st Healy b Warne	24
VJ Wells c Ponting b Reiffel	38
J Ormond b Warne	1
TJ Mason c Julian b Reiffel	4
ARK Pierson c Langer b Warne	0
AD Mullally not out	2
Extras (b 1, lb 1, w 1, nb 10)	13
Total (all out, 51.4 overs)	**179**

FW: 1–21 (Maddy), 2–66 (Sutcliffe), 3–68 (Macmillan), 4–92 (Whitaker), 5–118 (Habib), 6–155 (Nixon), 7–157 (Ormond), 8–168 (Mason), 9–177 (Wells), 10–179 (Pierson).

Bowling: McGrath 14–5–40–1 (1nb); Reiffel 12–3–49–3; Julian 8–1–35–1 (1w, 2nb); Warne 16.4–2–42–5 (2nb); Bevan 1–0–11–0

Umpires: DJ Constant and JH Harris

Australians won by 84 runs

SECOND TEST LORD'S, LONDON

19–23 JUNE 1997 — TOSS: AUSTRALIA

England 1st innings

MA Butcher c Blewett b McGrath	5
*MA Atherton c Taylor b McGrath	1
+AJ Stewart b McGrath	1
N Hussain lbw b McGrath	19
GP Thorpe c Blewett b Reiffel	21
JP Crawley c Healy b McGrath	1
MA Ealham c Elliott b Reiffel	7
RDB Croft c Healy b McGrath	2
D Gough c Healy b McGrath	10
AR Caddick lbw b McGrath	1
DE Malcolm not out	0
Extras (b 4, nb 5)	9
Total (all out, 42.3 overs)	**77**

FW: 1–11 (Butcher), 2–12 (Atherton), 3–13 (Stewart), 4–47 (Thorpe), 5–56 (Crawley), 6–62 (Hussain), 7–66 (Croft), 8–76 (Gough), 9–77 (Ealham), 10–77 (Caddick).

Bowling: McGrath 20.3–8–38–8; Reiffel 15–9–17–2 (3nb); Kasprowicz 5–1–9–0 (2nb); Warne 2–0–9–0.

Australia 1st innings

*MA Taylor b Gough	1
MTG Elliott c Crawley b Caddick	112
GS Blewett c Hussain b Croft	45
ME Waugh c Malcolm b Caddick	33
SK Warne c Hussain b Gough	0
SR Waugh lbw b Caddick	0
MG Bevan c Stewart b Caddick	4
+IA Healy not out	13
PR Reiffel not out	1
Extras (b 1, lb 3)	4
Total (7 wickets declared, 61 overs)	**213**

DNB: MS Kasprowicz, GD McGrath.

FW: 1–4 (Taylor), 2–73 (Blewett), 3–147 (ME Waugh), 4–147 (Warne), 5–147 (SR Waugh), 6–159 (Bevan), 7–212 (Elliott).

Bowling: Gough 20–4–82–2; Caddick 22–6–71–4; Malcolm 7–1–26–0; Croft 12–5–30–1.

England 2nd innings

MA Butcher b Warne	87
*MA Atherton hit wicket b Kasprowicz	77
+AJ Stewart c Kasprowicz b McGrath	13
N Hussain c & b Warne	0
GP Thorpe not out	30
JP Crawley not out	29
Extras (b 8, lb 14, w 1, nb 7)	30
Total (4 wickets declared, 79 overs)	**266**

FW: 1–162 (Atherton), 2–189 (Stewart), 3–197 (Hussain), 4–202 (Butcher).

Bowling: McGrath 20–5–65–1 (2nb); Reiffel 13–5–29–0 (2nb); Kasprowicz 15–3–54–1 (4nb); Warne 19–4–47–2 (1w); Bevan 8–1–29–0; SR Waugh 4–0–20–0

Umpires: DR Shepherd and S Venkataraghavan (India)
Third Umpire: DJ Constant
Match Referee: RS Madugalle (Sri Lanka)

Man of the Match: GD McGrath

Match drawn

AUSTRALIANS V HAMPSHIRE COUNTY GROUND, SOUTHAMPTON
28–30 JUNE 1997 — TOSS: HAMPSHIRE

Hampshire 1st innings
JS Laney lbw b Kasprowicz	6
ML Hayden c Blewett b Kasprowicz	6
M Keech c & b Reiffel	17
RA Smith c Healy b Warne	22
WS Kendall c ME Waugh b Reiffel	0
*JP Stephenson c Taylor b Gillespie	0
+AN Aymes not out	31
SD Udal c Healy b Warne	2
SJ Renshaw lbw b Warne	4
JNB Bovill lbw b Gillespie	9
SM Milburn b Kasprowicz	23
Extras (b 1, lb 10, w 1, nb 24)	36
Total (all out, 49.1 overs)	**156**

FW: 1–9 (Hayden), 2–30 (Laney), 3–45 (Keech),
4–57 (Kendall), 5–79 (Stephenson), 6–83 (Smith),
7–85 (Udal), 8–93 (Renshaw), 9–112 (Bovill),
10–156 (Milburn).

Bowling: Kasprowicz 11.1–2–33–3 (4nb);
Gillespie 16–2–65–2 (5nb);
Reiffel 7–1–17–2 (1w, 3nb); Warne 15–4–30–3

Australians 1st innings
MTG Elliott c Keech b Udal	61
*MA Taylor c Bovill b Stephenson	109
GS Blewett run out	2
ME Waugh c Hayden b Renshaw	173
SR Waugh c Udal b Renshaw	11
MG Bevan b Renshaw	24
+IA Healy not out	29
SK Warne lbw b Stephenson	38
PR Reiffel lbw b Renshaw	1
MS Kasprowicz not out	6
Extras (lb 8, w 1, nb 2)	11
Total (8 wickets declared, 121 overs)	**465**

DNB: JN Gillespie.

FW: 1–95 (Elliott), 2–118 (Blewett), 3–275 (Taylor),
4–294 (SR Waugh), 5–377 (Bevan), 6–404
(ME Waugh), 7–446 (Warne), 8–447 (Reiffel).

Bowling: Renshaw 27–5–107–4 (1w);
Bovill 26–7–87–0; Milburn 21–3–96–0 (1nb);
Stephenson 27–3–82–2; Udal 20–1–85–1

Hampshire 2nd innings
JS Laney c Healy b Reiffel	30
ML Hayden b Gillespie	2
M Keech c Kasprowicz b Gillespie	6
RA Smith c Warne b Gillespie	44
WS Kendall lbw b Gillespie	18
*JP Stephenson b Gillespie	0
+AN Aymes c Blewett b Kasprowicz	18
SD Udal b Warne	21
SJ Renshaw not out	13
JNB Bovill c Healy b Kasprowicz	1
SM Milburn b Kasprowicz	3
Extras (lb 6, nb 14)	20
Total (all out, 61.4 overs)	**176**

FW: 1–4 (Hayden), 2–14 (Keech), 3–91 (Laney),
4–111 (Kendall), 5–111 (Stephenson), 6–114
(Smith), 7–143 (Aymes), 8–159 (Udal), 9–160
(Bovill), 10–176 (Milburn).

Bowling: Kasprowicz 14.4–1–69–3 (3nb);
Gillespie 13–6–33–5 (1nb); Warne 19–3–26–1;
Reiffel 8–1–27–1 (3nb); Bevan 7–3–15–0

Umpires: HD Bird and B Leadbeater

Australians won by an innings and 133 runs

THIRD TEST OLD TRAFFORD, MANCHESTER
3–7 JULY 1997 — TOSS: AUSTRALIA

Australia 1st innings

*MA Taylor c Thorpe b Headley	2
MTG Elliott c Stewart b Headley	40
GS Blewett b Gough	8
ME Waugh c Stewart b Ealham	12
SR Waugh b Gough	108
MG Bevan c Stewart b Headley	7
+IA Healy c Stewart b Caddick	9
SK Warne c Stewart b Ealham	3
PR Reiffel b Gough	31
JN Gillespie c Stewart b Headley	0
GD McGrath not out	0
Extras (b 8, lb 4, nb 3)	15
Total (all out, 77.3 overs)	**235**

FW: 1–9 (Taylor), 2–22 (Blewett), 3–42
(ME Waugh), 4–85 (Elliott), 5–113 (Bevan), 6–150
(Healy), 7–160 (Warne), 8–230 (Reiffel), 9–235
(SR Waugh), 10–235 (Gillespie).

Bowling: Gough 21–7–52–3 (1nb); Headley
27.3–4–72–4 (1nb); Caddick 14–2–52–1; Ealham
11–2–34–2 (1nb); Croft 4–0–13–0

England 1st innings

MA Butcher st Healy b Bevan	51
*MA Atherton c Healy b McGrath	5
+AJ Stewart c Taylor b Warne	30
N Hussain c Healy b Warne	13
GP Thorpe c Taylor b Warne	3
JP Crawley c Healy b Warne	4
MA Ealham not out	24
RDB Croft c SR Waugh b McGrath	7
D Gough lbw b Warne	1
AR Caddick c ME Waugh b Warne	15
DW Headley b McGrath	0
Extras (b 4, lb 3, nb 2)	9
Total (all out, 84.4 overs)	**162**

FW: 1–8 (Atherton), 2–74 (Stewart), 3–94
(Butcher), 4–101 (Thorpe), 5–110 (Hussain), 6–111
(Crawley), 7–122 (Croft), 8–123 (Gough), 9–161
(Caddick), 10–162 (Headley).

Bowling: McGrath 23.4–9–40–3; Reiffel 9–3–14–0
(2nb); Warne 30–14–48–6; Gillespie 14–3–39–0;
Bevan 8–3–14–1

Australia 2nd innings

MTG Elliott c Butcher b Headley	11
*MA Taylor c Butcher b Headley	1
GS Blewett c Hussain b Croft	19
ME Waugh b Ealham	55
SR Waugh c Stewart b Headley	116
MG Bevan c Atherton b Headley	0
+IA Healy c Butcher b Croft	47
SK Warne c Stewart b Caddick	53
PR Reiffel not out	45
JN Gillespie not out	28
Extras (b 1, lb 13, nb 6)	20
Total (8 wickets declared, 122 overs)	**395**

FW: 1–5 (Taylor), 2–33 (Blewett), 3–39 (Elliott),
4–131 (ME Waugh), 5–132 (Bevan), 6–210 (Healy),
7–298 (Warne), 8–333 (SR Waugh).

Bowling: Gough 20–3–62–0 (2nb);
Headley 29–4–104–4 (2nb); Croft 39–12–105–2;
Ealham 13–3–41–1; Caddick 21–0–69–1 (2nb);

England 2nd innings

MA Butcher c McGrath b Gillespie	28
*MA Atherton lbw b Gillespie	21
+AJ Stewart b Warne	1
N Hussain lbw b Gillespie	1
GP Thorpe c Healy b Warne	7
JP Crawley hit wicket b McGrath	83
MA Ealham c Healy b McGrath	9
RDB Croft c Reiffel b McGrath	7
D Gough b McGrath	6
AR Caddick c Gillespie b Warne	17
DW Headley not out	0
Extras (b 14, lb 4, w 1, nb 1)	20
Total (all out, 73.4 overs)	**200**

FW: 1–44 (Atherton), 2–45 (Stewart),
3–50 (Hussain), 4–55 (Butcher), 5–84 (Thorpe),
6–158 (Ealham), 7–170 (Croft), 8–177 (Crawley),
9–188 (Gough), 10–200 (Caddick).

Bowling: McGrath 21–4–46–4;
Gillespie 12–4–31–3; Reiffel 2–0–8–0 (1nb);
Warne 30.4–8–63–3; Bevan 8–2–34–0 (1w)

Umpires: G Sharp and S Venkataraghavan (India)
Third Umpire: JH Hampshire
Match Referee: RS Madugalle (Sri Lanka)
Man of the Match: SR Waugh

Australia won by 268 runs

AUSTRALIANS V MINOR COUNTIES OSBORNE AVENUE, JESMOND

8 JULY 1997 — TOSS: AUSTRALIANS

Australians

MJ Slater c Pell b Sharp	27
JL Langer c Humphries b Richardson	12
RT Ponting lbw b Sharp	1
BP Julian b Oakes	106
MG Bevan st Humphries b Dalton	32
GS Blewett c Cockbain b Oakes	3
+DS Berry b Richardson	34
MTG Elliott not out	35
MS Kasprowicz not out	7
Extras (b 4, lb 15, w 14)	33
Total (7 wickets, 50 overs)	**290**

DNB: *SR Waugh, PR Reiffel.

FW: 1–35 (Langer), 2–36 (Ponting), 3–53 (Slater), 4–146 (Bevan), 5–202 (Blewett), 6–205 (Julian), 7–256 (Berry).

Bowling: Oakes 10–0–43–2 (5w); Sharp 10–2–29–2 (1w); Richardson 10–0–51–2 (3w); Dalton 9–0–63–1 (2w); Fielding 4–0–45–0; Myles 7–0–40–0 (3w)

Australians won by 9 runs

Minor Counties

SJ Dean c & b Julian	38
GW Ecclestone b Reiffel	21
MA Fell c Berry b Reiffel	20
SD Myles c Julian b Bevan	27
*I Cockbain c Bevan b Langer	82
RN Dalton b Kasprowicz	33
+MI Humphries c & b Ponting	5
JM Fielding c Reiffel b Slater	4
MA Sharp c Slater b Ponting	0
S Oakes not out	15
A Richardson not out	0
Extras (b 4, lb 6, w 10, nb 16)	36
Total (9 wickets, 50 overs)	**281**

FW: 1–61 (Dean), 2–92 (Ecclestone), 3–104 (Fell), 4–150 (Myles), 5–218 (Dalton), 6–241 (Humphries), 7–249 (Fielding), 8–254 (Sharp), 9–267 (Cockbain).

Bowling: Kasprowicz 10–0–58–1 (3w, 2nb); Julian 7–1–34–1 (1w, 6nb); Blewett 2–0–7–0; Reiffel 6–0–16–2 (1w); Bevan 10–0–39–1 (3w); Elliott 6–0–49–0; Ponting 7–0–42–2 (2w); Slater 1–0–7–1; Langer 1–0–19–1

Umpires: DL Burden and JM Tythcott

AUSTRALIANS V SCOTLAND EDINBURGH

12 JULY 1997 — TOSS: SCOTLAND

Australians

MJ Slater c Lockhart b Stanger	95
JL Langer c Salmond b Beven	46
RT Ponting c Salmond b Williamson	33
GS Blewett c Steindl b Sheridan	30
ME Waugh c Steindl b Sheridan	11
*SR Waugh b Sheridan	2
BP Julian c Salmond b Sheridan	5
+IA Healy c Stanger b Sheridan	2
JN Gillespie b Williamson	4
MS Kasprowicz not out	15
GD McGrath not out	7
Extras (lb 2, w 6, nb 20)	28
Total (9 wickets, 50 overs)	**278**

FW: 1–143 (Slater), 2–174 (Langer), 3–226 (Blewett), 4–235 (Ponting), 5–239 (SR Waugh), 6–250 (ME Waugh), 7–250 (Julian), 8–252 (Healy), 9–261 (Gillespie).

Bowling: Steindl 6–0–43–0 (1w, 1nb); Thomson 9–0–29–0 (1w, 2nb); Stanger 8–0–48–1 (4w, 7nb); Williamson 7–0–47–2; Beven 10–0–44–1; Sheridan 10–0–65–5

Scotland

BMW Patterson c Healy b Kasprowicz	14
IL Philip b McGrath	3
MJ Smith c ME Waugh b Julian	15
*G Salmond c Healy b Kasprowicz	0
JG Williamson c Julian b Kasprowicz	2
+DR Lockhart c Julian b Gillespie	5
IM Stanger not out	10
PD Steindl not out	0
Extras (lb 5, w 17, nb 24)	46
Total (6 wickets, 21.5 overs)	**95**

DNB: IR Beven, KLP Sheridan, K Thomson.

FW: 1–31 (Patterson), 2–31 (Philip), 3–32 (Salmond), 4–39 (Williamson), 5–69 (Smith), 6–95 (Lockhart).

Bowling: McGrath 6–2–17–1 (3w, 3nb); Kasprowicz 6–0–28–3 (1w, 6nb); Julian 5–0–32–1 (11w, 3nb); Gillespie 4.5–0–13–1 (2w)

Umpires: J Breslin and DM Potter

No result

AUSTRALIANS V JOHN PAUL GETTY INVITATION XI IBSTONE

14 JULY 1997 — TOSS: AUSTRALIANS

Australians

MJ Slater c Krikken b Brown	10
MTG Elliott st Krikken b Whittall	93
JL Langer b Brown	0
RT Ponting c Krikken b Hollioake	36
MG Bevan c Strang b Whittall	54
*MA Taylor not out	38
+DS Berry not out	22
Extras (lb 6, nb 6)	12
Total (5 wickets declared, 44 overs)	**267**

DNB: BP Julian, PR Reiffel, JN Gillespie, GD McGrath.

FW: 1–21, 2–26, 3–102, 4–167, 5–216.

Bowling: Tudor 10–0–47–0 (6nb); Brown 9–2–28–2; Hollioake 5–0–36–1; Strang 8–0–58–0; Whittall 9–1–65–2; Hick 1–0–5–0; Crowe 2–0–22–0

John Paul Getty Invitation XI

RA Smith b Bevan	57
MD Crowe not out	115
BC Hollioake c sub (MS Kasprowicz) b Bevan	6
GA Hick c Julian b Bevan	26
DW Randall c Taylor b Bevan	22
M Nicholas not out	2
Extras (lb 5, nb 4)	9
Total (4 wickets, 37 overs)	**237**

DNB: A Whittall, +KM Krikken, PA Strang, D Brown, AJ Tudor.

FW: 1–144, 2–150, 3–209, 4–234.

Bowling: McGrath 10–2–41–0 (1nb); Reiffel 7–3–17–0 (2nb); Julian 6–0–54–0; Gillespie 5–0–35–0; Bevan 9–0–85–4 (1nb)

Umpires: HD Bird and NT Plews
Scorers: WH Frindall and MK Walsh

Match drawn

AUSTRALIANS V GLAMORGAN SOPHIA GARDENS, CARDIFF
16–18 JULY 1997 — TOSS: GLAMORGAN

Australians 1st innings

*MA Taylor c Morris b Cosker	71
MTG Elliott c Maynard b Butcher	26
GS Blewett b Butcher	54
RT Ponting not out	126
MJ Slater c Metson b Cosker	26
JL Langer not out	50
Extras (b 4, lb 8, w 2, nb 2)	16
Total (4 wickets declared, 88 overs)	**369**

DNB: MG Bevan, +DS Berry, BP Julian, PR Reiffel, MS Kasprowicz.

FW: 1–72 (Elliott), 2–132 (Taylor), 3–197 (Blewett), 4–246 (Slater).

Bowling: Thomas 16–1–73–0; Parkin 19–4–78–0 (1w); Dale 13–2–49–0 (1w); Butcher 13–1–52–2 (1nb); Cosker 24–5–95–2; Maynard 3–0–10–0

Glamorgan 1st innings

SP James c Kasprowicz b Bevan	91
H Morris lbw b Bevan	13
A Dale c Blewett b Bevan	0
*MP Maynard c Berry b Kasprowicz	19
MJ Powell lbw b Kasprowicz	24
GP Butcher c Blewett b Reiffel	23
PA Cottey c Berry b Reiffel	22
SD Thomas c Taylor b Reiffel	10
+CP Metson b Reiffel	0
DA Cosker b Reiffel	2
OT Parkin not out	0
Extras (b 4, lb 17, w 5, nb 24)	50
Total (all out, 68.3 overs)	**254**

FW: 1–88 (Morris), 2–88 (Dale), 3–127 (Maynard), 4–178 (Powell), 5–182 (James), 6–218 (Butcher), 7–233 (Thomas), 8–237 (Metson), 9–249 (Cottey), 10–254 (Cosker).

Bowling: Reiffel 18.3–5–61–5 (1w, 5nb); Kasprowicz 18–5–56–2 (1w, 6nb); Bevan 20–2–73–3 (3w, 1nb); Julian 9–2–34–0; Ponting 3–0–9–0

Australians 2nd innings

MJ Slater lbw b Thomas	7
JL Langer b Parkin	10
MG Bevan c Metson b Thomas	1
BP Julian c & b Parkin	12
+DS Berry c Metson b Parkin	9
PR Reiffel b Thomas	56
MTG Elliott st Metson b Cosker	37
GS Blewett not out	50
RT Ponting not out	28
Extras (b 1, lb 4, nb 2)	7
Total (7 wickets declared, 69 overs)	**217**

FW: 1–14 (Slater), 2–18 (Bevan), 3–26 (Langer), 4–37 (Julian), 5–42 (Berry), 6–122 (Reiffel), 7–147 (Elliott).

Bowling: Thomas 14–3–42–3; Parkin 15–3–38–3; Cosker 17–3–36–1; Butcher 10–1–36–0 (1nb); Dale 9–1–43–0; Maynard 4–0–17–0

Glamorgan 2nd innings

SP James c Julian b Bevan	79
H Morris c Berry b Kasprowicz	42
SD Thomas st Berry b Bevan	15
*MP Maynard not out	45
A Dale not out	20
Extras (lb 2, nb 8)	10
Total (3 wickets, 51 overs)	**211**

FW: 1–96 (Morris), 2–139 (Thomas), 3–160 (James).

Bowling: Kasprowicz 15–2–63–1; Reiffel 11–2–46–0; Julian 9–1–26–0 (4nb); Bevan 16–1–74–2

Umpires: JC Balderstone and TE Jesty

Match drawn

AUSTRALIANS V MIDDLESEX LORD'S, LONDON
19–21 JULY 1997 — TOSS: MIDDLESEX

Middlesex 1st innings

PN Weekes run out		19
JC Pooley c SR Waugh b McGrath		17
*MR Ramprakash c Healy b Gillespie		76
MW Gatting b McGrath		85
OA Shah c ME Waugh b Warne		28
+KR Brown c Healy b Kasprowicz		18
KP Dutch c Healy b Gillespie		10
RL Johnson c Blewett b Kasprowicz		1
ARC Fraser c Elliott b McGrath		15
PCR Tufnell not out		11
TF Bloomfield c Healy b McGrath		4
Extras (lb 6, w 3, nb 12)		21
Total (all out, 97.4 overs)		**305**

FW: 1–23 (Pooley), 2–49 (Weekes), 3–169
(Ramprakash), 4–241 (Gatting), 5–243 (Shah),
6–268 (Dutch), 7–275 (Johnson), 8–280 (Brown),
9–295 (Fraser), 10–305 (Bloomfield).

Bowling: Gillespie 23–2–67–2 (2w, 1nb);
McGrath 21.4–7–61–4 (1nb); Warne 23–4–76–1
(3nb); Blewett 5–1–12–0;
Kasprowicz 13–2–47–2 (1nb);
ME Waugh 12–0–36–0

Australians 1st innings

MTG Elliott st Brown b Dutch		83
*MA Taylor b Dutch		27
GS Blewett b Tufnell		40
ME Waugh not out		142
SR Waugh c Gatting b Johnson		57
RT Ponting c Shah b Tufnell		5
+IA Healy c Pooley b Bloomfield		16
SK Warne c Pooley b Dutch		39
Extras (b 2, lb 10, w 1, nb 10)		23
Total (7 wickets declared, 116 overs)		**432**

DNB: JN Gillespie, MS Kasprowicz, GD McGrath.

FW: 1–75 (Taylor), 2–154 (Elliott), 3–168 (Blewett),
4–271 (SR Waugh), 5–299 (Ponting), 6–341
(Healy), 7–432 (Warne).

Bowling: Fraser 29–6–115–0 (2nb);
Bloomfield 17–1–57–1 (1w); Johnson 17–2–63–1
(1nb); Tufnell 38–8–106–2 (2nb); Dutch 15–3–79–3

Middlesex 2nd innings

PN Weekes c & b Warne		28
JC Pooley b Warne		20
*MR Ramprakash c Healy b Warne		16
MW Gatting lbw b SR Waugh		47
OA Shah lbw b Kasprowicz		0
+KR Brown not out		48
KP Dutch b ME Waugh		4
RL Johnson not out		27
Extras (b 4, lb 5, nb 2)		11
Total (6 wickets, 59 overs)		**201**

DNB: ARC Fraser, PCR Tufnell, TF Bloomfield.

FW: 1–45 (Weekes), 2–50 (Pooley), 3–71
(Ramprakash), 4–72 (Shah), 5–156 (Gatting), 6–163
(Dutch).

Bowling: McGrath 11–3–37–0 (1nb);
Gillespie 13–6–32–0; Warne 16–4–55–3;
Kasprowicz 6–1–10–1; ME Waugh 7–1–37–1;
SR Waugh 5–2–13–1; Elliott 1–0–8–0

Umpires: AA Jones and AGT Whitehead

Match drawn

FOURTH TEST HEADINGLEY, LEEDS

24–28 JULY — TOSS: AUSTRALIA

England 1st innings

MA Butcher c Blewett b Reiffel		24
*MA Atherton c Gillespie b McGrath		41
+AJ Stewart c Blewett b Gillespie		7
N Hussain c Taylor b McGrath		26
DW Headley c SR Waugh b Gillespie		22
GP Thorpe b Gillespie		15
JP Crawley c Blewett b Gillespie		2
MA Ealham not out		8
RDB Croft c Ponting b Gillespie		6
D Gough b Gillespie		0
AM Smith b Gillespie		0
Extras (b 4, lb 4, w 1, nb 12)		21
Total (all out, 59.4 overs)		**172**

FW: 1–43 (Butcher), 2–58 (Stewart), 3–103 (Hussain), 4–138 (Headley), 5–154 (Atherton), 6–154 (Thorpe), 7–163 (Crawley), 8–172 (Croft), 9–172 (Gough), 10–172 (Smith).

Bowling: McGrath 22–5–67–2 (2nb, 1w); Reiffel 20–4–41–1 (10nb); Gillespie 13.4–1–37–7; Blewett 3–0–17–0; Warne 1–0–2–0

Australia 1st innings

*MA Taylor c Stewart b Gough		0
MTG Elliott b Gough		199
GS Blewett c Stewart b Gough		1
ME Waugh c&b Headley		8
SR Waugh c Crawley b Headley		4
RT Ponting c Ealham b Gough		127
+IA Healy b Ealham		31
SK Warne c Thorpe b Ealham		0
PR Reiffel not out		54
JN Gillespie b Gough		3
GD McGrath not out		20
Extras (b 9, lb 10, nb 35)		54
Total (9 wickets declared, 123 overs)		**501**

FW: 1–0 (Taylor), 2–16 (Blewett), 3–43 (ME Waugh), 4–50 (SR Waugh), 5–318 (Ponting), 6–382 (Healy), 7–383 (Warne), 8–444 (Elliott), 9–461 (Gillespie).

Bowling: Gough 36–5–149–5 (8nb); Headley 25–2–125–2 (12nb); Smith 23–2–89–0 (7nb); Ealham 19–3–56–2 (2nb); Croft 18–1–49–0; Butcher 2–0–14–0 (6nb)

England 2nd innings

MA Butcher c Healy b McGrath		19
*MA Atherton c Warne b McGrath		2
+AJ Stewart b Reiffel		16
N Hussain c Gillespie b Warne		105
GP Thorpe c ME Waugh b Gillespie		15
JP Crawley b Reiffel		72
MA Ealham c ME Waugh b Reiffel		4
DW Headley lbw b Reiffel		3
RDB Croft c Healy b Reiffel		5
D Gough c ME Waugh b Gillespie		0
AM Smith not out		4
Extras (b 6, lb 4, nb 13)		23
Total (all out, 91.1 overs)		**268**

FW: 1–23 (Butcher), 2–28 (Atherton), 3–57 (Stewart), 4–89 (Thorpe), 5–222 (Hussain), 6–252 (Ealham), 7–256 (Crawley), 8–263 (Headley), 9–264 (Gough), 10–268 (Croft).

Bowling: McGrath 22–5–80–2 (2nb); Reiffel 21.1–2–49–5 (6nb); Gillespie 23–8–65–2 (2nb); Warne 21–6–53–1 (2nb); SR Waugh 4–1–11–0 (1nb).

Umpires: MJ Kitchen and CJ Mitchley (South Africa)
Third Umpire: R Julian
Match Referee: CW Smith (West Indies)
Man of the Match: JN Gillespie

Australia won by an innings and 61 runs

AUSTRALIANS V SOMERSET COUNTY GROUND, TAUNTON
1–4 AUGUST 1997 — TOSS: SOMERSET

Somerset 1st innings

KA Parsons c Blewett b Kasprowicz	71
PCL Holloway c Healy b McGrath	11
*SC Ecclestone lbw b Warne	12
MN Lathwell c ME Waugh b Warne	18
ME Trescothick b Warne	8
+RJ Turner c Slater b Julian	58
GD Rose c Slater b McGrath	4
S Herzberg b Kasprowicz	18
AR Caddick c McGrath b Warne	16
AP van Troost not out	12
PS Jones lbw b Warne	4
Extras (b 10, nb 42)	52
Total (all out, 65.3 overs)	**284**

FW: 1–95 (Holloway), 2–122 (Ecclestone), 3–122 (Parsons), 4–143 (Trescothick), 5–154 (Lathwell), 6–167 (Rose), 7–240 (Turner), 8–258 (Herzberg), 9–262 (Caddick), 10–284 (Jones).

Bowling: Kasprowicz 14–2–95–2 (10nb); Julian 14–2–52–1 (7nb); McGrath 11–2–31–2 (2nb); Warne 18.3–7–57–5 (1nb); Bevan 8–2–39–0 (1nb)

Australians 1st innings

MJ Slater c Turner b Caddick	18
JL Langer b Caddick	30
GS Blewett b Caddick	20
ME Waugh c Turner b Rose	37
*SR Waugh c Lathwell b Caddick	62
MG Bevan c Trescothick b Caddick	16
+IA Healy c Trescothick b Jones	33
BP Julian c Turner b Jones	71
SK Warne c Rose b van Troost	1
MS Kasprowicz not out	1
GD McGrath lbw b van Troost	0
Extras (lb 2, nb 32)	34
Total (all out, 59.3 overs)	**323**

FW: 1–40 (Slater), 2–63 (Blewett), 3–82 (Langer), 4–145 (ME Waugh), 5–188 (Bevan), 6–211 (SR Waugh), 7–317 (Healy), 8–320 (Warne), 9–320 (Julian), 10–323 (McGrath).

Bowling: Caddick 16–2–54–5 (1nb); van Troost 15.3–0–132–2 (12nb); Jones 5–1–32–2; Rose 14–3–50–1; Parsons 2–0–4–0 (1nb); Herzberg 5–0–36–0; Trescothick 2–0–13–0

Somerset 2nd innings

+RJ Turner not out	65
PCL Holloway c Langer b McGrath	17
*SC Ecclestone c McGrath b ME Waugh	47
MN Lathwell st Healy b Warne	11
PS Jones not out	5
Extras (nb 2)	2
Total (3 wickets, 41 overs)	**147**

DNB: KA Parsons, ME Trescothick, GD Rose, S Herzberg, AR Caddick, AP van Troost.

FW: 1–33 (Holloway), 2–118 (Ecclestone), 3–138 (Lathwell).

Bowling: Kasprowicz 5–2–11–0; Julian 5–1–22–0; McGrath 7–1–24–1 (1nb); Blewett 4–0–33–0; Warne 11–3–26–1; ME Waugh 9–1–31–1

Umpires: NT Plews and JF Steele

Match drawn

FIFTH TEST TRENT BRIDGE, NOTTINGHAM
7–10 AUGUST 1997 — TOSS: AUSTRALIA

Australia 1st innings
MTG Elliott c Stewart b Headley	69
*MA Taylor b Caddick	76
GS Blewett c Stewart b BC Hollioake	50
ME Waugh lbw b Caddick	68
SR Waugh b Malcolm	75
RT Ponting b Headley	9
+IA Healy c AJ Hollioake b Malcolm	16
SK Warne c Thorpe b Malcolm	0
PR Reiffel c Thorpe b Headley	26
JN Gillespie not out	18
GD McGrath b Headley	1
Extras (b 4, lb 10, w 1, nb 4)	19
Total (all out, 121.5 overs)	**427**

FW: 1–117 (Elliott), 2–160 (Taylor), 3–225
(Blewett), 4–311 (ME Waugh), 5–325 (Ponting),
6–355 (Healy), 7–363 (Warne), 8–386 (SR Waugh),
9–419 (Reiffel), 10–427 (McGrath).

Bowling: Malcolm 25–4–100–3 (1w);
Headley 30.5–7–87–4 (3nb); Caddick 30–4–102–2
(1nb); BC Hollioake 10–1–57–1; Croft 19–7–43–0;
AJ Hollioake 7–0–24–0

England 1st innings
*MA Atherton c Healy b Warne	27
+AJ Stewart c Healy b Warne	87
JP Crawley c Healy b McGrath	18
N Hussain b Warne	2
GP Thorpe c Blewett b Warne	53
AJ Hollioake c Taylor b Reiffel	45
BC Hollioake c ME Waugh b Reiffel	28
RDB Croft c Blewett b McGrath	18
AR Caddick c Healy b McGrath	0
DW Headley not out	10
DE Malcolm b McGrath	12
Extras (b 2, lb 6, nb 5)	13
Total (all out, 93.5 overs)	**313**

FW: 1–106 (Atherton), 2–129 (Stewart), 3–135
(Hussain), 4–141 (Crawley), 5–243 (AJ Hollioake),
6–243 (Thorpe), 7–272 (Croft), 8–290 (BC
Hollioake), 9–290 (Caddick), 10–313 (Malcolm).

Bowling: McGrath 29.5–9–71–4;
Reiffel 21–2–101–2 (3nb);
Gillespie 11–3–47–0 (1nb);
Warne 32–8–86–4 (1nb)

Australia 2nd innings
*MA Taylor c Hussain b BC Hollioake	45
MTG Elliott c Crawley b Caddick	37
GS Blewett c Stewart b Caddick	60
ME Waugh lbw b Headley	7
SR Waugh c AJ Hollioake b Caddick	14
RT Ponting c Stewart b AJ Hollioake	45
+IA Healy c Stewart b AJ Hollioake	63
SK Warne c Thorpe b Croft	20
PR Reiffel c BC Hollioake b Croft	22
JN Gillespie c Thorpe b Headley	4
GD McGrath not out	1
Extras (b 1, lb 11, nb 6)	18
Total (all out, 98.5 overs)	**336**

FW: 1–51 (Elliott), 2–105 (Taylor), 3–134 (ME
Waugh), 4–156 (Blewett), 5–171 (SR Waugh),
6–276 (Healy), 7–292 (Ponting), 8–314 (Warne),
9–326 (Gillespie), 10–336 (Reiffel).

Bowling: Malcolm 16–4–52–0; Headley 19–3–56–2
(1nb); Croft 26.5–6–74–2; Caddick 20–2–85–3
(4nb); BC Hollioake 5–1–26–1; AJ Hollioake
12–2–31–2 (1nb)

England 2nd innings
*MA Atherton c Healy b McGrath	8
+AJ Stewart c SR Waugh b Reiffel	16
JP Crawley c Healy b Gillespie	33
N Hussain b Gillespie	21
GP Thorpe not out	82
AJ Hollioake lbw b Gillespie	2
BC Hollioake lbw b Warne	2
RDB Croft c McGrath b Warne	6
AR Caddick lbw b Warne	0
DW Headley c Healy b McGrath	4
DE Malcolm c ME Waugh b McGrath	0
Extras (b 6, lb 2, nb 4)	12
Total (all out, 48.5 overs)	**186**

FW: 1–25 (Atherton), 2–25 (Stewart), 3–78
(Hussain), 4–99 (Crawley), 5–121 (AJ Hollioake),
6–144 (BC Hollioake), 7–150 (Croft), 8–166
(Caddick), 9–186 (Headley), 10–186 (Malcolm).

Bowling: McGrath 13.5–4–36–3 (1nb);
Reiffel 11–3–34–1 (1nb); Gillespie 8–0–65–3 (2nb);
Warne 16–4–43–3

Umpires: CJ Mitchley (South Africa) and
DR Shepherd
Third Umpire: AA Jones
Match Referee: CW Smith (West Indies)
Man of the Match: IA Healy

Australia won by 264 runs

AUSTRALIANS V IRELAND EGLINTON
14 AUGUST 1997 — TOSS: AUSTRALIANS

Australians

MTG Elliott c Patterson b Cooke	28
MJ Slater c Lewis b Cooke	0
GS Blewett c Joyce b Heasley	44
ME Waugh st Rutherford b Molins	32
MG Bevan c Molins b Heasley	2
JL Langer c Patterson b Curry	57
RT Ponting not out	117
*MA Taylor c Molins b Curry	9
+DS Berry not out	1
Extras (lb 2, w 6, nb 5)	13
Total (7 wickets, 50 overs)	**303**

DNB: MS Kasprowicz, GD McGrath.

FW: 1–2, 2–52, 3–92, 4–114, 5–116, 6–265, 7–289.

Bowling: Cooke 10–0–65–2; Davy 7–0–53–0; Molins 10–0–36–1; Heasley 10–0–57–2; Curry 10–0–60–2; Joyce 3–0–30–0

Ireland

JD Curry c Berry b McGrath	12
AD Patterson b McGrath	0
DA Lewis c Berry b Kasprowicz	12
EC Joyce c Langer b Blewett	6
*JDR Benson c Berry b Ponting	9
WK McCallan not out	64
D Heasley c Berry b Ponting	7
JO Davy c Berry b Ponting	0
G Cooke c Waugh b Langer	26
+AT Rutherford b Slater	0
GL Molins st Berry b Taylor	0
Extras (b 4, lb 6, w 12, nb 6)	28
Total (all out, 45.3 overs)	164

FW: 1–16, 2–20, 3–33, 4–44, 5–65, 6–84, 7–86, 8–161, 9–163, 10–164.

Bowling: McGrath 4–0–12–2; Kasprowicz 8–0–26–1; Blewett 7–1–19–1; Bevan 5–0–13–0; Ponting 7–0–14–3; Elliott 3–0–15–0; Slater 7–0–31–1; Langer 4–0–23–1; Taylor 0.3–0–1–1

Umpires: H Henderson and P White

Australians won by 139 runs

AUSTRALIANS V KENT ST LAWRENCE, CANTERBURY
16–18 AUGUST 1997 — TOSS: KENT

Kent 1st innings

TR Ward c Berry b Kasprowicz	0
ET Smith c Lee b Kasprowicz	0
AP Wells c Berry b Kasprowic	0
WJ House c Langer b Kasprowicz	16
BJ Phillips c ME Waugh b Young	25
MA Ealham c SR Waugh b Bevan	30
MV Fleming c Berry b Lee	67
*+SA Marsh not out	35
PA Strang c Langer b Lee	0
JBdeC Thompson c Ponting b Lee	0
AP Igglesden c Berry b Lee	0
Extras (lb 2, nb 26)	28
Total (all out, 50.3 overs)	**201**

FW: 1–2 (Ward), 2–6 (Wells), 3–15 (Smith), 4–46 (House), 5–77 (Phillips), 6–107 (Ealham), 7–197 (Fleming), 8–201 (Strang), 9–201 (Thompson), 10–201 (Igglesden).

Bowling: Kasprowicz 15–4–72–4 (8nb); Young 11–3–46–1 (3nb); Lee 10.3–4–27–4; Bevan 11–1–49–1 (2nb); Blewett 3–1–5–0

Australians 1st innings

MJ Slater lbw b Igglesden	14
JL Langer c Marsh b Igglesden	20
GS Blewett run out	0
ME Waugh c Marsh b Igglesden	1
*SR Waugh c Marsh b Strang	154
RT Ponting b Ealham	32
MG Bevan c Ward b Phillips	55
S Young c Marsh b Phillips	0
S Lee c Marsh b Phillips	1
+DS Berry c House b Thompson	12
MS Kasprowicz not out	12
Extras (b 7, w 1, nb 6)	14
Total (all out, 81.1 overs)	**315**

FW: 1–29 (Slater), 2–31 (Blewett), 3–35 (Langer), 4–40 (ME Waugh), 5–106 (Ponting), 6–264 (Bevan), 7–266 (Young), 8–268 (Lee), 9–288 (Berry), 10–315 (SR Waugh).

Bowling: Igglesden 16–2–56–3 (1w); Phillips 15–1–57–3; Ealham 14–3–63–1 (3nb); Thompson 11–1–61–1; Strang 20.1–4–44–1; Fleming 5–0–27–0

Kent 2nd innings

TR Ward c Blewett b Bevan	68
ET Smith lbw b ME Waugh	46
AP Wells c Berry b Young	65
WJ House b Lee	20
MA Ealham c Ponting b Kasprowicz	85
BJ Phillips c SR Waugh b Kasprowicz	0
MV Fleming c Berry b Lee	29
*+SA Marsh c Kasprowicz b Lee	5
PA Strang c Ponting b Lee	2
JBdeC Thompson c Ponting b Kasprowicz	3
AP Igglesden not out	2
Extras (b 4, lb 2, nb 12)	18
Total (all out, 98 overs)	**343**

FW: 1–99 (Smith), 2–159 (Ward), 3–200 (House), 4–233 (Wells), 5–234 (Phillips), 6–285 (Fleming), 7–303 (Marsh), 8–307 (Strang), 9–318 (Thompson), 10–343 (Ealham).

Bowling: Kasprowicz 24–4–89–3 (5nb); Young 15–7–40–1 (1nb); Lee 25–7–86–4; Blewett 5–2–26–0; ME Waugh 12–5–30–1; Bevan 17–2–66–1

Australians 2nd innings

JL Langer c Marsh b Thompson	22
MJ Slater b Fleming	47
GS Blewett c Marsh b Thompson	18
ME Waugh c Smith b Strang	35
RT Ponting not out	56
MG Bevan not out	47
Extras (lb 2, nb 4)	6
Total (4 wickets, 51.5 overs)	**231**

FW: 1–67 (Langer), 2–91 (Blewett), 3–95 (Slater), 4–141 (ME Waugh).

Bowling: Igglesden 5–0–28–0; Ealham 5–1–19–0 (2nb); Phillips 6–2–36–0; Thompson 12–3–58–2; Fleming 11–2–22–1; Strang 10–0–42–1; House 2.5–0–24–0

Umpires: JW Holder and MJ Harris

Australians won by 6 wickets

SIXTH TEST THE OVAL, LONDON

21–23 AUGUST 1997 — TOSS: ENGLAND

England 1st innings
MA Butcher b McGrath	5
*MA Atherton c Healy b McGrath	8
+AJ Stewart lbw b McGrath	36
N Hussain c Elliott b McGrath	35
GP Thorpe b McGrath	27
MR Ramprakash c Blewett b McGrath	4
AJ Hollioake b Warne	0
AR Caddick not out	26
PJ Martin b McGrath	20
PCR Tufnell c Blewett b Warne	1
DE Malcolm lbw b Kasprowicz	0
Extras (b 2, lb 6, nb 10)	18
Total (all out, 56.4 overs)	**180**

FW: 1–18 (Butcher), 2–24 (Atherton), 3–97 (Stewart), 4–128 (Hussain), 5–131 (Thorpe), 6–132 (Hollioake), 7–132 (Ramprakash), 8–158 (Martin), 9–175 (Tufnell), 10–180 (Malcolm).

Bowling: McGrath 21–4–76–7 (3nb); Kasprowicz 11.4–2–56–1 (6nb); Warne 17–8–32–2 (1nb); Young 7–3–8–0

Australia 1st innings
MTG Elliott b Tufnell	12
*MA Taylor c Hollioake b Tufnell	38
GS Blewett c Stewart b Tufnell	47
ME Waugh c Butcher b Tufnell	19
SR Waugh lbw b Caddick	22
RT Ponting c Hussain b Tufnell	40
+IA Healy c Stewart b Tufnell	2
S Young c Stewart b Tufnell	0
SK Warne b Caddick	30
MS Kasprowicz lbw b Caddick	0
GD McGrath not out	1
Extras (lb 3, w 1, nb 5)	9
Total (all out, 79.3 overs)	**220**

FW: 1–49 (Elliott), 2–54 (Taylor), 3–94 (ME Waugh), 4–140 (SR Waugh), 5–150 (Blewett), 6–164 (Healy), 7–164 (Young), 8–205 (Warne), 9–205 (Kasprowicz), 10–220 (Ponting).

Bowling: Malcolm 11–2–37–0 (1nb); Martin 15–5–38–0 (1nb, 1w); Caddick 19–4–76–3 (1nb); Tufnell 34.3–16–66–7 (2nb)

England 2nd innings
MA Butcher lbw b ME Waugh	13
*MA Atherton c SR Waugh b Kasprowicz	8
+AJ Stewart lbw b Kasprowicz	3
N Hussain c Elliott b Warne	2
GP Thorpe c Taylor b Kasprowicz	62
MR Ramprakash st Healy b Warne	48
AJ Hollioake lbw b Kasprowicz	4
AR Caddick not out	0
PJ Martin c & b Kasprowicz	3
PCR Tufnell c Healy b Kasprowicz	0
DE Malcolm b Kasprowicz	0
Extras (b 6, lb 10, nb 4)	20
Total (all out, 66.5 overs)	**163**

FW: 1–20 (Atherton), 2–24 (Stewart), 3–26 (Butcher), 4–52 (Hussain), 5–131 (Thorpe), 6–138 (Hollioake), 7–160 (Ramprakash), 8–163 (Martin), 9–163 (Tufnell), 10–163 (Malcolm).

Bowling: McGrath 17–5–33–0; Kasprowicz 15.5–5–36–7 (2nb); Warne 26–9–57–2 (2nb); ME Waugh 7–3–16–1; Young 1–0–5–0

Australia 2nd innings
*MA Taylor lbw b Caddick	18
MTG Elliott lbw b Malcolm	4
GS Blewett c Stewart b Caddick	19
ME Waugh c Hussain b Tufnell	1
SR Waugh c Thorpe b Caddick	6
RT Ponting lbw b Tufnell	20
+IA Healy c & b Caddick	14
S Young not out	4
SK Warne c Martin b Tufnell	3
MS Kasprowicz c Hollioake b Caddick	4
GD McGrath c Thorpe b Tufnell	1
Extras (b 3, lb 4, w 1, nb 2)	10
Total (all out, 32.1 overs)	**104**

FW: 1–5 (Elliott), 2–36 (Taylor), 3–42 (ME Waugh), 4–49 (Blewett), 5–54 (SR Waugh), 6–88 (Ponting), 7–92 (Healy), 8–95 (Warne), 9–99 (Kasprowicz), 10–104 (McGrath).

Bowling: Malcolm 3–0–15–1; Martin 4–0–13–0 (1w); Tufnell 13.1–6–27–4 (2nb); Caddick 12–2–42–5

Umpires: LH Barker (West Indies) and P Willey
Third Umpire: KE Palmer
Match Referee: CW Smith (West Indies)
Man of the Match: PCR Tufnell

Men of the Series: GD McGrath and GP Thorpe

England won by 19 runs

AUSTRALIAN FIRST-CLASS TOUR AVERAGES

Batting	Matches	Innings	Not Out	Runs	Highest Score	50s	100s	Average	Caught	Stumped
RT Ponting	8	12	3	571	127	2	2	63.44	7	–
MTG Elliott	12	19	–	1091	199	5	4	57.42	7	–
SR Waugh	13	17	–	924	154	4	4	54.35	9	–
PR Reiffel	8	9	4	242	56	2	–	48.40	2	–
JL Langer	6	10	3	312	152*	1	1	44.57	5	–
ME Waugh	13	20	3	746	173	3	2	43.88	11	–
BP Julian	5	5	1	162	71	2	–	40.50	4	–
GS Blewett	12	18	1	686	125	4	2	40.35	17	–
MA Taylor	12	19	–	680	129	4	2	35.79	8	–
MG Bevan	11	16	3	463	104*	3	1	35.62	6	–
IA Healy	12	16	4	407	63	1	–	33.92	38	4
MJ Slater	5	8	–	159	47	–	–	19.88	3	–
SK Warne	12	17	1	293	53	1	–	18.31	5	–
MS Kasprowicz	10	8	3	56	17	–	–	11.20	8	–
DS Berry	2	2	–	21	12	–	–	10.50	9	1
JN Gillespie	8	9	2	67	28*	–	–	9.57	5	–
GD McGrath	11	10	6	25	20*	–	–	6.25	4	–
S Young	2	3	1	4	4*	–	–	2.00	1	–
S Lee	1	1	–	1	1	–	–	1.00	1	–
AC Gilchrist	1	1	1	9	9*	–	–	–	3	–
AJ Bichel	1	–	–	–	–	–	–	–	–	–

Bowling	Matches	Overs	Maidens	Runs	Wickets	Average	5 Wickets	10 Wickets	Best
S Lee	1	35.3	11	113	8	14.13	–	–	4/27
PR Reiffel	8	188.4	49	520	28	18.57	2	–	5/49
SK Warne	12	433.4	111	1154	57	20.25	4	–	7/103
GD McGrath	11	363.4	105	1012	49	20.65	2	–	8/38
JN Gillespie	8	198.4	43	692	29	23.86	2	–	7/37
MS Kasprowicz	10	267.2	50	1010	39	25.90	1	–	7/36
ME Waugh	13	47.0	10	150	4	37.50	–	–	1/16
S Young	2	34.0	13	99	2	49.50	–	–	1/40
BP Julian	5	108.0	17	455	9	50.56	–	–	3/88
MG Bevan	11	152.4	23	606	11	55.09	–	–	3/73
SR Waugh	13	26.0	5	97	1	97.00	–	–	1/13
AJ Bichel	1	5.0	1	28	–	–	–	–	–
GS Blewett	12	20.0	4	93	–	–	–	–	–
RT Ponting	8	3.0	–	9	–	–	–	–	–
MTG Elliott	12	9.0	–	43	–	–	–	–	–

Batting	Matches	Innings	Not Out	Runs	Highest Score	50s	100s	Average	Caught	Stumped
PR Reiffel	4	6	3	179	54*	1	–	59.67	1	–
MTG Elliott	6	10	–	556	199	2	2	55.60	4	–
RT Ponting	3	5	–	241	127	–	1	48.20	1	–
SR Waugh	6	10	–	390	116	1	2	39.00	4	–
GS Blewett	6	10	–	381	125	2	1	38.10	9	–
MA Taylor	6	10	–	317	129	1	1	31.70	6	–
IA Healy	6	10	1	225	63	1	–	25.00	25	2
ME Waugh	6	10	–	209	68	2	–	20.90	6	–
SK Warne	6	10	–	188	53	1	–	18.80	2	–
GD McGrath	6	8	6	25	20*	–	–	12.50	2	–
JN Gillespie	4	7	2	57	28*	–	–	12.50	2	–
MG Bevan	3	5	–	43	24	–	–	8.60	1	–
MS Kasprowicz	3	4	–	21	17	–	–	5.25	2	–
S Young	1	2	1	4	4*	–	–	4.00	–	–

Bowling	Matches	Overs	Maidens	Runs	Wickets	Average	5 Wickets	10 Wickets	Best
ME Waugh	6	7.0	3	16	1	16.00	–	–	1/16
GD McGrath	6	249.5	68	701	36	19.47	2	–	8/38
JN Gillespie	4	91.4	20	332	16	20.75	1	–	7/37
MS Kasprowicz	3	93.3	19	310	14	22.14	1	–	7/36
SK Warne	6	237.1	69	577	24	24.04	1	–	6/48
PR Reiffel	4	112.1	28	293	11	26.64	1	–	5/49
MG Bevan	3	34.4	6	121	2	60.50	–	–	1/14
GS Blewett	6	3.0	–	17	–	–	–	–	–
SR Waugh	6	20.0	3	76	–	–	–	–	–
S Young	1	8.0	3	13	–	–	–	–	–

1997 ASHES TOUR — TEST AVERAGES
ENGLAND

Batting	Matches	Innings	Not Out	Runs	Highest Score	50s	100s	Average	Caught	Stumped
GP Thorpe	6	11	2	453	138	3	1	50.33	8	–
N Hussain	6	11	–	431	207	–	2	39.18	8	–
MA Ealham	4	6	3	105	53*	1	–	35.00	3	–
JP Crawley	5	9	1	243	83	2	–	30.38	3	–
MR Ramprakash	1	2	–	52	48	–	–	26.00	–	–
MA Butcher	5	10	–	254	87	2	–	25.40	8	–
AJ Stewart	6	12	1	268	87	1	–	24.36	23	–
MA Atherton	6	12	1	257	77	2	–	23.36	2	–
BC Hollioake	1	2	–	30	28	–	–	15.00	1	–
AJ Hollioake	2	4	–	51	45	–	–	12.75	4	–
PJ Martin	1	2	–	23	20	–	–	11.50	1	–
AR Caddick	5	8	2	59	26*	–	–	9.83	1	–
DW Headley	3	6	2	39	22	–	–	9.75	1	–
RDB Croft	5	8	–	75	24	–	–	9.38	1	–
AM Smith	1	2	1	4	4*	–	–	4.00	–	–
DE Malcolm	4	5	1	12	12	–	–	3.00	2	–
D Gough	4	6	–	17	10	–	–	2.83	–	–
PCR Tufnell	1	2	–	1	1	–	–	0.50	–	–

Bowling	Matches	Overs	Maidens	Runs	Wickets	Average	5 Wickets	10 Wickets	Best
PCR Tufnell	1	47.4	22	93	11	8.45	1	1	7/66
MA Ealham	4	58.4	11	191	8	23.88	–	–	3/60
AR Caddick	5	179.5	27	634	24	26.42	2	–	5/42
AJ Hollioake	2	19.0	2	55	2	27.50	–	–	2/31
DW Headley	3	131.2	20	444	14	27.75	–	–	4/72
D Gough	4	142.0	27	511	16	31.94	1	–	5/149
BC Hollioake	1	15.0	2	83	2	41.50	–	–	1/26
DE Malcolm	4	93.0	20	307	6	51.17	–	–	3/100
RDB Croft	5	161.5	41	439	8	54.88	–	–	3/125
MA Butcher	5	2.0	–	14	–	–	–	–	–
AM Smith	1	23.0	2	89	–	–	–	–	–
PJ Martin	1	19.0	5	51	–	–	–	–	–

STATISTICAL NOTES
ON THE TEST SERIES

BY IAN RUSSELL

First Test

Test Debut
Mark Butcher (England)

Centuries

Batsman	Runs	Mins	Balls	Fours	Sixes
Nasser Hussain	207	437	336	38	–
Graham Thorpe	138	293	245	19	–
Mark Taylor	129	398	296	13	1
Greg Blewett	125	302	228	19	1

Greg Blewett's hundred was his third hundred in his third Ashes Test, after scoring centuries in each of his first two Ashes Tests, in 1994–95. He is the only man to score a century in each of his first three Ashes Tests.

This was Blewett's fourth Test hundred in all, in 17 Tests. He became the second Australian to score centuries in his first Ashes Test in Australia and in England, after Harry Graham (107 at Lord's in 1893, 105 at Sydney in 1894–95).

Mark Taylor's century was his 15th hundred in Test cricket, in 82 Tests, and first Test century since November 1995 (123 v Pakistan in Hobart), 15 Tests and 26 Test innings previously. It was the first time Taylor had passed 50 in a Test innings since December 1995, when he scored 96 against Sri Lanka in Perth.

Taylor has scored Test centuries on five different English grounds (Headingley and Trent Bridge in 1989, Old Trafford and Lord's in 1993, Edgbaston in 1997) and in the opening Test of the Ashes series of 1989, 1993 and 1997. No other Australian has performed either feat. When he reached 42, Taylor became the 13th Australian to score 2000 runs against England in his 23rd Ashes Test.

Nasser Hussain's double century was his first century against Australia, in his fifth Ashes Test, and his fourth Test hundred, in his 18th Test.

Hussain's innings was the highest individual score for England against Australia since David Gower's 215 at Edgbaston in 1985.

Graham Thorpe's century was his third against Australia, in his fifth Ashes Test, and his fifth Test hundred, in his 38th Test match.

The 288 runs partnership between Nasser Hussain and Graham Thorpe established a new record for England's fourth wicket against Australia (the previous record was 222 by Wally Hammond and Eddie Paynter, Lord's, 1938).

Prior to the Test, English bookmakers were offering 3–1 against about an English victory in the match. By lunch on the first day, the home team were 4–1 on.

Andy Caddick's figures of 5–50 in Australia's first innings was the first time he had taken five wickets in an innings against Australia. This was his fifth Ashes Test. In the 1993 Ashes series, Caddick had played in four Tests and taken a total of five wickets, at an average of 97.60. It was his third five-wicket return in Test cricket, in his 12th Test.

England's first innings total of 478 was their highest innings total against Australia since the second Test of the 1986–87 series, in Perth, when they scored 8–592 (declared).

Both Australian opening bowlers (Glenn McGrath and Michael Kasprowicz) were playing in their first Test in England. This was first instance of two such 'debutants' opening the Australian attack in an Ashes Test in England since 1972, when Dennis Lillee and David Colley played their first Tests in England at Manchester.

The 133-runs opening partnership in Australia's second innings, between Mark Taylor and Matthew Elliott, was Australia's first century opening stand since the Test against Sri Lanka in Perth in December 1995.

This was the first time since 1986–87 that England had won the first Test of an Ashes series.

This was the first time since 1986–87 that England had held the lead in an Ashes series.

This was the first time since 1986–87 that England had won a Test before the Ashes were decided.

Second Test

Century

Batsman	Runs	Mins	Balls	Fours	Sixes
Matthew Elliott	112	242	180	20	–

Matthew Elliott's hundred was his first century in Test cricket, in his seventh test.

Michael Atherton captained England for a record 42nd time, passing Peter May's previous record, set between 1955 and 1961.

England's 77 is their lowest completed innings total against Australia since 1948 (52 at The Oval). This was England's lowest innings total at Lord's since 1888, when they scored 53 and 62 and lost to Australia by 61 runs. Those two innings in 1888 are the only lower totals ever by England in a Test match at Lord's

Glenn McGrath's 8–38 is the best bowling analysis in an innings by an Australian at Lord's. It is the second best ever at Lord's, after Ian Botham's 8–34 against Pakistan in 1978, the best by an Australian in England besides Frank Laver's 8–31 at Manchester in 1909, and the third best ever by an Australian in Test cricket, after Arthur Mailey's 9–121 against England at the MCG in 1920–21 and Laver's 8–31. It was McGrath's first return of five wickets in an innings against England, and his seventh in Test cricket, in his 30th Test.

In one spell during England's first innings, McGrath took five wickets for 12 runs from 34 balls.

On the third day, during Australia's innings, John Crawley substituted for Alec Stewart as England's wicketkeeper.

This was Australia's first draw in 19 Tests, since the second Test against the West Indies, in Antigua, in 1995. In between, they had won 11, lost seven. The only comparable sequence this century was also 18 Tests, between (and including) the fifth Ashes Test of 1930 and the second Ashes Test of 1934. However, 15 of those matches were played in Australia, where Tests were played to a finish.

England have won only one Ashes Test at Lord's this century (in 1934). Australia has won 10 and drawn 13.

Third Test

Dean Headley (England).

Headley became the first Test cricketer whose grandfather (George Headley: 22 Tests for the West Indies between 1930 and 1954) and father (Ron Headley: 2 Tests for the West Indies in 1973) also played Test cricket. The only previous instance of 'grandfather–grandson' Test cricketers was Australia's Victor Richardson (1924–36) and the Chappell brothers, Ian, Greg and Trevor.

With Dean Headley's selection, the England team included three sons of Test cricketers. Alec Stewart's father, Micky, played eight Tests for England between 1962 and 1964, Mark Butcher's father Alan played one Test for England in 1979.

Centuries

Batsman	Runs	Mins	Balls	Fours	Sixes
Steve Waugh	108	243	175	13	–
Steve Waugh	116	380	281	10	–

These were Waugh's 13th and 14th centuries in Test cricket, in his 92nd Test. He became the sixth batsman, third Australian and first Australian right-hander to score a century in each innings of an Ashes Test. The other two Australians were Warren Bardsley (136 and 130 at The Oval in 1909) and Arthur Morris (122 and 124* at Adelaide in 1946–47). The three Englishmen to achieve this feat are Wally Hammond, Herbert Sutcliffe and Denis Compton. This was Waugh's fifth hundred against England, all scored in England. Only Sir Donald Bradman (11) among Australians has scored more Test centuries in England (Allan Border and Mark Taylor also have five; Warren Bardsley scored five, too, but two of them came against South Africa in the 'Triangular' series in 1912). Waugh became the fourth Australian, after Bradman (1930, 1934, 1938, 1948), Bill Lawry (1961, 1964, 1968) and Taylor (like Waugh, 1989, 1993, 1997), to score centuries on three consecutive Ashes tours.

Shane Warne's 6–48 are his best bowling figures in a Test innings against England, his fourth return of five wickets or more against England and his 11th return of five wickets or more in Test cricket. His 6–48 came in his 14th Ashes Test and 55th Test.

Ian Healy, by stumping Mark Butcher, reached 100 dismissals in Ashes cricket, in his 25th Ashes Test. He became the third keeper, after Rod Marsh (Australia, 148 dismissals in 42 Tests) and Alan Knott (England, 105 dismissals in 34 Tests), to reach the mark.

Shane Warne's dismissal of Alec Stewart in England's second innings was the 250th of his Test career.

CAPTURING YOUR OPPONENT'S PIECES: In chess, captures are never made by moving over an opponent's piece. Instead, captures are always made by moving your piece to a space that is occupied by your opponent's piece. Since two pieces can never occupy the same space at the same time, your opponent's piece is now captured and removed from the board.

CASTLING : This is an exceptional move, made once by each player at any time during the game to bring a Rook into play and strengthen the King's defenses. The King moves two places either left or right and the Rook is placed on the opposite side of the King. Castling is allowed only when:

Both King and Rook are on their original squares.
There are no pieces between the King and the Rook.
The King is not under attack and does not pass a square under attack.

CHECK: When the King is threatened he is said to be "in check" and must be so warned by his opponent. To get out of check, the player may:

Capture the attacking piece. The defending player must immediately move the King or get out of check by taking the attacking piece or interposing another.
Move the King out of danger.
Put another piece between the attacking piece and the King.

CHECKMATE: When the King is unable to escape from check in any of these ways, this is checkmate - the final object of the game - and the attacking player wins.

DRAW: A game is drawn when:

One player cannot checkmate the other.
Both players agree to end the game.
There is a "stalemate." This happens when a King is not in check, but when his only move puts him into check. This differs from a checkmate, where the King is already in check before moving.

Fourth Test

Test Debut

Mike Smith (England).

Centuries

Batsman	Runs	Mins	Balls	Fours	Sixes
Matthew Elliott	199	455	351	23	3
Ricky Ponting	127	264	202	19	1
Nasser Hussain	105	251	181	14	–

Matthew Elliott's century was his second in Test cricket, in nine Tests. He was the third batsman to be dismissed in Test cricket for 199 — the others are Mudassar Nazar, for Pakistan v India in Faisalabad in 1984–85, and Mohammad Azharuddin, for India v Sri Lanka in Kanpur in 1986–87. The previous closest to 200 for Australia, without actually making it, were Lindsay Hassett (198* v India in Adelaide in 1947–48), Arthur Morris (196 v England at The Oval in 1948), Ian Chappell (196 v Pakistan in Adelaide in 1972–73) and Allan Border (196 v England at Lord's in 1985).

Ricky Ponting's century was his first in Test cricket, in his seventh Test. He became the 19th Australian to score a hundred in his debut Ashes Test.

Nasser Hussain's century was his second century against Australia, in his eighth Ashes Test.

Jason Gillespie's 7–37 was his second return of five wickets in a Test innings, in his eighth Test. They are the best bowling figures ever taken by an Australian bowler at Leeds, beating Charlie Macartney's 7–58 in 1909.

This was the third Headingley Test in a row that Australia had passed 500 in their first innings. In 1989 they scored 7–601 (declared), in 1993 they managed 4–653 (declared).

Darren Gough's 5–149 was his second return of five wickets in an innings against Australia, in his seventh Ashes Test, and his third in Tests, in his 21st Test.

Paul Reiffel's 5–49 was his fifth return of five or more wickets in a Test innings, in his 28th Test. He has now taken 14 wickets at Leeds, in two Tests (in 1993 he took 5–65 and 3–87).

This was the 50th Test match together for the Waugh twins. The previous best by brothers is 43 Tests together, by Ian and Greg Chappell between 1970 and 1980. Steve and Mark Waugh remain the only twins to play Test cricket.

Fifth Test

Test Debuts
Adam Hollioake (England)
Ben Hollioake (England)

This was the fifth occasion that brothers have made their Test debuts in the same match (after Dave and Ned Gregory for Australia in 1877, WG, Edward and Fred Grace for England in 1880, Syed Wazir Ali and Syed Nazir Ali for India in 1932, and Andy and Grant Flower for Zimbabwe in 1992).

The only other occasion this century when brothers appeared together for England in a Test match was in 1957, when Peter and Derek Richardson played against the West Indies.

This was the first Test in Ashes history where each side included a pair of brothers.

Six members of the England starting XI were born outside England — Andy Caddick (Christchurch, New Zealand), Robert Croft (Morriston, Wales), Adam and Ben Hollioake (Melbourne, Australia), Nasser Hussain (Madras, India) and Devon Malcolm (Kingston, Jamaica).

When Mark Taylor reached 15 in Australia's first innings he also reached 6000 runs in Test cricket, in his 86th Test. He joined Allan Border (11,174 runs in 156 Tests), David Boon (7422 in 107 Tests), Greg Chappell (7110 in 87 Tests), Sir Donald Bradman (6996 runs in 52 Tests) and Neil Harvey (6149 runs in 79 Tests) as the only Australians to achieve this feat.

When Steve Waugh reached 41 in Australia's first innings, he became the 14th Australian to score 2000 runs in Ashes Tests, in his 31st match.

Ian Healy, by catching Alec Stewart in England's first innings, reached 300 catches in his Test career, in his 93rd Test. He became the second keeper to reach this milestone, after Rod Marsh (343 catches in 96 Tests).

This catch also made Healy the second keeper, after Rod Marsh, to complete 100 catches in Ashes Tests.

This was Australia's third consecutive Test win. The only other Australian team to achieve this on a tour of England was Warwick Armstrong's 1921 team, which won the first three Tests of that series.

This was the fifth time an Australian team had won three Tests during an Ashes series in England, after 1921, 1948, 1989 and 1993.

Sixth Test

Test Debut
Shaun Young (Australia)

Had Young not made his debut in this match, this would have been the first Ashes series since 1905 when not one Australian made his Test debut during an Ashes rubber (this does not include three 'one-off* Tests — the 1977 and 1980 Centenary Tests and the 1988 Bicentenary Test — or the 1979–80 three-Test series in Australia, when the Ashes were not being played for).

England won the toss for the first time in the series.

Glenn McGrath, by dismissing Mike Atherton in England's first innings, reached 150 Test wickets, in his 34th Test.

When Shane Warne reached 6 in Australia's first innings he became the ninth Australian to score 1000 Test runs and take 100 Test wickets, the fourth to score 1000 Test runs and take 200 Test wickets (after Richie Benaud, Ray Lindwall and Merv Hughes) and the first to score 1000 Test runs and take 250 Test wickets.

Phil Tufnell's 7–66 was his second return of five wickets in an innings against Australia, in his 11th Ashes Test, and his fifth in Test cricket, in his 28th Test.

Michael Kasprowicz, in his fifth Test, took five wickets in an innings for the first time in Test cricket. His 7–36 were the best bowling figures in an innings by an Australian bowler at The Oval since 1902 (when Hugh Trumble took 8–65).

No Australian scored a half-century in the match, the first time this has occurred in Test cricket since the Test against the West Indies in Melbourne in December 1988, when Australia scored 242 (Steve Waugh top scored with 42) and 114.

England were dismissed for under 200 in each innings but still won the Test. The last time this happened in an Ashes Test was in 1950–51, at the Melbourne Cricket Ground, when Australia (194 and 181) defeated England (197 and 150) by 28 runs.

Australia's second innings 104 is their lowest completed score in a Test since 1986, when they totalled 103 against New Zealand in Auckland, and their lowest against England since 1977, when they managed 103 at Leeds.

Australia have not won at The Oval since 1972. In seven Tests since then they have lost three and drawn four.

This was the third Test series in succession where Australia lost the final Test of the series, having already won the series (after West Indies in Australia and South Africa in South Africa).

The Series

Australia have now played 141 Tests against England in England: they have won 41, lost 40, and drawn 60. This is the first time Australia has held the 'lead'.

Australia has never previously won three consecutive series in England.

Australia has never previously won five consecutive series against England. The previous best was four, in 1897–98, 1899, 1901–02 and 1902.

Mark Taylor has now captained Australia on 33 occasions, for 18 wins, 10 losses and five draws. Only Allan Border (32 wins in 93 Tests) and Greg Chappell (21 wins in 48 Tests) have led Australia to more Test victories. Only Border, whose 93 Tests were in succession, has captained Australia in more consecutive Tests than Taylor's 33.

Australia used 14 players in the Tests, their most in an Ashes series in England since 1985 (when they used 16). England used 18, their least in an Ashes series in England since 1985 (when they used 17).

Andy Caddick, with 24 wickets in five Tests, became England's most successful bowler in an Ashes series since 1985 (when Ian Botham took 31 wickets).

Glenn McGrath's 36 wickets for the series was the fourth best return by an Australian bowler in an Ashes series in England, after Terry Alderman (42 wickets in 1981, 41 in 1989) and Dennis Lillee (39 wickets in 1981).

Matthew Elliott's series batting aggregate of 556 runs was the eighth best ever by an Australian in an Ashes series in England. Those with higher totals are: Sir Donald Bradman (974 in 1930, 758 in 1934), Mark Taylor (839 in 1989), Arthur Morris (696 in 1948), Allan Border (597 in 1985), Bill Ponsford (569 in 1934) and Dean Jones (566 in 1989).

During the third Test, Shane Warne became the third Australian, after Dennis Lillee (355 Test wickets) and Craig McDermott (291 Test wickets), to take 250 Test wickets. In the first innings of that Test, he had passed Richie Benaud's previous highest number of wickets by a leg spinner in Test cricket of 248. Only the off spinner Lance Gibbs (West Indies, 309 Test wickets) and the left-arm finger spinners, Derek Underwood (England, 297 wickets) and Bishen Bedi (India, 266 wickets), among slow bowlers, remained ahead of Warne, who finished the series with 264 Test wickets, on the all-time Test wicket-taking list.

AUSTRALIANS IN TEST CRICKET

(AS AT NOVEMBER 1, 1997)

Most Appearances

Rank	Player	Tests	Eng	SA	WI	NZ	India	Pak	SL
						Opponents			
1.	AR Border	156	47	6	31	23	20	22	7
2.	DC Boon	107	31	6	22	17	11	11	9
3.	RW Marsh	96	42	–	17	14	3	20	–
4.	**SR Waugh**	**95**	**32**	**7**	**20**	**14**	**6**	**11**	**5**
5.	**IA Healy**	**94**	**28**	**9**	**24**	**8**	**6**	**11**	**8**
6.	GS Chappell	87	35	–	17	14	3	17	1
6.	**MA Taylor**	**87**	**28**	**8**	**20**	**8**	**6**	**9**	**8**
8.	RN Harvey	79	37	14	14	–	10	4	–
9.	IM Chappell	75	30	9	17	6	9	4	–
10.	KD Walters	74	36	4	9	11	10	4	–
14.	**ME Waugh**	**69**	**19**	**9**	**19**	**5**	**5**	**6**	**6**
23.	**SK Warne**	**58**	**17**	**9**	**13**	**6**	**2**	**6**	**5**
58.	**MJ Slater**	**34**	**11**	**6**	**4**	**3**	**1**	**6**	**3**
58.	**GD McGrath**	**34**	**8**	**6**	**9**	**2**	**1**	**5**	**3**
69.	**PR Reiffel**	**29**	**7**	**3**	**7**	**5**	**2**	**3**	**2**
91.	**GS Blewett**	**22**	**8**	**3**	**8**	**–**	**–**	**3**	**–**

Less than 20 Tests
MG Bevan 17, MTG Elliott 11, JN Gillespie 9, RT Ponting 9, JL Langer 8, BP Julian 7, MS Kasprowicz 5, AJ Bichel 2, S Young 1.

Notes 1. *372 men have played Test cricket for Australia, in 572 Tests.*
2. *DS Berry, AC Gilchrist and S Lee are yet to make their Test debuts.*

Most Runs

Rank	Batsman	Runs	Tests	Innings	Not Out	Highest Score	100s	Avge
1.	AR Border	11,174	156	265	44	205	27	50.56
2.	DC Boon	7422	107	190	20	200	21	43.65
3.	GS Chappell	7110	87	151	19	247*	24	53.86
4.	DG Bradman	6996	52	80	10	334	29	99.94
5.	**MA Taylor**	**6162**	**87**	**155**	**9**	**219**	**15**	**42.20**
6.	RN Harvey	6149	79	137	10	205	21	48.41
7.	**SR Waugh**	**5960**	**95**	**148**	**28**	**200**	**14**	**49.66**
8.	KD Walters	5357	74	125	14	250	15	48.26
9.	IM Chappell	5345	75	136	10	196	14	42.42
10.	WM Lawry	5234	67	123	12	210	13	47.15
13.	**ME Waugh**	**4464**	**69**	**112**	**4**	**140**	**11**	**41.33**
18.	**IA Healy**	**3470**	**94**	**143**	**19**	**161***	**3**	**27.98**
31.	**MJ Slater**	**2655**	**34**	**59**	**3**	**219**	**7**	**47.41**
54.	**GS Blewett**	**1421**	**22**	**37**	**2**	**214**	**4**	**40.60**
73.	**SK Warne**	**1027**	**58**	**80**	**9**	**74***	**–**	**14.46**

Less than 1000 runs

MTG Elliott 866 at 48.11, MG Bevan 773 at 29.73, PR Reiffel 648 at 22.34,
RT Ponting 571 at 38.06, JL Langer 272 at 22.66, BP Julian 128 at 16.00,
GD McGrath 106 at 3.92, JN Gillespie 86 at 12.28, MS Kasprowicz 48 at 8.00,
AJ Bichel 40 at 13.33, S Young 4 at 4.00.

Most Wickets

Rank	Bowler	Wickets	Tests	Balls	Runs	Best	5 wicket Innings	Avge
1.	DK Lillee	355	70	18467	8493	7–83	23	23.92
2.	CJ McDermott	291	71	16586	8332	8–97	14	28.63
3.	**SK Warne**	**264**	**58**	**16642**	**6323**	**8–71**	**11**	**23.95**
4.	R Benaud	248	63	19108	6704	7–72	16	27.03
5.	GD McKenzie	246	60	17681	7328	8–71	16	29.78
6.	RR Lindwall	228	61	13650	5251	7–38	12	23.03
7.	CV Grimmett	216	37	14513	5231	7–40	21	24.21
8.	MG Hughes	212	53	12285	6017	8–87	7	28.38
9.	JR Thomson	200	51	10535	5601	6–46	8	28.00
10.	AK Davidson	186	44	11587	3819	7–93	14	20.53
15.	**GD McGrath**	**155**	**34**	**8133**	**3636**	**8–38**	**8**	**23.45**
31.	**PR Reiffel**	**91**	**29**	**5293**	**2401**	**6–71**	**5**	**26.38**
36.	**SR Waugh**	**80**	**95**	**6515**	**2894**	**5–28**	**3**	**36.17**

Less than 50 wickets
ME Waugh 41 at 36.31, JN Gillespie 32 at 22.28, MG Bevan 27 at 23.29,
BP Julian 15 at 39.93, MS Kasprowicz 14 at 31.14, GS Blewett 4 at 69.25,
RT Ponting 2 at 4.00, MA Taylor 1 at 26.00, MJ Slater 1 at 4.00, AJ Bichel 1 at 143.00.

Most Dismissals by a Wicketkeeper

Rank	Keeper	Dismissals	Tests	Caught	Stumped
1.	RW Marsh	355	96	343	12
2.	**IA Healy**	**329**	**94**	**307**	**22**
3.	ATW Grout	187	51	163	24
4.	WAS Oldfield	130	54	78	52
5.	GRA Langley	98	26	83	15
6.	H Carter	65	28	44	21
7.	JJ Kelly	63	36	43	20
8.	HB Taber	60	16	56	4
8.	JM Blackham	60	35	36	24
10.	D Tallon	58	21	50	8

Most Catches

(by fieldsmen; excluding wicketkeepers)

Rank	Fieldsman	Catches	Tests	Rank	Fieldsman	Catches	Tests
1.	AR Border	156	156	7.	**ME Waugh**	**87**	**69**
2.	**MA Taylor**	**123**	**187**	8.	IR Redpath	83	66
3.	GS Chappell	122	187	**9.**	**SR Waugh**	**70**	**95**
4.	RB Simpson	110	162	10.	R Benaud	65	63
5.	IM Chappell	105	175	**19.**	**SK Warne**	**41**	**58**
6.	DC Boon	199	107	**37.**	**GS Blewett**	**26**	**22**

Less than 20 catches
PR Reiffel 14, MJ Slater 11, RT Ponting 10, MG Bevan 8, GD McGrath 8, MTG Elliott 7, BP Julian 4, JN Gillespie 3, JL Langer 2, MS Kasprowicz 2.

Note 1. This list excludes catches taken while fielding as a substitute.